DREAMING
RENAISSANCE

DREAMING THE ENGLISH RENAISSANCE

POLITICS AND DESIRE IN COURT AND CULTURE

Carole Levin

palgrave
macmillan

First published in 2008 by PALGRAVE MACMILLAN® in the US - a division of St. Martin's Press LLC, 175 Fifth Avenue, New York, NY 10010.

Where this book is distributed in the UK, Europe and the rest of the world, this is by Palgrave Macmillan, a division of Macmillan Publishers Limited, registered in England, company number 785998, of Houndmills, Basingstoke, Hampshire RG21 6XS.

Palgrave Macmillan is the global academic imprint of the above companies and has companies and representatives throughout the world.

Palgrave® and Macmillan® are registered trademarks in the United States, the United Kingdom, Europe and other countries.

ISBN-13: 978-1-4039-6089-4 (hardcover)
ISBN-10: 1-4039-6089-5 (hardcover)
ISBN-13: 978-0-230-60261-8 (paperback)
ISBN-10: 0-230-60261-4 (paperback)

Library of Congress Cataloging-in-Publication Data

Levin, Carole, 1948–
   Dreaming the English Renaissance : politics and desire in court and culture / Carole Levin.—1st ed.
      p.   cm.
   Includes bibliographical references and index.
   ISBN-13: 978-1-4039-6089-4
   ISBN-10: 1-4039-6089-5
   ISBN-13: 978-0-230-60261-8 (pbk.)
   ISBN-10: 0-230-60261-4 (pbk.)
      1. Dreams—England—History—16th century.   2. Dreams—England—History—17th century.   3. England—History—16th century.   4. England—History—17th century.   I. Title.
   BF1078.L469   2008
   154.6'3094209032—dc22   2008012159

A catalogue record for this book is available from the British Library.

Design by Westchester Book Group

First edition: October 2008

10 9 8 7 6 5 4 3 2 1

Printed in the United States of America.
Transferred to Digital Printing in 2009

Dream of family tree.

Private collection.

A dream will tell the truth, but not to everyone.
Russian proverb

This book is for

John Watkins, dear friend and intellectual companion, and for

Anya, Alexander, and April Riehl and HtB, who help me have sweet dreams

Contents

LIST OF ILLUSTRATIONS

ACKNOWLEDGMENTS

I first started thinking about this book in the early 1990s when I was completing my study of Elizabeth I, *The Heart and Stomach of a King,* and came across dreams about the queen. I decided I wanted to do a book on dreams in the English Renaissance, and to make the material accessible, the spelling of early modern sources has been modernized. I have had much help in creating this book. John Watkins, Jo Carney, and Linda Shenk each read the entire manuscript. Lynn Botelho, Debbie Barrett-Graves, and Al Geritz read portions. I appreciate their generous and helpful feedback. I want to especially thank Ruth Elwell for her professional index.

Indeed, so many people have been so generous that I have thought all I had to do for research was tell people my project and then wait for the wonderful examples that they shared with me. I was fortunate to be able to do research for this book at the Newberry Library in Chicago in 2003. I want to thank Carla Zecher and the staff of the Renaissance Studies Program for their help and support. Fellow scholars Susan Sleeper-Smith, Jeanie Brink, Stephanie Leitch, and especially Tilar Mazzeo and Anna-Lisa Cox helped create a wonderful working environment. Above all, I am grateful to Dina Kalman Spoerl, who made working at the Newberry a delight. I was also so fortunate that year to have time with Robert Bucholz, Gina Buccola, and Jonathan Walker, who not only provided help and support on the project but great friendship as well. The summer of 2004, I held a short-term fellowship at the Folger Shakespeare Library in Washington, D.C. I was indeed fortunate that Lynn Botelho was there at the same time; she helped me in the reading of manuscripts and has been a wonderful friend ever since.

The 2006–2007 year at the Folger Shakespeare Library allowed me to complete the research and much of the writing of this book. My year at the Folger was magical. Georgianna Ziegler is the queen of reference librarians. Carol Brobeck takes great care of the fellows. I am deeply grateful to other readers and fellows, most especially Tim Harris and Paul Hammer who read sections of the manuscript and provided me with fascinating dream references. Also, Andrew Fleck, Melissa Smith, Julian Yates, Rebecca Winer, Jim Bono, Susan Wabuda, Kimberly Hossain, Kim Coles, Denise Walen, Margaret Hunt, Patrick Tuite, Katie Crawford, Marissa Greenburg, and Jay Zysk offered me wonderful friendship and great dream references. Those on the Folger staff generously do the work that allows those of us who come as readers to produce our scholarship. Gail Kern Paster is a great scholar who understands what scholars need. Betsy Walsh makes the reading room the best place in the world for scholars, with the help of Harold Batie, LuEllen Dehaven, Dragan Gill, Karen Kettnich, Rosalind Larry, Nicole Murray, and Camille Seerattan.

I am so deeply grateful to the National Endowment for the Humanities for the two long-term fellowships that allowed me to do research and writing at these two premiere libraries.

I also wish to thank Charles Beem, Patricia Crawford, Susan Doran, Erin Kelly, Tom Freeman, Tom Hanks, Bruce Janacek, Gwynne Kennedy, Karolyn Kinare, Rebecca Larouche, Sara Mendelson, Andrew Murphy, Susan O'Malley, Lois Schwoerr, Martha Skeeters, Pamela Starr, and Retha Warnicke for offering me dream references or encouragement when I needed it, or sometimes both. I presented my research at a number of scholarly conferences and universities and am grateful for the questions and comments that allowed me to refine my arguments.

My current, former, and future graduate students graciously listened to many accounts of dreams, and I am particularly grateful to Amy Gant, Matthew Hansen, Joy Currie, Michael Hewitt, Shawndra Holderby, Hesham Khadawardi, Amber Harris Leichner, Nathan Martin, Shannon Meyer, Cassie Olsen, Nate Probasco, Mark Reuter, Lisa Schuelke, Christine Stewart-Nuñez, and most especially Timothy Elston, who even shared with me his dream about the game show "Name That Monarch," hosted by Henry VII. Carolyn Biltoft spent her year before entering graduate school helping me with research.

I am deeply grateful to my home institution, the University of Nebraska, for all the support I have received for this project. Love Library's holdings are excellent, and the Interlibrary Loan office at Love Library also facilitated research I needed with efficiency and grace. Kathy Johnson is a gifted reference librarian who truly loves books and seems to know everything. I particularly wish to thank Prem Paul, the Vice Chancellor for Research, and Laura Damuth, the director of the undergraduate research program, UCARE. My UCARE research assistants Jarrod Brand, Lindsay Kerns, Natasha Luepke, Cassie Olsen, and Erica Wright not only provided great help to the project, but also are wonderful, brilliant students with whom I was greatly privileged to work.

The staff at Palgrave treat their authors really well; I am especially grateful to Michael Flamini, who believed in this project at the beginning, and to Chris Chappell, who shepherded it through at the end.

Certain people have been steadfast in their support of this project and no one could dream of better friends than Pamela Nickless, Lena Orlin, Michele Osherow, Anya Riehl, Lynn Spangler, Pat Sullivan, Rick Cypert, Jody Stoneking, and especially Elaine Kruse. My thanks to all of you.

INTRODUCTION

Why do dreams matter so much to us? Dreams themselves, and the way we interpret them, take us into the deepest part of our individual as well as cultural psyches. Dreams indicate to us the ways in which we are fundamentally the same as peoples of earlier times and also the ways in which we are deeply different. Dreams—and discussions of dreams—can give us information about the most significant issues of a historical period, especially the sites where religion and politics, as well as death and power, intersect. Popular literature and historical documents from early modern England include a remarkable number of recorded dreams and a considerable discourse on their meanings. But if we have difficulties in understanding our own dreams and those of our contemporaries, we have to be especially careful in our investigations of the dreams of peoples from centuries ago. Anthony Stevens cautions that interpreting "the dream of someone long dead presents impressive difficulty because one cannot ask the dreamer for his associations or the products of his active imagination." Clearly, we must deal carefully with dreams as cultural evidence since "dreams are," as Charles Carlton notes in his own work on the dream life of seventeenth-century Archbishop William Laud, "ephemeral" sources.[1]

Some early modern dreams sound strikingly similar to those we have today. The dream that so many academics admit to having of finding themselves in a classroom completely unprepared to teach parallels a dream the seventeenth-century clergyman Ralph Josselin had of a similar lack of preparation. Dreaming that he was in the pulpit wearing neither his collar nor his surplice, Josselin found himself, to his horror, completely unable to sing the psalms or locate the biblical passages he needed.[2] Unlike this kind of dream that speaks across the centuries, some dreams are much more tied to a specific time and place. Dreams can impress us or frighten us; sometimes they can change lives. As William Dement argues, "the emotional impact of our dreams can be so powerful that they might as well really have occurred." He suggests that such dreams have "fascinated people since at least the beginning of recorded history."[3]

As fascinating as our own dreams might be, their meaning is often elusive, and because they fade and are hard to interpret, it is even more difficult to have a thorough and accurate account of them. This challenge proves yet greater because the linear format of narrative itself defies the nonlinearity of a dream world where, for example, a person can be two people at once or where time and place shift suddenly and radically. Each person's dream world is highly individual. The minister Philip Goodwin, a writer in the mid-seventeenth century, noted that "all men, says an obscure writer, while awake, are together in one common world, but when they sleep, each man goes into a single world by himself." This theme, clearly common in the early modern period, echoes the ancient writer Heraclitus: "The world of the waking is unique and common, but each sleeper returns unto himself." Thomas Nashe pointed out that "how many sorts there be of [dreams] no man can rightly set down, since it scarce hath been heard, there were ever two men that dreamed alike."[4] Forever isolated by the individuality of our dream worlds, we cannot turn to others to help us piece together our hazy recollections. We can never completely and accurately remember those individual worlds we inhabited even when we are awake. What we have of dreams are, as Jean-Claude Schmitt describes, a "fleeting memory and reconstructed account."[5]

Throughout the early modern period, the question whether truth could be found in dreams was hotly debated. Often, people would recount how they had dreamed that someone they loved would die. When the narrators mentioned the dream to friends or relatives, their fears would frequently be dismissed with the comforting reminder that there was no truth in dreams. This scenario appears to be the early modern equivalent of the moment in the horror movie when, right before characters get attacked, one character assures the other that, despite the one's premonition of danger, it is perfectly safe to walk through the graveyard or to explore the haunted house. Such refusal to acknowledge the ability of dreams to foretell the future usually portends that the dream's validity will prove true all-too-soon.

A particularly indicative example specific to sixteenth-century England occurred in 1558, late in the reign of Catholic Queen Mary I. The Protestant minister John Rough was "sore troubled" when he dreamed "that he saw two of the Guard leading Cutbert Simson," the deacon of his own congregation away to be interrogated. Rough was so disturbed because, in his dream Simson was carrying a book that listed the members of the underground Protestant congregation, and this document, if found, would have put the entire group at risk. Deeply upset, he related the dream to his wife and asked her to light a candle so that he could read for a while. Before she could comply, however, Rough went back to sleep and "dreamed the like dream again." Now even more distraught, Rough resolved to visit Simson, but before he could, Simson came to see him. With relief, Rough told him, "Cutbert, you are welcome, for I have been sore troubled with you this night" and then related his dream. Concerned about the consequences should the authorities seize the book, Rough begged Simson to stop carrying it with him, yet Cutbert dismissed his fears, saying "dreams . . . were but fantasies, and not to be credited." When Rough told Cutbert to obey him in the name of the Lord, Cutbert gave the book to Rough's wife. This move was fortunate indeed: Simson was arrested soon after. Because of Rough's premonitory dream, the Protestant congregation narrowly escaped exposure.

As a result of this experience, Cutbert apparently had a change of heart and decided to take dreams more seriously. He had one of his own dreams after he had been put on the rack, and then another only a day or so before he was burned at the stake. In his book about the Protestant martyrs, John Foxe described these events some years after they happened; however, Foxe admitted uncertainty, writing that if Cutbert was "in a slumber, or being awake I cannot say." It was about 11 o'clock at night, and the prison was in complete darkness. A presence came through the door, and while it had "nor candle or torch that he could see," it gave forth "a brightness and light." All it said to Cutbert was "hah!" before it departed, but the next day Cutbert told how it had brought him "joyful comfort."[6] For Rough, as we will see in chapter 3, more of his dreams and those of members of his family were recorded before he, too, was arrested and burned for heresy.

Rough's dream took place in the politically precarious world of an underground Protestant living and worshipping in a Catholic regime, and his dream alerted him to a true danger. Some people were warned of dangers through a vision while they were awake or while they were in a trance. Although these visions are fascinating and historically revealing, they are not within the scope of this book. The distinction between dreams and visions, however, is sometimes difficult to discern, as Foxe's uncertainty about Cutbert's experience demonstrates. As medievalist Jacques le Goff observes, "The frontier between sleep and wakefulness is not always apparent."[7] In keeping with this same sense of indeterminacy, Zacharie Jones's early seventeenth-century translation of Pierre de Loyer's treatise on specters and apparitions describes a trance as "that which is between sleeping and waking."[8]

People in the early modern world had some incidents that they believed were not dreams: For example, many described an experience in which a person, while lying in bed (often at night) would see an angel, spirit, or ghost appear before them. While the early modern subject was apt to describe this experience as a visitation, we in the post–Enlightenment, twenty-first century are more apt to conclude that it was a vivid dream. The author of the seventeenth-century text, *Wonderful Prodigies of Judgment and Mercy*, related that James V of Scotland was greatly frightened in what the author described as a dream. James himself may not have been sure what it was, "for whilst he lay sleeping, he thought that Sir James Hamilton . . . came to him with a drawn sword in his hand, and therewith cut off both his arms . . . with which he awaked, and as he lay musing what this dream should signify, news was brought him of the death of his two sons, James and Arthur."[9]

In *Leviathan* (1651), Thomas Hobbes demonstrated a particular interest in clarifying what distinguishes waking visions from sleeping dreams. He stressed that it is difficult to make this distinction, especially when the person "sleeps, without the circumstances of going to bed."[10] Hobbes argued that it was much better for someone to "industriously lay himself to sleep, in case of any uncouth and exorbitant fancy comes unto him, [he] cannot easily think it other than a dream." Hobbes sought to separate dreams from visions because he did not believe that dreams had any value as prognostication. Conversely, Hobbes's contemporary Gervase Holles believed strongly in prophetic dreams, and he expressed scorn for "Hobbes and atheistic philosophy."[11] To add to the difficulties in distinguishing between a dream and a waking experience, the terms "dream" and "vision" were often used interchangeably. As Nigel Smith and David Como have pointed out, this practice was particularly prevalent among certain religious groups of the early modern period. Keith Thomas adds that "most of the 'visions' and 'revelations' which were so common during the Interregnum were probably what we should call dreams."[12]

Thus, in this study I focus on dreams linked with sleep—specifically with experiences that people labeled as their own dreams and which do not appear to be the products of their waking minds. I do address some liminal experiences of strange happenings that took place when someone was in bed either in the middle of the night or because of serious illness. Such events could well have been a dream even if the person at the time considered it to be a visitation by a ghost, spirit, or angel. Some writers in the early modern period tried to articulate the difference between these experiences. In his text, the minister Goodwin made a clear distinction between what he classifies as an awake vision and a dream, arguing that, when St. Paul had a vision in the night, it was a dream. "We may imagine 'twas a dream in his sleep being a vision in the night. Though visions in the day, were when men were awake, yet visions in the night were ordinary in sleep."[13]

The definition of a dream in the 1641 text *The Divine Dreamer* by an author known only as Gonzalo is a useful one: "A dream is that which appears to us while we are sleeping; not by the function of the eyes, but by the imagination. Some dreams leave a man joyful and well disposed at a thing. Contrarily, there are others sad and offensive that for diverse days after such dreams, procure a melancholy languishing both in soul and body, making a man unable to receive delight."[14] The seventeenth-century author William Vaughan also gave an interesting definition, arguing that "dreams are either tokens of things past, or significant of things to come."[15] Goodwin explained that "though sleep be a plain image of death, yet dreams are the signs of men alive . . .'Tis living men who do commemorate, meditate, excogitate matters in their minds both awake and asleep. Even sleeping their minds are in motion which we call dreams."[16]

Goodwin reminds his readers that dreams are helped by both fantasy and memory. This study also must take into account how memory over time can reorganize the order of events and the emotional resonances of experiences, especially such intangible ones as dreams. It is often difficult to remember a dream accurately, even immediately upon waking because, as our dreams recede into the past, our memory of the contents can shift. Some of the dreams I discuss in this book were reported many years after they occurred; therefore, the chronology of events and the significance of the dream may have been transmuted over time. It is not only the distance from the time of the dream to its reporting that can cause us to wonder at its veracity. At times we do not even know if a documented dream actually happened. We have to examine where and how and why the dream is reported. A dream recorded in a diary does not have the expectation of audience that a dream described in a letter does. Conversely, a letter detailing a dream to a private person is quite different from one sent to the government as a warning. Yet more different still, a dream recounted in a pamphlet not only has a very different and much wider audience but also raises additional questions of credibility because dreams, in pamphlets, were often used as justification for readers to take a certain action. In some cases, whether the dream actually occurred—or occurred as described—may be far less important than how people responded to it. The various audiences of a recorded dream helped shape both the narrative and the way the dream was used to make a point or prove a position. Sometimes, of course, dreams were initially recorded for one reason but then used later for an entirely different purpose. For example, William Laud kept a private journal that, among much else, detailed a number of his dreams. One that he recorded from 21 August 1625 described his dream about George Villiers, the Duke of Buckingham.

> That night, in my sleep, it seemed to me that the Duke of Buckingham came into bed with me; where he behaved himself with great kindness towards me. . . . Many seemed to me to enter the chamber who saw this.[17]

While Laud recorded this dream for his own private use, its utility changed after his arrest for treason on 18 December 1640. After his imprisonment, he asked to return to Lambeth to retrieve some of his papers as well as his diary, and in this diary, he continued to write. In May 1643, after Laud had been moved to the Tower, William Prynne, with a retinue of soldiers, entered Laud's cell and confiscated twenty-two bundles of papers, including the diary. In 1644 Prynne published an account of this dream in his *Breviate of the life of William Laud . . . extracted for the most part verbatim out of his Diary.* For Prynne this dream proved that Laud was guilty of "uncleanness"—but I think the dream has a multiplicity of possible meanings, not all of which are sexual. Buckingham was very powerful in 1625, and the expression of politicians getting into bed together was a common one then as now.

It is also necessary for any scholar exploring dreams to be clear about the theoretical context of the dream analyses. While both Sigmund Freud and Carl Jung have made many contributions to a modern understanding of dreams, their philosophies will not factor greatly into this book. Instead, I will build a theoretical framework using primarily early modern writers on dreams. In some cases, such as the seventeenth-century French theologian Moise Amyraut, the ideas of these writers sound eerily similar to "modern" theories on dreams. In one particular instance, Amyraut sounds as if he is describing Freud's theory of dreams' oppositional import when he states "those who undertake to give rules of their interpretation . . . tell us that we ought sometimes to take the direct contrary to the dream for its interpretation."[18] Many early modern dream books detailed the meaning of opposites in dreams. For example, "to weep in sleep" means joy, and "to see the dead, long life."[19] Thomas Nashe was highly skeptical of this oppositional structure, arguing "What sense is there that the yolk of an egg should signify gold, or dreaming of Bears, or fire, or water, debate and anger, that everything must be interpreted backward as Witches say their Pater-noster, good being the character of bad, and bad of good."[20] Nashe, however, did agree that dreams were caused by guilt or by the fragments of the day. Thomas Cooper also argued that some dreams inform us "of the sins of the heart" because "what we conceive or practice in the day will be corruptly dreamed of in the night, to make us more inexcusable."[21] For the purposes of this book, examining what the early modern people themselves thought about dreams is far more useful than subjecting their dreams to modern theory. While people of the premodern period believed dreams provided them with a variety of meanings, they were not considering them as a key to the unconscious. As Stéphane Moses points out, premodern dreams were often read as prophetic "and were thus oriented toward the future, in Freud's eyes they refer to the dreamer's past."[22]

It is important to recognize that, just as today, there are many different views of dreams and what they mean, so, too, in early modern England, there were many different perspectives—some of which were meant to be taken more seriously than others. Today we might check our horoscope in the morning paper, but that does not mean we truly believe the stars control us. Or we might pick up an inexpensive guide to dream interpretations at the checkout line, but we peruse it more out of idle curiosity than hope for true insight. Likewise, some books on the meaning of dreams published in the early modern period were scholarly tomes; others, such as *A Book of Secrets,* were entertaining but clearly not highly regarded texts.

Dream books of the early modern period catalogued many specific interpretations for certain objects or events depicted in a dream. Some of these interpretations contradicted each other, and sometimes, the interpretation of an object or event depended on the context. For example, to dream of asparagus gathered up and tied in bundles was an omen of tears, but seeing it growing wild predicted good fortune. An artichoke in a dream meant that dreamers would soon receive a favor from someone from whom they least expected it. Picking green apples off the top of the tree foretold advancement. On the other hand, a cauliflower was a terrible thing to see in a dream. It meant that all the dreamer's friends would slight him or her, and then to make matters worse, when the dreamer descended into poverty, this person would get no pity or aid. Dreaming of an egg suggested that the dreamer would hear angry voices the next day. Violets were ominous to the unmarried dreamer, foretelling great evil, but these same flowers promised joy to the married dreamer. Flowers in general, however, signified a funeral. If one ate lettuce in one's dream, death would follow. Dreams of serpents meant friends would turn into the bitterest of enemies, but killing a serpent in a dream foretold victory for the dreamer in waking life. Dreams about teeth always had distressing implications and seemed to be quite common, possibly suggesting the problems early modern people had with dental care. Losing a tooth meant the death of a friend, but bloody teeth foretold one's own death. One of the worst dreams would be of drinking mustard thinned to a liquid consistency: It meant being accused of murder.[23]

Recognizing that dreams can inform us in new ways about a historical period, a number of scholars have recently produced important, thoughtful works on the subject. Such studies have given us new insights into the intertwining of politics and religion in the Middle Ages, into Catholic and Buddhist conversion experience in China, into the development of a new nation in the American colonial and revolutionary periods, and into the terrifying political trauma inflicted under such regimes as Nazi Germany and Stalinist Russia.[24]

For this book, I am interested both in the early modern period's wide range of theories about dreams as well as dreams that were recorded in diaries, described in letters, narrated in family history, reported in chronicle histories, and included in political and religious tracts. Some of the dreams were clearly reported honestly as actual dreams whereas others were very clearly invented to make a political or religious point. These latter "dreams" are still well worth scrutinizing because they demonstrate how seriously dreams were taken in the period—so seriously that they could be leveraged to support an agenda. George Steiner has noted that, historically, "dreams, both private and public, play their part."[25] Some people in the early modern period were very aware that couching a suggestion as if it came from a dream was a way to have the idea taken seriously. Henry Howard, Earl of Northampton, made exactly that point when he wrote to discredit dreams as prophecies. He described how the city walls were crumbling in ancient Rome, so a citizen "dreamed or in deed, or rather feigned (as I think) to dream, that unless the walls of the city were repaired with some diligence, the town would be brought (ere it were long) into great jeopardy." The earl suggests that since the walls of any town were "esteemed as the strongest guard" and since it would be a terrible thing if some enemies were "to make their profit of their neighbors negligence," then "I cannot otherwise conceive, but that some cunning fellow, finding the magistrates too careless of the public state, and too much addicted to their private gain; under the mask of a dreaming oracle, gave warning to the counsel, of their careless oversight in matters of most moment."[26]

Dreams and their cultural, religious, and political significance are explored in the five chapters of this book. At the core of the book is the importance of dreams in the court and then throughout the culture. To highlight that significance, the study is bookended with the first and last chapters focused on the court. Chapter 1 outlines some of the different ways dreams could be used at court and in legal cases, centering on three examples all of which occurred in 1605. From this specific focus that illuminates a number of the book's themes, chapter 2 then widely ranges over the many different ways dreams were understood and interpreted in the early modern period. In chapter 3, I examine the role dreams played in religious beliefs as well as the roles they played in fears about witchcraft. Chapter 4 focuses on dreams that were part of the questions of sexuality and power in the reigns of the Tudors. Chapter 5 centers on dreams about sacred blood and monarchy, ones about earlier rulers as reported in the Tudor and early Stuart period and others about sixteenth-century monarchs. The first chapter begins with the court of James I; the final chapter brings us back to dreams about Elizabeth and James's mother, Mary Stuart.

Examining the actual dreams, purported dreams, and beliefs about dreams of early modern English men and women is another way to study and comprehend sixteenth- and seventeenth-century England as a fault line between medieval and modern.[27] Dreams and the beliefs about them provide a window into understanding this fault line because they suggest a development toward the individual and interiority, which helps move us closer to a modern sensibility. The frequent changes in state religion and in the nature of monarchy caused a time of great instability in which the religious, cultural, and social boundaries of identity became more permeable. Dreams, both actual and created for use as propaganda, give us greater insight into how these insecurities were felt. This study of early modern English dreams centers on questions of gender, culture, and power as well as on how we can better understand a very different age even as we elucidate something about our own.

CHAPTER 1

1605, THE YEAR OF THREE DREAMS

In November 1605, Guy Fawkes, under the alias John Johnson, was living in a small house adjacent to the House of Lords and was Thomas Percy's supposed servant and caretaker. Percy had leased the house the year before and in March of that year had also leased a storeroom located on the ground floor directly under the House of Lords. Thirty-six barrels of gunpowder were stored in that room in the spring and summer of 1605. With that gunpowder, Fawkes was planning an act of terrorism against the Crown—an act so extreme that it would give rise to both a popular and political rhetoric saturated with the language of dreams and nightmares.

The opening day of Parliament was scheduled for November 5, and Fawkes was planning to blow up the Houses of Parliament with the king, his wife, and eldest son present. An obscure letter sent on October 26 to William Parker, Lord Mounteagle,[1] warned him not to attend the opening of Parliament "for though there be no appearance of any stir, yet I say they shall receive a terrible blow this Parliament, and yet shall not see whom hurts them." Mounteagle immediately took the strange letter to Whitehall to show to Sir Robert Cecil, Earl of Salisbury. He found Salisbury with Thomas Howard, Earl of Suffolk; Edward Somerset, Earl of Worcester; and Henry Howard, Earl of Northampton, all about to have dinner together. Mounteagle asked to speak with Salisbury privately. Although Salisbury praised Mounteagle for bringing the letter to his attention, he was skeptical that it was significant. Not wanting to take chances, however, Salisbury showed it to the members of the Privy Council at court that same night. With James I away hunting, the councilors decided to wait until his return to take action. James returned and was informed of the letter on November 1. According to later official accounts, James immediately suspected that "blow" meant "blow up," as in a gunpowder explosion.

James may have been so quick to discern the meaning of "blow" because, as Henry Paul has suggested, "the king's idea of hunting was a little different from that of other people," as is especially clear with his first hunting trip of

1605 back in January. On the twenty-sixth of that month, John Erskine, the Earl of Mar, wrote to Robert Cecil: "We are here continually busied either at hunting or examining of witches, and although I like the first better than the last, yet I must confess both uncertain sports." James himself wrote to Cecil in March to apologize for not keeping up with their correspondence: "I have been out of privy intelligence with you since my last paring, for having been ever kept so busy with hunting of witches, prophets, puritans, dead cats, and hares."[2] James was accustomed to examining odd circumstances and figuring out meaning, though Joel Hurstfield doubts that it took "any great analytical skill to detect that this language almost certainly meant a plan to blow up Parliament by means of gunpowder." Hurstfield argues that Cecil had already figured it out but "went through the pantomime . . . of leaving it to that kingly Solomon to unravel its meaning to the admiration of his ministers and courtiers." G.P.V. Akrigg describes the "Jacobean rhetoric" that credited James with saving the kingdom by unmasking the meaning of the letter as "so much poppycock."[3]

On the evening of November 4, the king ordered the area around the palace of Westminster searched. The Earl of Suffolk led the investigation, and Mounteagle asked to be part of the group. After looking through the chamber of the House of Lords, the search party went to inspect the ground-floor vaults that ran the length of the building. They saw a very large store of firewood in one of the cellar rooms. The man looking after it, Guy Fawkes, was later described as very tall and desperate looking. When asked, he said the room belonged to his master, Thomas Percy. Suffolk did not want to make the man aware that he considered the firewood suspicious, so they hurriedly moved on. Suffolk's concerns intensified after Mounteagle informed him that Percy was an old friend of his and that he had had no idea Percy had rented property in Westminster. He also mentioned that Percy was a Catholic. When James was informed of these facts, he decided a more intensive search was needed.

Later that night, by order of the king, Sir Thomas Knyvett, Keeper of the Whitehall Palace, a member of the King's Privy Chamber, and a Justice of the Peace for Westminster, returned with men to search the house and storeroom. Knyvett ordered the arrest of the caretaker, who was dressed in cloak and boots ready for immediate departure. Looking in the storeroom among the firewood, Knyvett found the barrels of gunpowder. Searching the man he had arrested, Knyvett also found fuses to be used to cause an explosion. This, of course, was the Gunpowder Plot[4]—one of the most famous failed conspiracies of history, and Guy Fawkes and Thomas Percy were two of the conspirators.

Had this plan succeeded, it would have been a seventeenth-century nightmare of terrorism similar in scope and intent to our own 9/11. Recent scientists estimate that such a blast would have obliterated the Palace of Westminster, Westminster Hall, Westminster Abbey, as well as the surrounding streets. The king himself told the Venetian Ambassador "had the scheme been carried out thirty thousand persons would have perished at a stroke, the city would have been sacked, and the rich would have suffered more than the poor; in short, the world would have seen a spectacle so terrible and terrifying that its like has never been heard of."[5]

People at the time were terrified at the thought of what would have happened had the explosion occurred. An anonymous ballad composed soon after described in nightmarish terms how it would have been:

> . . . royal and noble shapes
>
> Blown up in the whisking air—
>
> Here arms, there legs, dissevered quite,
>
> Lie mangled everywhere.
>
> . . .
>
> And every street be purplefied
>
> With gores coagulate.[6]

The King's chaplain, William Hubbard, argued that the conspirators intended "to destroy root, and branch: and fruit, parent, and child in one day: to kill dam and young in one nest." The nightmare metaphor was suggested in the anonymous *The Returne of the Knight of the Post from Hell*, which refers to the conspirators as "monsters and monstrous men," which sounds like those whom one might meet in a horrible dream. Five days after the plot was discovered, on November 10, William Barlow, bishop of Rochester, also described the event in rhetoric that suggested terrifying dreams: "the shortness of time . . . the dreadfulness of the danger . . . could not but leave an impression of horror." Barlow described what Fawkes intended: "the horses and bodies flying up; he living and laughing at it." In 1606, Lancelot Andrewes, at the time bishop of Chichester, preached a sermon about the plot that argued "our age brings forth strange children," who are "monster-like."[7]

One wonders whether Fawkes was able to sleep while he stayed there those last nights before the plan was to be put in motion and, if he slept, whether that slumber was disturbed by dreams of what he planned to do. While we can never know what Fawkes's dreams were, we do know that the people of early modern England dreamed and that many dreams were recorded. One such dreamer was Robert Wintour, one of the Gunpowder Plot conspirators, and his dream received a high-level of publicity because it was mentioned at his trial. There were two other events that year, though they are far less well known, that directly related to beliefs about dreams and the changing nature of politics and religion, law, and belief in the supernatural: the investigation into a man named Richard Haydock, known as the "sleeping preacher," and the series of recurring dreams that helped solve a violent murder case. These events reveal concerns of particular urgency to early modern English court and culture, and they touched one figure most nearly: King James himself.

In 1605, the perceptive James I not only exposed the Gunpowder Plot but also revealed that Haydock, "the sleeping preacher," was actually a fraud.

Though this latter instance hardly weighed as heavily as the Plot, it also received substantial attention: Haydock made a public apology at Paul's Cross and then a second, less public apology when he dedicated his manuscript on dreams to James. The other major event, taking place as Haydock was back in Salisbury penning his text, was the love affair of Anne Waters and Giles Haworth in Lancashire. This liaison led to the murder of Waters's husband. The recurring dreams of their neighbor—and possible relative—Thomas Haworth led to the exposure of that murder. We will examine both of these other dreams before returning to that of the plotter Robert Wintour and the seriousness with which that dream was taken.

In early modern England, dreams were explained in a variety of ways: Some were considered natural or caused, for example, by eating the wrong foods; others were believed to be simply the fragments of the day retold. Some were seen as diabolic, perhaps the result of being bewitched, and still others might be the means by which God or the angels spoke to humans. Some people believed that dreams held different meanings depending on astrological sign, social status, or marital status, or depending on the time of night or the time of the year in which the dream occurred, or on one's balance of the four humours. Books dealing with the meaning of dreams ranged from heavy tomes to brief broadsides; many of them offered specific ways in which to interpret dreams.

DID KING JAMES BELIEVE IN DREAMS?

Despite these different approaches to dreams, one of the most widely held interests concerned their power of prognostication: If one could only understand the symbolism, one would know the future foretold by the dream. But this was not a belief that King James supported in his scholarly writings. James appears to have had no belief in the ability of dreams to predict the future or to be used in magic. While still king of Scotland, James believed strongly in the supernatural, particularly in the power of witches. A strand that runs through witchcraft trials and pamphlets is the belief in the power witches have from their own dreams as well as from their ability to bewitch others through the dreams they cause their victims to have. But while James's text *Daemonology* (1597) expressed many of his beliefs about the power of witches, he expressed doubt about dreams having supernatural powers. He discarded the idea of a demon truly coming to someone when he sleeps. James claimed, instead, that what felt like such a visitation "is but a natural sickness . . . being a thick fleume, falling into our breast upon the heart, while we are sleeping, intercludes so our vital spirits, and takes all power from us, as makes us think that there were some unnatural burden or spirit, lying upon us and holding us down." While many medical texts supported James's position, a number of other learned works did not. Lewes (sometimes called Ludwig) Lavater's *Of Ghostes and Spirites Walking By Nyght* was published in Latin in Zurich in 1569 and subsequently translated into German, French, Spanish, and Italian until, finally, the English translation was published in

1572. It argued that "incubi and succubi, (which we call mares) are night spirits, or rather devils, which leap upon men in their sleep."[8] Succubi were female demons who stole men's seed, then turned into incubi to impregnate women. All this happened, people believed, while the poor men and women slept.

James is even more dismissive of the power of dreams in *Basilikon Doron, Or His Majesties Instructions to His Dearest Sonne, Henrie the Prince* (1599), the text he wrote for his oldest son on how to be a good ruler. James warned Henry to "take no heed to any of your dreams, for all prophecies, visions, and prophetic dreams are accomplished and ceased in Christ: And therefore take no heed to fret either in dreams, or any other things; for that error proceeds of ignorance, and is unworthy of a Christian." Both *Daemonology* and *Basilikon Doron* were originally published in Edinburgh while James was king of Scotland. They were republished in London beginning in 1603, so the concepts in them were widely available to the English people at the time.[9]

Once James became king of England, he grew far more skeptical about the supernatural in general and often expressed great delight in exposing potential cases of the supernatural as frauds.[10] As Arthur Wilson, writing about James in the decades after his death, put it: "The King took delight by the line of his reason to fund the depths of such brutish impostors, and he discovered many."[11] The same year as Haydock the "sleeping preacher" mesmerized his audiences, twenty-one-year-old Anne Gunter claimed to be bewitched with bizarre symptoms such as vomiting and sneezing pins. A few months after Haydock was at court, Gunter had her turn, and James also proved her to be a fraud. There are odd connections between Gunter and Haydock. Both Gunter's bewitchment and the case of the "sleeping preacher" caused a brief sensation at court, and there are several cross currents that tie the two events together. We have no evidence that James was even aware of the Waters murder, though he did read Stow's *Annales,* which mentions the case.

THE SLEEPING PREACHER

In the spring of 1605, news came to court of one of those bizarre events or "strange marvels" of which James was so fond and which he liked to explore. There was a medical doctor, one Richard Haydock, who apparently gave excellent sermons only while he was deeply asleep. This strange phenomenon had begun while Haydock was studying at Oxford. People claimed that even if people called to him or pulled at his hands and feet, Haydock would not awake but would continue preaching in his sleep.[12] Though Thomas Sackville, Earl of Dorset, was certainly busy as Lord Treasurer and Chancellor of Oxford University, at the king's request he went to Oxford to bring the sleeping preacher to court. But, as Dorset wrote to Robert Cecil, "Mr. Haydok is gone from Oxford a good while . . . and for certain that Mr. Haydok is at this present settled and lodged . . . in the close at Salisbury where he practices physic and is in good regard."[13]

Haydock's choice to play the role of "sleeping preacher" has its roots in his personal history. He was born about 1570 in the county of Hampshire and attended Wykeham's school in Winchester. In July 1588, he matriculated at New College, Oxford. Elected a fellow in 1590, he received his Bachelor of Arts in 1592 and his Master of Arts in 1595. (Haydock's wide-ranging interests even included art; he was himself an artist.) His maternal grandfather, Thomas Bill, had been a physician to Henry VIII and Edward VI. This family history may have influenced Haydock in choosing to study medicine, but whatever his main reason, he did not pursue his passion for preaching. Haydock had a stutter, and he felt that it would prevent him from becoming a preacher.[14] He traveled on the continent for a while before returning to Oxford. Though he was studying medicine, in 1598 he published a translation of Giovanni Paolo Lomazzo's *Trattato dell' arte della Pittura,* which had been published in Milan in 1584. Haydock's translation was called *A Tracte containing the Artes of curious Paintinge, Carvinge, & Buildinge written first in Italian JO: PAUL LOMATIUS painter of Milan and englished by R. H. student in Physick.* Haydock also made an impressive number of engraved plates including the self-portrait on the title page.[15] Despite this turn toward art, he continued with his medical studies and received his Bachelor of Medicine in 1601. He stayed on at Oxford for another four years; in 1605, he moved to Salisbury, where he set up his medical practice. (figure 1.1)

Only a few weeks after he arrived in Salisbury, Haydock's path crossed with Gunter's. Two of the three women accused of bewitching her had been tried for witchcraft—the third had run away. Although the women had been acquitted, Gunter's bizarre symptoms continued, and many people were talking about her case. Since the diocese of North Moreton was under the purview of Henry Cotton, bishop of Salisbury, he decided to investigate. In the spring of 1605, he had Gunter taken from her parents' house and lodged in the Cotton's residence at Salisbury. Apparently Haydock, who had been in Salisbury only a few weeks himself, was asked to examine her. We do not know the result of this examination, but we do know that Haydock's servant, fifty-year-old widow Joan Greene was asked to look after Gunter while she lived in the Cotton residence. Also looking after Gunter was twenty-eight-year-old Joan Spratt. Because of his own exposed fraud, Haydock was not called to testify before the Star Chamber in the Gunter case, but both of the women were. Greene and Spratt testified how they had become convinced that Gunter was simulating her symptoms and that they had told her it was a dreadful thing to be doing something that led to false accusations of witchcraft against innocent women. While Joan Greene encouraged Gunter to confess everything to the bishop, Gunter was deeply afraid of what might happen to her father as a result, so she did not take the advice. Evidently, neither of the women confided their suspicions, and Gunter appears to have returned to her father's house without being examined for fraud. That spring, the connection between Anne Gunter and Richard Haydock was broken, at least for the time.

Figure 1.1 Richard Haydock.
Lomazzo's A tracte containing the artes of curious paintinge, Englished by R. H. student in physick by permission of the Folger Shakespeare Library.

When James visited Oxford in August 1605, Brian Gunter took Anne to meet the king. James was skeptical and had a team examine her. On 10 October 1605, James wrote to Robert Cecil that he "spent some time this day in the examination of her. . . . and we find by her confession . . . that she was never possessed with any devil nor bewitched."[16] Anne admitted that her father had pressured her into feigning her symptoms, and they were both brought before the Star Chamber in February of 1606; there appears to have been no punishment given to Anne, probably, as J. A. Sharpe hypothesizes, because she had confessed so thoroughly. Her father Brian Gunter was imprisoned for about two years but then "was able to return to North Moreton and continue the life of a gentleman."[17]

Months before Anne Gunter made the acquaintance of James I, he had already met and exposed Haydock. When Haydock left Oxford for Salisbury, he was already known for his preaching while asleep, and he continued to do so in his new home. John Gordon, the dean of Salisbury, and Michael Hyde, chancellor of Salisbury Cathedral, sent Haydock to Cecil in mid-April with a letter describing how they had listened to Haydock preach in his sleep since "Our intention was to hear him more amply and then to bring him to the King, as he can witness himself; and seeing that he is now sent for by the Lords of the Council." Gordon and Hyde explained that when Haydock had come to practice medicine in Salisbury, they had heard about his preaching in his sleep. They said that, the previous Wednesday at about three in the morning, they had gone into his chamber when they were told he was preaching in his sleep. While there, they listened to him for about an hour and a half. When Gordon and Hyde approached the bed, they "perceived that his eyes did not move at all. His hands and his arms remained closed within his sheets, without any moving; his lips and his tongue only moved, as did his belly by the respiration of his lungs; and the end of his prayer and his Amen savored a sleeping man's speech." Gordon and Hyde added that it was a pity Haydock could not preach so well when he was awake.

> His language was much better in sleeping preaching than it is in his discourse when he is awaked; his method very formal, and in the expounding of his text his preaching very full of learned discourses, his metaphors very fit for his text; the notes gathered out of his text very well appropriated to the matter, and the applications of the doctrine conveniently performed in allegations of Scriptures and sentences of the poets and of the fathers very apt for his purpose.

The king would have particularly appreciated the way Haydock ended his sermon: "In the end he made a Prosopopeia to the King's Majesty, wherein he represented the machinations of Satan by the papists of this kingdom to erect up again idolatry and popery, and ended with a godly prayer."[18]

THE SLEEPING PREACHER COMES TO COURT

By the end of April, Haydock was at court causing a brief sensation. It was known that two or three times a week he was preaching in his sleep, so a variety of people stayed up different nights to see if they would have the chance to hear this strange marvel. When people talked with Haydock while he was awake, they found him to appear honest, and he was not allowed a place to study or books to consult. One night Giles Thompson, the dean of Windsor, and Sir Thomas Chaloner witnessed Haydock's preaching. On another night, Robert Cecil had a bed set up in his drawing room at court, and when Haydock started preaching, he sent for a number of colleagues including William Herbert, Lord Pembroke; Grey Brydges, Lord Chandos; Henry, Lord Danvers; and John Erskine, Lord Mar. All were very impressed by the sermon's organization and clarity. When the sermon was over, Haydock woke up, stretched, and said he remembered nothing about it. The real test, of course, was when James listened to the sleeping preacher.[19] James sat up most of the night so that he could witness the extraordinary event. Haydock appeared deeply asleep at which point he began to pray, with his sermon inveighing against the pope and praising the king as God's representative. When his sermon ended, he continued to sleep.

While others at court declared themselves amazed and accepted Haydock for what he appeared to be, James had doubts. He decided to allow Haydock to get his sleep after the exertion of the sermon, but the next morning, he had the sleeping preacher brought into his presence where he privately quizzed Haydock about the preaching in his sleep, "handling him so like a cunning surgeon," that Haydock finally confessed.[20] Later the story evolved so that it was reported that while James listened to Haydock preaching, to check that he was truly asleep, James pretended to be offended by something Haydock said and threatened to cut off his head with a sword at which Haydock leaped up.[21] On April 30, Edmund Lascelles wrote to the Earl of Shrewsbury: "I have no news to write to your Lordship, but that the admirable strange preacher in his sleep confessed himself to the King's Majesty to be a counterfeit." The same day, John Chamberlain wrote to Dudley Carleton: "Then Haddocke . . . so much followed and admired in Oxford and every where, being sent for to the Court and there plain his [fraud] was discovered and confessed himself an impostor."[22] Haydock explained to the king that while he was still a student at Oxford he regretted that his stutter had kept him from training to be a minister, so he had gone into medicine instead. Haydock remembered that while at Wykeham's School he had been told he spoke in his sleep and that when he did so, the stutter that greatly disturbed his waking speech was refreshingly absent. Haydock had always wanted to be a preacher, but his stutter had stopped him. He wondered whether, if he could wake himself up after his first sleep and speak when no one was with him, he would be able to speak without impediment. The first few nights he attempted this, Haydock spoke to himself about medical practices. When this went smoothly, he began to preach. One night the student in the adjacent room was also awake and heard him, telling people the next day how Haydock had preached brilliantly in his sleep. Instead of confessing that he had actually been awake, Haydock accepted the commendations and continued to preach while supposedly asleep. Once the subterfuge had begun, Haydock explained, he did not know how to end it. Haydock assured James that when he was called to court he told himself he should confess the truth at once, but he was so proud of the reputation that he had established among the learned and judicial men who had heard him preach that he was embarrassed to admit that he was a fraud until the king had taxed him with it.

As he confessed, Haydock went down on his knees and begged the king's forgiveness. James was apparently very proud of himself for exposing Haydock and had liked the pro-monarchy nature of his sermons, so he granted his pardon but demanded that Haydock should write a proper confession that addressed his motives for the fraud, why he continued it, and "if he had been dismissed without discovery he minded to have continued that course of preaching at night."[23] He also required Haydock to preach, where all could observe he was doing it awake, at St. Paul's. Haydock had to acknowledge his offense openly since so many people believed "that his nightly preaching was either by inspiration, or by vision."[24] Haydock later admitted "that I had perfect knowledge of what I spoke, that it was voluntary and waking." He wanted to assure the king and others "that I was led along in this error upon the commendation of others, who hearing me attributed more to those night discourses . . . would needs impute it to sleep, which vainly I winked at, when in my wisdom I should have disclaimed it." Haydock needed the king to know there was nothing treasonous about his pretence: "I never acquainted any with concealment: and therefore could have no combination, plot, or purpose with anyone."[25]

The king also had Cecil write to those in charge of the church at Salisbury and have them search Haydock's rooms. As soon as they got the letter, Thomas Hyde "went to Mr. Haddock's lodging, which by your appointment was sealed up; and find the seals whole as they were left we entered the chamber and opened two of his trunks and a chest of his man's, and perused all the books and papers we could find in the chamber."[26] Hyde could find only one small note that pertained to "divinity," and this he sent on to Cecil. Meanwhile, people kept talking about the wonder that James had exposed as a fraud. Tobie Matthew, the archbishop of York, was told, "You have heard of Haddock though you never ate any. It stinks. The sleeping preacher stinks worse by this time."[27]

King James obviously enjoyed unmasking fakes, and the many astrological responses to the solar eclipse of October 2 caused him to ridicule them in a letter to Cecil. James thought back to the two frauds he had exposed earlier that year since on account of the eclipse, "diverse great mysteries and secrets are discovered and brought to light this year. First a great dreaming divine hath closed his prophetical mouth and taken up his clyster spout again." The king also refers to Anne Gunter and suggests that she and Haydock would make a great couple: "And therefore if any man knows any lawful impediment why this dreaming prophet and possessed maid may not be joined together in the bonds of matrimony let him declare in time."[28] In a more sober fashion, Sir Roger Wilbraham, solicitor general for Ireland, also linked the two cases together. He recorded in his diary the following January that "the king's majesty, since his happy coming, by his own skill hath discovered two notorious impostures: one of a physician that made Latin and learned sermons in the sleep: which he did by secret premeditation: the other of a woman pretended to be bewitched, that cast up at her mouth pins, and pins were taken by diverse in her fits out of her breast."[29]

As one narrates the affair of the sleeping preacher, one thing that becomes apparent is the amount of time, effort, and expense that was expended on it by the order of the king. As Henry Paul points out, by 1605, James "instead of persecuting witches, was trying to find the nature of the strange malady which underlines such delusions,"[30] and this can be said of a number of odd behaviors and experiences. James's interest was so well known that this same year Zacharie Jones translated Pierre de Loyer's *A Treatise of Specters or Straunge Sights, Visions and Apparitions Appearing Sensibly unto Men* and dedicated it to James.[31] James's interests and expenses based on them say a great deal about the nature of his kingship and also, given the affair of the sleeping preacher, of the significance of sleep and dreams.

THOMAS HAWORTH DREAMS OF MURDER

Also in the year 1605 and recorded in both Sir Richard Baker's *A Chronicle of the Kings of England* and in Edmund Howe's continuation of John Stow's *Annales* was a somewhat sensational murder case that was solved because of a dream.[32] The scandal took place in Darwen, a township located in the parish of Blackburn in Lancashire. Darwen was divided into two districts, known at the time as Upper Darwen, or Over Darwen, and Lower Darwen. While Darwen was part of the Blackburn parish, the townspeople felt themselves fiercely independent of the larger neighbor Blackburn. In Darwen in the early modern period, the textile trade developed, with workers spinning and weaving the cloth in their own homes. The major families of town included the Aspinals and the Haworths. Of the thirty-four people listed as major landholders and merchants in Lower Darwen in James's reign, four were Haworths. In 1567, Richard Haworth of Lower Darwen became one of the original governors of the new Grammar School in Blackburn; nearly twenty years later, Lawrence Haworth became one of the governors.[33]

A gardener in Lower Darwen, John Waters often traveled for his work, leaving behind his wife Anne and their six-month-old twins. With her husband away so much, Anne became involved in an affair with Giles Haworth, a landholder. He suggested to Anne that, if they could murder her husband upon his return and bury the body where no one would know, they could claim he had just never come home. Anne agreed, and Haworth hired a poor man named Ribchester to help him. When Waters returned and went to bed, Anne brought Ribchester into the room where her husband slept. The two babies were also asleep in the bed one on either side of John. The sight of the children was too much for the proposed assassin, who went back into the other room and said he could not commit the murder. Giles himself went in and killed John, either by dashing out his brains with an axe or by strangling him—differing accounts describe both methods. Amazingly, the two children were said not to have wakened, though even if they had, they were far too young to know what was happening. With Ribchester's help, Haworth then buried the body under a dunghill in a nearby cow house.

Eventually, the neighbors began to question Anne about the whereabouts of her husband, but Anne claimed he had never returned home and that she had no idea where he was. Concerned townspeople went out on search parties, afraid that John might have fallen into one of the pits that surrounded the town. Their searches were fruitless.

One of Anne's neighbors, Thomas Haworth, listed in the records as a yeoman, found that he had a lot of trouble sleeping; within two weeks of John Waters's disappearance, he started dreaming that the man had been murdered. Thomas told his wife, but she implored him not to tell other people or get involved. Haworth had to pass the Waters' house every day on his way to work, and he would often stop in and ask if there was any news. One day about two months after the murder, he was at the Waters' house at the same time as one of the neighbors who was highly suspicious of Anne; the neighbor said that she thought Waters was dead and buried under the hearthstone. Taken aback, Haworth replied, "And I have dreamed that he is under a stone not far distant." Also in the Waters house at the time was the town constable, Myles Aspinall, who begged Haworth to tell him more about his dreams. Haworth related "I have many a time within this eight weeks dreamed very restlessly, that Waters was murdered and buried under a broad stone in the Cow-house; I have told my troubled dreams to my Wife alone." Though his wife did not want him to tell others his dreams, Haworth explained, "I am not able to conceal my dreams any longer, my sleep departs from me, I am pressed and troubled with fearful dreams which I cannot bear any longer, and they increase upon me." Certainly a recurrent dream of a body buried in a dunghill in the cow house would make anyone lose sleep.[34]

One might wonder if Thomas Haworth had been reading his Chaucer around that time. There had been several editions of *The Canterbury Tales* in the late fifteenth and early sixteenth centuries, and a "complete works" had just been published in 1602. In the "Nun's Priest's Tale," the cock Chanticleer's terrible dream of his own murder by a fox leads to a long discussion between him and his favorite wife, the hen Pertelote. Pertelote is appalled that his dream caused him such fear, telling him he has lost her heart because she cannot love a coward.

> Alas, and can you be afraid of dreams?

Pertelote describes dreams as caused by vapors from the belly and discusses the humoral theory of dreams from such ancient authorities as Cato. Chanticleer proves that a cock can be as well read as a hen and describes a story he read of two comrades off on a pilgrimage together. One night, they came to a town where they could not find lodging together, so they separated for the night. One found lodging in a yard with oxen and plough; the other went elsewhere and that night had a dream:

> This man met in his bed, there as he lay,
> Now that his fellow upon him called,
> And said "Alas, for in an ox's stall,

This night shall I be murdered, there I lie:
Now help me dear brother, or I die."

The dreamer awoke in terror, but once awake, he paid no attention to the dream, rolled over, and went back to sleep. He kept having the dream until it changed. This time, his friend came to him to tell him that he had been killed for his money. He advised his friend that he must rise early and go to the west gate, where he would there see

A cart full of dung there shall you see,
In which my body is hid full prively,
Do thou that cart arrest boldly.

At dawn, the friend went to where his friend had spent the night and called for him, but the innkeeper assured him that his friend had already left. Thinking of his dream, the man rushed off to the western gate and saw a dung cart. The man shouted

"My fellow murdered this same night,
And in this cart he lies, gaping upright."
. . . .
The people cast the cart to ground,
And in the middle of the dung they found
The dead man, that murdered was all new.[35]

The town officers arrested the carter and the innkeeper; both confessed to the murder and were subsequently hanged. Chanticleer was convinced that God had revealed the murder in the dream because "Murder will out." Chaucer's *The Canterbury Tales* was certainly well known at the time of the Waters murder, and specifically that story of a murdered body in a dung heap. Thomas Walkington, in his discussion of dreams in *The Optick Glasse of Humors,* refers to "the merry tale of the Nuns priest." William Vaughan alludes to the same story when he states that, of the many examples of foretelling dreams he has read about, "this one seems the most strange." Josiah Dare's *Counsellor Manners: His Last Legacy to His Son* relates the same story as an example "that divine justice will not suffer murder to go undiscovered."[36]

In 1605, the Constable took Haworth's dream just as seriously, and he immediately searched the cow house where he did indeed discover the murdered body of John Waters. Ribchester and Giles Haworth managed to flee and were never found. Anne, however, was arrested. At first, she denied having anything to do with her husband's death, but realizing how dire her situation was, "she saw no hope of life and then became penitent."[37] Anne confessed to the murder and was convicted of petty treason. Legally in late medieval and early modern England, the murder of a husband by a wife and a servant of a master was carefully distinguished from other forms of murder and was considered equivalent to high treason. Anne Waters was burned to death on 22 August 1608; the punishment for petty treason was a far more horrific death than the methods, such as hanging or beheading, used to execute other murderers.

Unlike manslaughter, murder—the premeditated death of someone—was relatively rare in Elizabethan and Jacobean England. Only about 5 percent of all persons on trial for felony were suspected murderers, and of those only a bit over one quarter were women, though if the suspect was a woman, overwhelmingly her victim was male.[38] Statistics of domestic murders suggest that husbands were more than twice as likely to murder their wives as wives their husbands.[39] But there were more than a dozen recorded cases of wives murdering husbands that were described in murder pamphlets, recorded in chronicles such as Holinshed's or Stow's *Annales,* or even dramatized, such as the 1592 play, *The Lamentable and True Tragedy of M. Arden of Feversham.*[40] The description of the Waters murder in Stow's and Baker's histories is, therefore, not all that unusual, but the murderer being discovered through a dream is.

DREAMS CAUSE MURDERS

In a sermon Cardinal Reginald Pole preached on 2 December 1554, he stated that "in sleep men dream sometimes of killing."[41] And indeed, it was more likely for a dream to cause someone to commit murder than for someone to be able to discover a murderer through a dream. In 1572 when John Kynnestar explained why he stabbed his wife to death, he said that before they went to bed they had been merry and there had been no quarreling. But as he slept, he said, a thought came into his head that told him, "Arise go kill thy wife." Kynnestar said he then awoke in a "marvelous rage," went downstairs, got a knife, came back to the bedroom, and stabbed his wife many times in the heart. As the constable was taking him to jail later that night, he asked Kynnestar why he had committed this dreadful crime. Kynnestar freely explained how the idea had come to him in his sleep. Found guilty of murder, Kynnestar was hanged.[42]

A murder pamphlet also published in 1605, the year of the Waters murder, described the "tragic and desperate end of Sir John Fites." Fites lived in Wistocke in Devonshire about ten miles from the city of Plymouth. He was the much-loved son of an older man who made sure his child was well educated. The father did his best to give his son every possible advantage, including arranging a marriage for him with a wealthy, sweet-tempered woman. Yet Fites lived a dissipated life of violence, drunkenness, and womanizing. After turning his wife out of his house, he became convinced that his father-in-law was out to destroy him. He fled his home and stopped at an inn on his way to London. While sleeping there that night, "in his dreams he muttered fearful words, grievous sighs, and deep-fetched groans: most fearful were his visions, and so terrible unto him, that where he lay in rest he suddenly start[ed] up, and called for his horses, intending to post presently away."

Later that night, he stopped at a house and begged a bed from a laborer who kindly gave up his own conjugal bed and sat up with him. Fites killed the man and wounded the man's wife before killing himself.[43] Not only did dreams prompt violence against others, they could also lead to self-murder. Philip Goodwin wrote, "I have read of a man, who dreaming he had lost his money, awaked in a fright and immediately went and murdered himself."[44]

Just as dreams could cause people to commit murder and allow murders to be discovered, they could also prevent murder as well. In the mid-seventeenth century, the minister Vavasour Powell compiled a book describing the spiritual experiences of a number of believers from his congregation, including a woman known only by her initials M. K. She stated, "When I take a view of my life upon the stage of this world, I may very well compare it to a comic tragedy, or a tragic comedy." M. K. may well have been cryptically referring to her plan to murder someone. She had gone through a spiritual conversion as a child and was devastated by the death of first her mother and then her father. She later married and moved to a house in Westminster. M. K. and particularly her husband began spending time "with some company which did not only cause much time to be spent in idleness, but also almost all our means." The worst of the group was a man "who gave his mind to drinking, and other vices . . . [he] was never well contented without my husband's company." M. K., afraid of what would happen to her and her husband if they continued to live their lives in this fashion, kept begging her husband, often on her knees, not to spend time with his friend, "or at least not to suffer him to come so often home to our house." Her husband refused to listen. M. K., later thinking that she had let the devil into her heart or she would never even have considered this plan, decided to murder her husband's friend, and began looking for an opportunity. "Then one night (in my sleep) I thought I was in a very large chamber, sitting behind a table covered with a green carpet, upon which lay all manner of instruments which proclaim death; suddenly the man came into the chamber, whom so soon as I espied to be alone, catching up a weapon in my hand, I resolved there to commit the horrid act of murder upon his body." Then the dream changed and M. K. heard God tell her to desist. God stated, " 'Vengeance is mine'; to which voice I answered aloud, 'And thou wilt repay, O Lord.' " Upon awaking, M. K. gave up all thought of murder.[45]

Most people who dreamed of murder did not solve murders, commit murders, or resist committing murder because of dreams. Margaret Charlton Baxter had several such dreams. Samuel Clark, who was a friend both to her and her husband, the minister Richard Baxter, wrote that Margaret "dreamed much of fire, and murders, and these dreams augmented her fears, so she could not endure the clapping of a door, nor any sudden noise." Margaret Charlton came from a long-established gentry family in Shropshire and was born at Apley Castle. Her father died in 1642, when she was only six and her younger brother three. To protect her family in a time of war, her mother Margaret soon after married the royalist Thomas Hanmer, and he moved into the family home. But in 1644, the Parliamentarians took the castle. The soldiers were "storming her mother's house, firing and burning down part of it; plundering and killing some, and threatening the rest." Margaret was a witness, and Clarke stated that Margaret "had a diseased fearfulness, against which she had little more free-will, or power, then a man in an ague fit, hath against shaking." Perhaps this condition was caused by the traumatic event of her youth as well as other traumas; these may have permanently affected her in both her waking and sleeping life.[46]

LANCASHIRE: A PLACE FOR SUPERNATURAL DREAMING

We know much more about the Waters murder than just the information found in accounts given in more contemporary chronicles. Almost fifty years after the scandal, Thomas Haworth's then aged widow and his son gave a thorough description of the event—a description that John Webster, a medical doctor, included in his *The Displaying of Supposed Witchcraft*. We might wonder about Thomas Haworth's dreams. Though none of the sources mention any relationship between Thomas and Anne's lover, the two men do have the same last name, a name that filled the records of early modern Lower Darwen. Possibly Giles was Thomas's cousin, and Thomas had heard something that made him suspicious when John Waters disappeared. Perhaps he had heard something that even suggested where the body had been buried. As we shall see throughout this book, many people at the time believed that dreams might come from natural causes, from demons, or from God and the angels. No one at the time believed in a natural cause for this particular dream. Webster was convinced that Haworth's dream could not be demonic in nature because a dream that exposed a murder was serving divine justice.

It might be significant that this case occurred in Lancashire, a county that had a high number of cases dealing with the supernatural. One reason for this fact may have been that, as Michael Mullett and J. A. Sharpe suggest, Lancashire lay on "religious fault lines." The contestation between Catholic and Protestant often showed itself in witchcraft accusations and efforts to deal with demonic possession.[47] Lancashire was the site of two famous cases of witchcraft trials. The Pendle Forest case of 1612 led to the execution of ten people, making it the first case that had such a high death rate in England. The accusations of the boy Edmund Robinson could have led to mass executions in 1634 if, first, the assize judge and then the Privy Council had not intervened. Altogether there were over one hundred and twenty accusations in Lancashire.[48] Thomas Cooper argued in *The Mystery of Witch-Craft,* published in 1617, that the Lancashire trials of five years earlier had occurred in a region of "gross ignorance and popery."[49]

HAYDOCK'S APOLOGY

While the murder case was going on in Lancashire, Richard Haydock returned to Salisbury to resume his medical practice and begin writing his tract on dreams that he would dedicate to James. Over the next months, he worked on this text so that he could, essentially, provide a more formal apology to the king. Haydock emphasized that he wished to show "my self prostrate in thankfulness" to James by presenting him with "my broken and distracted meditations of the nature of dreams." Haydock had certainly studied beliefs about dreams from antiquity forward, and his definitions and classification of dreams are useful as an introduction to understanding ideas about dreams in early modern England. These concepts are discussed in more detail in chapter 2.

Haydock argued that not everyone dreams, stating that "histories mention some never to be molested with dreams." He believed dreams were not necessary for one to enjoy good health. Moise Amyraut, however, countered that while some never dreamed, not all people remembered their dreams. When vapors in the body are "gross and in great plenty, the images of things recalled from the memory, are there so swallowed up," that people either do not dream, or if they do, "it is attended with so much weakness and obscurity, that when we awake, we remember nothing of what we dreamed." As a result of the nature of the vapors, "some, though very few, never dream at all; because the vapors that arise in their sleep, are always thick and darksome."[50] For those that do, he defined a dream as "consisting of a fantasy, so is this composed of images and shapes produced by motion, without which there can be no dream." He wanted to differentiate between dreams and reality: "If the things appearing were continually firm and fixed, there would be as much coherence and reason in dreams as in our waking meditations." But, of course, this is not the case. "It falls out in our dreams, as when a stone is cast into the water, from which arises presently a circle, which instantly begets another, and yet a third, and so more successively, until it comes to the bank, and so vanishes: so in sleep, does one image and form tread upon the heel of another, and the latter still supplant the former, till all the matter of it and sleep be spent, and we awake." He added that the "fantasy must be free, or else there can be no dream."

Haydock declares that there are three types of dreams. The first happens because of the predominant humor that a person has in his or her body. The four humours are as follows: choleric, which suggests a hot and fiery nature that causes someone to be inclined to be wrathful, irascible, hot-tempered, passionate, and easily enraged; sanguine, which means that one is courageous, hopeful, amorous, and confident of success but also delights in causing bloodshed; phlegmatic, which indicates that someone is without passion, not easily excited or moved to action, but also stolidly calm, self-possessed, and imperturbable; and finally melancholic, which means a pensive, thoughtful, meditative, and reflective personality but often disposed to depression, sorrow, and sullenness. An imbalance of humours could lead to nightmares. Haydock referred to dreams caused by humours as natural. Those who are choleric can be troubled by dreams of "apparitions of fire and flaming ensigns [tokens]," while the sanguine "hath often a confused imagination of Red Colors or blood." The phlegmatic dreams of water, rivers, and snow, but the melancholic has "fearful visions of darnes [secrets], tortures, etc." Haydock's descriptions of the various types of dreams are fairly typical, as we shall see over the course of the book.

One can assume that Haydock, eager to please his king, had read *Daemonology*. He echoed James's definition of the nightmare of the incubus as not being a demonic visitation but in fact a result of someone so oppressed by a multitude of "gross vapors" that he thinks he is "overlain by some hag." This idea was common at the time, and not at all original to the king, but it still suggests the connections between James's and Haydock's views of dreams.

The second type of dream comes from "the daily affairs about which we have been last busied and employed," what Thomas Nashe refers to as the "fragments of the day." Haydock categorized such dreams as animal and claimed that these are the most common type of dreams. Haydock argued that dreams that resemble waking events "in the same substance, method and order" as they actually happened "signify health," but if they are distorted and disturbing, they "argue distemper, and so much the greater, by how much they are more repugnant." Dreams can demonstrate health or sickness. "In an exact tempered body are found more coherent dreams, whereas in the contrary habit nothing but wild antic histories are adumbrated."

The third type is the most significant, as these dreams are "instilled and infused into the mind supernaturally." These dreams might be from God, but they could also be from the devil and "so must be a damnable illusion." In spite of their importance, these are also dreams that Haydock did not choose to discuss at any length "because these appertain more properly to divinity," and he "dares not presume to undergo so high a task." Perhaps because of James's disdain for the idea of supernatural dreams, Haydock did not wish to get involved in what he might consider an ideological quagmire. He ended his manuscript with the hope that God would "direct all our cogitations both waking and sleeping that neither willfully nor unawares we give any offence whatsoever."[51]

There is, as far as I have been able to discover, only one copy of Haydock's manuscript, and we have no evidence that James ever received it. Of course, the manuscript is dated 20 November 1605, and in November of 1605, James had far more serious issues to be concerned about than his "great dreaming divine" that he had joked about the month before. It appears from the manuscript that Haydock had written it not only for the king but also with an eye toward publication, since he stated early in his manuscript that he did "so desire I to reconcile the world to me again. . . . None can more condemn me, than I do my self." He also remarked, "If it seem difficult and obscure to the ordinary reader, it is not so much my fault as the matters which can hardly be explained, but to the learned and intelligent, especially in few words, which is my desire." This sounds a bit self-serving, but it might also have been a means to flatter James. In 1598, Haydock had published his translation of Lomazzo, so he did have some experience with the mechanics of publication. But whatever Haydock had planned, this manuscript never made it to print. It may have been his refusal to address supernatural dreams that made the manuscript, in the end, of less interest.

DREAMS AND THE GUNPOWDER PLOTTERS

Even if Haydock's text never sparked attention, dreams, as phenomena, were certainly being discussed in the aftermath of November 1605. The idea of blowing up Parliament was first bruited by Robin Catesby at a meeting on Sunday, 20 May 1604, at a London inn called the Duck and Drake, which was apparently also a Catholic safe house. Also at the meeting were Thomas Wintour, John Wright, Thomas Percy, and Guy Fawkes. While some were at first skeptical, Catesby, "a man of great charm, strength, and personal magnetism," in Joel Hurstfield's words, soon convinced them to go along with the plot.[52] Robert Keyes, a cousin of John Wright, joined the conspiracy in October 1604; in December, Thomas Bates, a retainer of Robin Catesby, agreed to participate. On Lady Day, March 25, then recognized as the first day of the new year 1605, more men were brought into the conspiracy: John Wright's brother Christopher, Tom Wintour's brother-in-law John Grant, and Tom's older brother Robert. In September, Ambrose Rookwood and Francis Tresham joined. The final conspirator was Sir Everard Digby, bringing the number up to an unfortunate thirteen. Some of those involved in the conspiracy had been on the edges of the plotting that took place with Robert Devereux, the Earl of Essex, only a few years previously; they had hoped that if Essex prevailed there would be more toleration for Catholics. The disillusionment after the failure of Essex's uprising may have led to this later plotting.[53]

Robert Wintour, who inherited Huddington Court near Worcester as well as a considerable fortune, was known for his generosity, but many considered him far less lively and clever than his dynamic younger brother Tom. They and their sister Dorothy, who married John Grant, were all devout Catholics. Their maternal uncle, the priest Francis Ingleby, a follower of Cardinal William Allen, was hanged, drawn, and quartered in 1586, which must have had a profound impact on the Wintours. With Robert as owner, Huddington Court became a refuge for priests, and mass was secretly celebrated there. Robert's wife was Gertrude Talbot whose family had suffered greatly as recusants; her father John had spent nearly twenty years in prison. By 1605, John Talbot was at liberty; he did not want to jeopardize his freedom, and claimed a strong allegiance to his king.[54]

After Fawkes and the gunpowder were discovered in the early hours of November 5, the members of the Privy Council were awakened and gathered in James's bedchamber. The prisoner, calling himself John Johnson, was brought there for questioning but refused to admit anything except what had already been established, that he worked for Thomas Percy and, had he not been discovered, would have blown up Parliament with the king there. It is said he told the king, in what must have sounded especially nightmarish in the early hours of the morning of the fifth, that if he could have, he would have been delighted to have blown both James and his Scottish courtiers all the way back to his mountainous first home.[55] James concluded that had the plot been successful, there would have been "a spectacle so terrible and terrifying that its like has never been heard." That the plot was to blow up James with gunpowder must have made it even more nightmarish because Henry Stuart, Lord Darnley, the father he never knew, had been killed when the house in which he was staying was blown up by gunpowder. When the Venetian Ambassador Nicolo Molin wrote home about the plot, he reported that, upon reading the Mounteagle letter, James stated, "I remember that my father died by gunpowder." Actually, Darnley had managed to escape the house before the explosion, only to be strangled in the garden. George Buchanan, who passionately believed Mary Stuart guilty of Darnley's murder, had been appointed James's tutor when he was only three years old, so James had been raised on stories of his father's death.[56]

The night that Fawkes was arrested, the government immediately issued a warrant for the arrest of Thomas Percy. James's government was desperate enough to send someone to the fashionable astrologer Simon Forman, asking him to discover through his knowledge of the stars where Thomas Percy might be. Forman was one of the most famous of a number of professional astrologers of the Elizabethan and Jacobean era who cast nativities and interpreted dreams for their clients. Forman had already been consulted about the outcome of the 1597 Parliament, the siege of Ostend, and the Earl of Essex's invasion of Ireland. While Forman did not in the end give information that allowed the government to find Percy, he did offer the prediction that "Saturn, being Lord of the Eighth house [of death] shows that the fugitive shall be taken by commandment of the Prince, and in being taken, shall be slain."[57]

Though Fawkes at first refused to name other conspirators, rumors were spreading not only in the Westminster area but also throughout the capital. Christopher Wright overheard Lord Worcester summoning Mounteagle to go with him and rushed to the Duck and Drake to tell Tom Wintour that "the matter is discovered."[58] The other conspirators in London fled the city. Ambrose Rookwood found Robin Catesby and some of the others in Bedfordshire and told him of the disaster. Tom Wintour headed to his brother Robert's house at Huddington. Catesby insisted that they still might triumph, and at that time several more Catholics they knew joined them, including Stephen Littleton and Henry Morgan. They all met up at Huddington in the afternoon of November 6. Though Fawkes had held out for two successive days as "he underwent the most excruciating torture without saying anything,"[59] by November 7 he began to talk, and that day a proclamation for the arrest of the other conspirators was issued. Also on November 7, the gunpowder discovered was transported to the Tower of London and stored within the office of Ordinance.

Robert Wintour was not sleeping well those days. In the early hours of November 7, all the conspirators went to confession, took the sacrament, and then rode off to Stephen Littleton's house, Holbeach House near Kingswinford, just inside Staffordshire. On their way, they stopped at

Whewell Grange, the home of Thomas, Lord Windsor, and seized a large store of arms, including more gunpowder, which they conveyed away in an open cart. The conspirators reached Holbeach House about ten o'clock at night. They believed this was a house they could fortify, and they would make their last stand there. Tom Wintour thought they should ask Robert's father-in-law, John Talbot, for help. Robert absolutely refused, saying that he knew Talbot could not be wooed away from his allegiance to the king. Tom decided to try anyway, and Stephen Littleton went with him.

The gunpowder the conspirators had brought with them had been drenched with rain. While Tom Wintour and Stephen Littleton were off on their errand, the others decided to attempt to dry it out. Without intending to, they finally got their gunpowder explosion. Clearly they were both exhausted and desperate, as it was the height of foolishness to spread the gunpowder out in front of the open fire to dry. A spark flew out of the fire and ignited the gunpowder. The violent blaze engulfed Robin Catesby, Ambrose Rookwood, John Grant, and Henry Morgan. Grant was blinded and Morgan fairly seriously injured; Rookwood was also scorched and shaken.

As Tom Wintour and Stephen Littleton were on their way back to Holbeach after John Talbot angrily dismissed them, a messenger reached them with the news that because of an explosion some of the conspirators were dead and the rest dispersed. Littleton fled, but Wintour decided to return to Holbeach House to see what had happened. While some, including Wintour's brother Robert, had left hurriedly, Tom found that the messenger had exaggerated—Robin Catesby and some others had remained. The next day, Sir Richard Walsh, Sheriff of Worcestershire, arrived with 200 men, and the conspirators made their last stand. Most of them were killed or died very soon after. Robin Catesby and Thomas Percy, standing together, were killed by a single bullet; Forman's prediction for Percy that, "in being taken," he would "be slain" turned out to be true. Tom Wintour, however, while seriously wounded, survived and was taken to the Tower. In the meanwhile, Robert Wintour met with Stephen Littleton and managed to elude capture until early January.

After he had been captured and was being examined, Robert Wintour spoke about a dream that he had had only a few nights before the explosion was to take place. Wintour described his disturbing dream that included churches that had been attacked, steeples falling down, and men with "strange and unknown faces inside the churches," also looking very damaged. After the accident at Holbeach House, Robert Wintour, who had not been injured, saw "much disfigured the faces and countenances of Grant, Rookwood, and others. Then did Winter call to mind his dream, and to his remembrance thought that the faces of his associates so scorched, resembled those which he had seen in his dream."[60] Attorney General Edward Coke argued at Wintour's trial that it was providential that the whole house did not go up in flames so that all inside perished, as that would have made it far more difficult to understand the plot with so many of the conspirators dead before they could be examined. Wintour's dream obviously appeared important to

the government in putting on its case against the accused. Coke discussed it
not only in Wintour's own trial but also in the trial of Henry Garnet.

> But by evident confession it appears, that the very night when the powder
> should have wrought the desperate effect, either the light of reason, the horror
> of vexation, or the power of revelation, presented to Robert Winter in a dream,
> the faces of his chief friends, and the highest traitors that should have acted exe-
> cution upon the bloody stage, in such a ghastly and ugly figure, more like to that
> "malus genius" which appeared on to Brutus the night before his death, or the
> face of Hector that appeared onto Andromache, or the countenance which they
> themselves held afterward upon the pinnacles of the parliament, than to that fig-
> ure of beatitude by which their own fantastical conceits and alluding apprehen-
> sions were too much flattered.[61]

Coke's description of the explosion at Holbeach House, as well as other
descriptions of the event, conveyed the strong sense that it was only right that
those who had wanted to use gunpowder to blow up the king should themselves be damaged by it: "the pit they dug, they fell in" is repeated again and
again in the discussion of Wintour's dream and the explosion of Holbeach
house, an echo of Psalm 35, verse 6: "They have dug a pit before me, into the
midst whereof they are fallen [themselves]."

While Coke argued that Wintour's dream may well have been a "revelation" of the future accident, an examination of the definitions of dreams in
Thomas Nashe's *The Terrors of the Night,* published in 1594, suggests a more
psychological explanation for Wintour's dream. Nashe claimed, "A dream is
nothing else but a bubbling scum or froth of the fancy, which the day hath
left undigested. . . . In the daytime we torment our thoughts and imaginations with sundry cares and devices; all the nighttime they quake and tremble
after the terror of their late suffering, and still continue thinking of the per-
plexities they have endured."[62] Nashe, in what we might consider a very
modern perspective, believed that all of our sins and the guilt on our consciences return to haunt us at night.

The Wintour dream continued to hold fascination for those in the seventeenth century who wrote about the plot. In 1641, John Vicar published
November 5 1605: The Quintessence of Cruelty, a rhyming translation of the
1606 Francis Herring *Pietas Pontificia.* Robert Wintour's dream plays a significant role. After stating that because of the explosion the conspirators "all
stood astonished, pale-faced, faint affright," Vicars then described the dream
in some detail:

> Yea, Robert Winter, but the day before
> This fearful chance (to make his horror more)
> Dreamt, that he churches saw, and as it were,
> Steeples to stand awry, and with much fear,
> That in those churches he strange faces saw;
> This sad event, these to his thoughts did draw,

And caused him, that, to his dream to mind to call,
And thereof, thus, made him resolve withall,
That sure those faces which did there appear,
Were right like these that now before him were;
And did unto him rightly show the frame,
And shapes of these whom thus the powder-flame
Had scorched and burnt. This him amazed, much,
And did his traitorous heart most deeply touch.[63]

WHY WERE DREAMS IMPORTANT?

Sixteenth- and seventeenth-century England was a time of great change in terms of religious beliefs, the concept of the individual, and the role of the monarch. Along with these changes were the multiplicity of beliefs and attitudes toward dreams and the working mind and spirit while asleep. The case of the sleeping preacher and the Waters murder of 1605 are not connected except for the coincidence that both happened in the same year and that both received substantial contemporary attention as significant events. Three seventeenth-century texts—chronicles by Richard Baker and John Stow, and John Webster's work on witchcraft—discuss these two incidents in close proximity to each other. The same year, Robert Wintour's dream received even more publicity, as it was discussed during the trials of the Gunpowder plotters, all of whom were, of course, executed. As the story of the discovery of the Gunpowder Plot developed in the days after Fawkes had been apprehended, James's role became more central. Thomas Egerton, Lord Ellesmere and Lord Chancellor, in a speech to Parliament on November 9 described the plot and gave full credit to the king for interpreting the cryptic warning in the letter Mounteagle received.[64]

As discussed earlier, William Barlow preached a sermon of thanksgiving at Paul's Cross the following day. He spoke about the horrors of the plot and of James's ability to understand the hidden meaning of the letter that betrayed it. Barlow praised King James's intuition in understanding the meaning of the Mounteagle letter, helping to cement the official story that it was the king's inspiration to divine the hidden meaning in the letter that allowed him to understand, and therefore expose, the plot. Barlow suggested that James's mind might have leapt to this conclusion because of remembering what had happened to his father. "By his Majesty's apprehension, who though he walks securely, in the sincerities of his conscience . . . yet his heart have him (by some words in that letter) that there might be some fiery engine, perhaps remembering his father's case, who was blown up with powder."[65] That James had already received much fame for his cleverness in unmasking the frauds of Richard Haydock and Anne Gunter may well have helped establish the belief that James could almost magically unlock any mystery—and of course some of the mysteries of the age were dreams.

During his reign, James had two other close experiences with dreams that people noted. In the spring of 1617, James decided to return to Scotland, but his wife Anna had a fearsome dream of James being in great danger if he were to go. But as we know, James claimed that, while dreams may have been prophetic before and up through the age of Christ, they no longer had that power. As Colonel Henderson wrote to Dudley Carleton, "The King will set out March 15, and be at Edinburgh May 15. Neither dreams nor predictions alter his resolution."[66] James was, however, far more willing to believe in the significance of a dream of his own that occurred a few years later. In March 1622, the Reverend Joseph Mead wrote to Sir Martin Stuteville to say he had heard from Mr. Downham, who had newly come from London, of a disturbing dream James had of his old childhood tutor George Buchanan. "His master, Buchanan, who seemed to check him severely, as he used to do; and his majesty . . . seemed desirous to pacify him." Buchanan, "with a frowning countenance," turned away from James, but said some verses, "which his majesty, perfectly remembering, repeated the next day, and many took notice of them." In September of the same year, the Venetian ambassador Girolamo Lando wrote in one of his dispatches that the people of England

> tell secretly of a dream his Majesty had some months ago, when his old tutor Buchanan appeared to him and predicted his fate in verse, that soon afterwards he would fall into ice, and then into fire that he would endure frequent pain, and die after two years. When the king awoke he had it put in writing by some of the most intimate gentlemen of his chamber. The two accidents of water and fire have actually occurred, although the last, in his own chamber, has been kept a profound secret.[67]

While James may have dismissed Anna's dream as foolishness, he apparently was shaken by his own, and so were many other people deeply moved by the dreams they encountered. This wide range of beliefs in dreams and their meanings permeated the lives of the people of early modern England, as we can see in the excitement over the sermons preached by Richard Haydock when he was supposedly asleep, in murder cases and pamphlets, as part of the testimony of the treason trials of Gunpowder plotters, and in the fear of an aging king. In chapter 2, there is further examination of just how many different ways dreams could be interpreted and expressed.

CHAPTER 2

THEORISTS AND PRACTITIONERS:
DREAMING ABOUT THE LIVING
AND THE DEAD

There were wide-ranging beliefs about dreams in early modern England. For some, at least, belief in the efficacy of dreams was the early modern version of believing one could win the lottery. One dream story current in the sixteenth and seventeenth centuries would have definitely encouraged people to believe in their dreams and to act on them. In 1693, Abraham de la Pryme recorded in his diary a description of a "constant tradition" that happened in "former times" in Swaffham, Norfolk. At that time, a peddler had the dream that if he went to London Bridge and stood at a specific place he "should hear very joyful news." At first the peddler ignored the dream, but after the third time he had it, he decided to go to London and see what would happen, even though London was ninety miles away. After standing for two or three days at the place on the bridge that most resembled the one in his dream, he began to wonder if he had wasted his time—a feeling that was soon reenforced, only to be exploded. A shopkeeper had noticed him standing there and asked him what he was doing. When the peddler told him, the shopkeeper laughed at him for being a fool. He added, "I'll tell thee, country fellow, last night I dreamed that I was at Sopham, in Norfolk, a place utterly unknown to me, where, I thought behind a peddler's house, in a certain orchard, and under a great oak tree, if I dug, I should find a vast treasure! Now think you that I am such a fool to take such a long journey upon me upon the instigation of a silly dream? No, no, I'm wiser. Therefore, good fellow, learn wit of me, and get you home, and mind your business."

While the peddler thanked the shopkeeper for his advice, he was secretly delighted to understand the real meaning of his dream. Now it all made sense: He immediately went home, dug in his garden, and found "a prodigious great treasure," which made him very wealthy. He decided to use some of his wealth to rebuild the crumbling church in his village. De la Pryme ended the story by writing, "to this day there is his statue therein, cut in stone, with his pack at his back, and his dog at his heels; and his memory is also preserved by the same form or picture in most of the old glass windows, taverns, and alehouses of that town, unto this day."[1]

Just as narrative and individuals take on many shapes in dreams, so too are there a number of different versions of this legend. In some, the peddler cannot feed his family and is so despondent that he is thinking of jumping off the bridge when the scoffing stranger relates his dream. In others, his wife scorns him for carrying out the dictates of a dream that wastes time and money for the London trip. Sometimes the man is not a peddler at all, but a tinker, someone who traveled about mending pots and pans. In other versions, he has to dig under an apple tree that is way out in the north of town.[2] In Swaffham today, the story from the Official Guide of the town's history states that the peddler was John Chapman and that he followed the instructions that had "reputed to have been given to him repeatedly in dreams." This version then details that Chapman went to London Bridge, heard from the shopkeeper who scorned his own dream, and returned to dig in his own garden where he found two large pots of gold.[3] There was a John Chapman in Swaffham in the fifteenth century who was probably a wool merchant and churchwarden of the Church of St. Peter and St. Paul. The Swaffham Black Book, an inventory of all the work done on the church between 1435 and 1474 and recorded by John Botewright, states that the rector, John Chapman paid for rebuilding the North Aisle. Chapman is buried in the church, which also has a statue of the "peddler of Swaffham," who provided so generously after he was enriched through the help of dreams.[4]

In early modern England, many people from all social strata believed in the importance of dreams. There was also a long history of belief about the different sources of dreams. Dreams might be simply the fragments of the day retold or the result of food or drink. They might also be occurrences "proceeding only from the constitution of the heavens, or dispositions of the air, or from previous cogitations, or from the temper of the body, or from the affection of the mind, or from the procuration of the devil, and only some few from the operation of good angels," as Isaac Ambrose explained in his book, *Ministrations of, and Communication with Angels.*[5] This belief system continued throughout the period. In 1700 a man named Andrew Perry wrote to Anthony Sharp, a noted Quaker, for advice. Though Perry himself was not a Quaker, he was deeply concerned about the potential religious significance of dreams. Sharpe responded that good dreams came from God, the evil ones from the flesh or the devil, and those that were neither good nor evil came from a "multitude of thoughts." The way to understand which was which, Sharpe explained, was to seek Christ and love and obey him.[6]

Some dream interpreters believed in all types of dreams, while many others were convinced of either the natural or supernatural nature of dreams. Many were convinced that if they could unlock the meaning of the dream, they could know the future. Scholars went back to much earlier dream books, especially the famous ancient dream book by Artemidorus, *Oneirocritica,* composed about 200 CE. It was available in England in a Latin translation in 1546. After the first edition of the English translation was published in 1606, it went through a number of subsequent editions in the seventeenth century.[7] Thomas Hill's *The Pleasant Art of the Interpretations of Dreams,* first published in 1576, was based in part on the famous earlier text, *Oneirocritica.* Hill popularized a variety of topics such as gardening, astronomy, and physiognomy, as well as dream interpretation.[8] Artemidorus's work had been a place where the theories of the learned and the suppositions of the populace converged. He told his readers that he used the works of the learned but also consulted with "the soothsayers of the marketplace."[9] Over a thousand years later, Hill did the same thing, and his book was apparently widely read (or at least widely purchased): It went through seven editions in the first fifty years. There were also editions of simply English translations of Artemidorus. The first, published in 1606, was based on a French translation of the Latin translation of the Greek original. Three more English editions of Artemidorus were published in the seventeenth century. Many argued that dreams were prognostications if one could only understand the symbolism. Some dreams, however, such as the one just recounted, were so straightforward that all one had to do was follow the instructions. In other cases, it was important to know the meaning of dreams so that one could evade the future the dreams seemed to portend. William Lilly published a list of what dreams foretold so "that a man partly knowing of any bad fortune that will befall him, may by prayer to Almighty God, and keeping himself in his chamber for that day, he may (through God's assistance) prevent the danger, which otherwise might have fallen on him."[10] But dreams could inform someone of terrible events to come, such as the death of a child, and there was nothing the dreamer could do to avoid the fate. Some such dreams were said to come to women during pregnancy.

MORNING DREAMS AND MOURNING DREAMS

In 1660, Alice Thornton recorded in her diary a dream that she had when she was pregnant and near her time. In the dream, the white sheets of her bed were sprinkled all over with blood. The dream "so frightened me that I told my aunt of it in the morning; but she put it off as well as she could, and said dreams were not to be regarded." However, Thornton could not get over her dream; "I kept it in my mind till my child died."[11] Seventy years earlier, in 1590, Margaret Russell, Countess of Cumberland, was already the mother of two sons when she became pregnant with her third child. She dreamed that a presence came to her, explaining that "she should be delivered a little while after of a daughter which should be the only child to her parents and live to inherit the ancient lands of her father's ancestors." As a child, Lady Anne Clifford frequently heard this story from her mother, who assured her "that the ancient lands of her father's inheritance would at last come to be hers, what opposition so ever was made to hinder it."[12] Margaret believed this so strongly because the first part of the prophecy had tragically come to pass; her elder son died only a month after her dream and her younger one when Anne was sixteen months old. For Anne, the recounting of this dream was important as evidence that *she,* not a male cousin, should have the family estates.

Dreams warning about the death of a child, a spouse, or a parent were all too common. In 1603 the playwright Ben Jonson and his friend and former teacher William Camden were staying at Sir Robert Cotton's house in Huntingdonshire. Jonson dreamed that his seven-year-old son Benjamin, who was in London at the time, came to him with the "Mark of a bloody cross on his forehead as if it had been cut with a sword." The next morning, highly distressed, Jonson went into Camden's room and related the dream; Camden attempted to reassure Jonson by telling him it was "but an apprehension of his fantasy at which he should not be dejected." Later that day, however, Jonson received a letter from his wife telling him that their son had died of the plague.[13] To put this story into perspective, we learn of it from William Drummond, to whom Ben Jonson told it when he visited him in Scotland in 1618, fifteen years later. We cannot know if it would have been presented differently right after the event. Memories, like dreams, can alter chronology and change both direction and meaning.

A commonly held belief was that, if one had "secret passages of sympathy" with someone, one could learn of their death through a dream. Francis Bacon, a man with a reputation for high intellect and rationality, wrote in *Novum Organum* that believing in dreams, as foretelling, was superstition and that people "take note of events where they are fulfilled, but where they are not (even if this happens much more often), they disregard them and pass them by." But even he argued that those who loved each other could know of each other's fortunes through dreams. "I myself remember, that being in Paris, and my father dying in London, two or three days before my father's death I had a dream, which I told to diverse English gentlemen, that my father's house in the country was plastered all over with black mortar."[14] Thomas Heywood gave another example of this secret sympathy. In 1635 he wrote that Alexander the Great, "a man known to be free from all superstition," one night dreamed that "he saw his mother's funeral solemnized, being then a day's journey distant thence: and waking, in great sorrow and many tears, he told this apparition to diverse of his familiars and friends." The very next day, Heywood assured his readers, news was brought to Alexander that "at the same hour of his dream his mother expired."[15] While it was certainly true that there was an extremely close bond between Alexander and his mother Olympias, she actually survived her son by seven years. The story, however, would have given great authority to the belief that a child would dream of the news of a parent's death before he or she were informed of it.

Gervase Holles also believed that "when there is between two a harmony in their affections, there is likewise between their souls an acquaintance and sometimes an intelligence." Holles married Dorothy Kirketon in June 1630, and their daughter was born November of the next year. She was named after Holles's mother Elizabeth, who had died before he turned two. Their son George was born two years later. Holles felt such love and happiness that "from the time of my marriage. . . . I found no cause to envy any person living." On 18 January 1635, Dorothy died while giving birth to their third child; the baby girl also died. Holles's foretelling dream two nights before, which he related in his memoirs, wove together his fear for his wife and his still strong feelings about the death of his mother when he was a toddler.

> I dreamt that my wife was brought to bed of a daughter and that she and the child were both dead, and that I (in a great deal of affliction) walking under the north wall of the close in the Friers Minorites at Grimesby (the place where I was born) my own mother walked on the other side her hand continually touching mine on the top of the wall; and so (my heart beating violently within me) I awakened.

Holles did not tell his wife of this nightmare about her, but the next day he told it to "her father and mother, who seeing me sad were importunate to know the reason. They, being rigid Puritans, made slight of it; but the day after made it too true in every syllable." Holles not only recorded the dream in his memoirs the day after he related it to his in-laws but he also expressed the "parallel she [his wife] made to my mother; my mother brought my father three children as she did unto me; my mother died in childbed of a daughter as she did; the daughter died likewise as hers did; my son was within about six weeks as old as I was at the departure of my mother."[16]

Of course we are always impressed—if saddened—when the dream of the death of someone comes to pass, while dreams foretelling the death of someone who continues on with a healthy life are far less interesting and therefore less mentioned. Author and lawyer Robert Ashley recorded some of his dreams, including one in about the year 1614. He dreamed of the death of his younger brother Francis, but Francis lived another twenty years and died at the ripe old age of sixty-six. At another time, Ashley wrote that he dreamed "that teeth fell out of my upper and lower jaw" and noted that there are "those who confirm that our brothers and relatives are symbolized by teeth in our dreams." As we know, the belief that dreaming of losing teeth meant losing people was indeed common. An early seventeenth-century commonplace book in a listing on dreams explained that to dream that "your teeth are drawn out" means "another's death," while for someone to dream that one's own "teeth are bloody" warns that the dreamer will soon die. This concept was echoed in *The Helpe to Discourse,* which maintained that "to lose an axle tooth or eye, the death of some friend: to dream of bloody teeth, the death of the dreamer."[17]

Even those who were convinced of the predictive nature of dreams did not believe that all dreams were prognostications. Hill argued that some people have "vain dreams" as well as "true" ones. Vain dreams provide "no true signifiers of matters to come but rather show of present affections and desirers of the body." Because some dreams were "vain," it was important, claimed Hill, that "this difference of true dreams from vain ought diligently to be noted." It was sometimes difficult to know when a dream should be dismissed or when it should be taken seriously. Richard Saunders, even though he presented numerous examples of what dreams meant, suggested that "many dreams are ambiguous, double sensed, uncertain, and doubtful."[18]

Some who wrote about the meaning of dreams argued that, at least with some dreams, they could have different meanings depending on the gender or social status of the person or their condition (another idea that can be traced back to Artemidorus). For example, Hill explained that a poor man's dream that he was being born again, whether it was of his own mother or not, meant great fortune to come. But this same kind of dream did not bode well if a rich man had it because it signified "that one shall have the rule and governance over him." The dream that had the potential for the greatest variety of meanings was that of being nursed, getting milk from a woman's breast. According to Hill, for a man it signified a long illness—unless the dreamer's wife was pregnant at the time and then it would mean that they would have a son who would survive and prosper. If a pregnant woman had this dream, she would have a daughter who would grow up to be like her. For a young woman who was not pregnant, this dream meant she would soon become pregnant, unless she was so young that she was not of marriageable age, and then it portended her death. For a woman past childbearing years, it was an excellent dream if she were poor because then it meant she would become rich. But if the elderly woman dreamer was already rich, it meant that she would lose money.

While the examples just given from *The Pleasant Art of the Interpretation of Dreams* based their interpretation on status or gender, some dream interpreters were convinced that it was the length of time asleep or the time of night the dream occurred that made the difference. In premodern Europe, it was common for people to sleep, wake for an hour or more, and then sleep again. Philip Goodwin argued that "short sleeps may be best for good dreams. In a long sleep many a heavenly dream die and be buried, so as never to rise or come up in remembrance. . . . But when a man suddenly awakes, he the sooner reflects, and reviews over what he thought in his sleep."[19] Many believed, however, that it was not length of time asleep but rather the time the sleep took place. Dreams that occurred in the first sleep before midnight were much less significant and accurate in predictive value than morning dreams, an idea that goes back to the writings of Macrobius in the late fourth century. As Roger Ekirch points out in his history of sleep, the fact that early modern people had the habit of awakening after their first sleep meant that many more dreams were remembered because of the time dreamed rather than whether they were believed to be true or not.[20] John Palsgrave wrote in 1540 that "After midnight men say, that dreams be true." Reginald Scot amplified this by suggesting that "Dreams in the dead of the night are commonly preposterous and monstrous; and in the morning when the gross humors be spent, there happen more pleasant and certain dreams, the blood being more pure than at other times." William Vaughan assured his readers that "surely if a man's mind be free from cares, and he dream in the morning, there is no doubt, but the affairs then dreamed of, will truly come to pass."[21]

There were medical doctors or astrologers, such as John Dee, Simon Forman, and Elias Ashmole, whose practices included dream interpretation. They often recorded their own dreams in their diaries and carefully noted if it was a morning dream or not. When Dee dreamed in August 1600 that he had successfully worked with a philosophers' stone—something that gave wealth, long life, and foreknowledge of the future through dreams—he noted "I had a dream after midnight of my enjoying and working of the philosophers' stone." He ended his diary entry by reiterating that "my dream was after midnight toward day." For an astrologer to work hard at alchemy and then dream of alchemical success was not, by the way, unusual. Forman also recorded a collection of dreams from 1587 to 1595 about the philosophers' stone, including one in November 1587 where he met a boy and a woman who discussed with him how to make one. Two other dreams in January 1594 and October 1595 were ones in which he bought a book on how to create a philosophers' stone.[22]

In September 1645, Ashmole, considered by Derek Parker as having "one of the most interesting and lively minds of his time,"[23] began to write down his dreams, carefully recording at what time of night or day his dreams took place. One morning dream that he had on 26 December 1645 was anything but "pleasant." At the time of this dream, Ashmole was twenty-eight and had only days earlier moved from Oxford (where he had been studying) to Worcester. Charles I, to whom he was extremely loyal in those tumultuous times, had just appointed him to the position of Commissioner of Excise for the city and county of Worcester. Earlier that year, he had met George Wharton, a leading royalist astrologer, who encouraged Ashmole's burgeoning interest in astrology, a field that was to be one of Ashmole's consuming passions for the rest of his life.[24]

Ashmole was a young widower. In 1638 when he was twenty-one, he had married Eleanor Manwearing, a woman fourteen years his senior with whom he was deeply in love. The same year he began a law practice. The marriage, however, was brief and tragic. Their first child was stillborn, and Eleanor, pregnant a second time, died in December 1641. Ashmole gave up law and began to study at Oxford. In October 1645, Ashmole began to consider marrying a second time. With this on his mind, as well as the difficult political situation and the impending fourth anniversary of Eleanor's death, Ashmole dreamed about his dead wife. He dreamed that he was walking in the churchyard of the town where her parents had lived and where she was buried. He came across many graves that had been opened. "I saw many carcasses and coming to one grave I thought it was my wife's and there being many children about it." Ashmole noted that her face was very much withered but he still stooped down to kiss her. As he did so, "she opened her eyes, and at which the children screeching I wakened."[25] Ashmole described the dream in far more detail than usual, but he did not give an interpretation. Reading it now in the twenty-first century, we might perceive elements of guilt and ambivalence. In the 1641 *The Divine Dreamer,* Gonzalo suggests that "men as have sustained some great loss, either in their honors, body, goods, parents, kindred or friends . . . oftentimes in their dreams they have very strange, fearful and mournful apparitions."[26]

We do not know what Ashmole himself made of this "morning" dream, but he was certainly aware of the widely accepted belief that such dreams were far more significant than ones occurring earlier in the night. Did he also know that some believed that it was the time of year that made the dream significant or not? While some thought the dream's importance depended on whether it occurred in the first or second sleep, others contended that what most determined the significance of the dream was the time of the week, month, or year the dream occurred.

If a Herefordshire young woman wanted to know whom she would marry, she would pluck a sprig of yew from a churchyard on Christmas Eve. If she put it under her pillow, her intended would appear to her in a dream.[27] In Dorsetshire, there was a strong belief that dreams occurring on a Friday night and recurring Saturday morning were true dreams. Some young women would especially hope that this was the case about Friday night dreams. There was a spell a woman could say before she went to sleep on a Friday to learn the identity of the man who would become her husband.

> This is the blessed Friday night
> I draw my left stocking into my right
> To dream of the living, not of the dead
> To dream of the young man I am to wed.[28]

The spell had to do with clothing as well as dreams, and Saunders stated that a dream of losing one's clothes, but especially one's shoes, meant great loss if the person was so unlucky as to have it occur on "the first days of the moon."[29] A very different theory suggested that people were far more likely to have true dreams in summer or winter than in spring or at harvest time because those are such changeable times: The "quiet seasons, do cause true dreams, but the wind, and boisterous weather, do work contrary, and the more boisterous, the rather falter."[30] Ashmole's nightmare was not only a morning dream but also one that had occurred in winter, a season of "true dreams."

DREAMS AND HUMOURS

More medically-minded people sought physiological or psychological explanations for dreams. Some believed that people should not look too deeply into the significance of dreams since their meanings were much more mundane. A medical book published at the end of the sixteenth century claimed that "This kind of dream happen[s] oftenest: for if we have seen, or thought upon, or talked of anything very earnestly in the day, the night following the same thing will offer itself unto us. The fisherman (say[s] Theocritus) dream[s] commonly of fishes, rivers and nets: the soldier of alarms, taking of towns, and the sounding of trumpets: the amorous rave of nothing in the night but of their love's object."[31] The apothecary Nicholas Culpeper explained that imagination "is always working, whether the man be sleeping or waking; and. . . . from a variety of cogitations, which, wanting the regulation of judgment, *when man sleepeth,* becomes a dream."[32] The Daniel Widdowes's 1631 translation of Wilhelm Adolf Scribonius's book, *Naturall Philosophy* presents a similar definition. "A dream is an inward act of the mind, the body sleeping: and the quieter that sleep is, the easier be dreams. . . . The clear and pleasant dreams are when the spirits of the brain, which the soul use[s] to imagine with, are most pure and thin, as towards morning."[33]

There were other medical beliefs about the nature of dreams, and many people were convinced, as we saw Richard Haydock was in the previous chapter, that one dreamed according to the body's predominant humour—sanguine, phlegmatic, choleric, or melancholic. Disturbing dreams could also be signs that the "humours" of the body were out of alignment, particularly that melancholy had taken over. Theories about dreams in the early modern period are also a means to further understand sixteenth- and seventeenth-century ideas about both physical and mental health. Some would argue that one's dominant humour caused the type of dreams people had. Thomas Wright argued in *The Passions of the Minde* that "dreams are caused by the spirits which ascend into the imagination, the which being purer or grosser, hotter or colder, more or less (which diversity depends upon the humors of the bodies) move diverse passions according to their nature."[34]

A number of early modern dream books described the different dreams caused by the dominant humour. Those of choleric disposition do not sleep well: They dream of fireworks, exhalations, comets, streaking and blazing meteors, fury, anger, stabbing, battles, and "matters of wrath," though they might also dream of "swiftly running or flying, sometimes also of thunder and tempests." The sanguine, however, sleep well and dream of beautiful women, gardens, flowing streams of blood, or of pure purple colors. The phlegmatic, however, dream of seas, rains, snow, rivers, and drownings. While the dreams of the phlegmatic may sound unpleasant, the melancholic's dreams are worse. These individuals dream of dark places, of graves and cells, of falls from high turrets, of living in caves in the earth, and of black, furious beasts. According to humoural theory, women "are by nature colder than men," which makes their sleep "deep and heavy."[35]

It is important to note that the term "melancholy" was used in this period to represent one of the four humours as well as the corresponding temperament and complexion it produced. It was also used to refer to a specific disease, particularly by those writing of diseases of the body and mind, such as the physician Timothy Bright in *A Treatise of Melancholie* (1586) and Robert Burton in *The Anatomy of Melancholy* (1621, with eight editions in the seventeenth century). M. Andreas Laurentius, principal physician to Henry IV of France, argued that someone could be "melancholic in the sense of his constitution, but not melancholic in the sense of a disease affecting the mind."[36] Those individuals primarily influenced by a different humour could also, as Burton carefully pointed out, suffer from the disease of melancholy, though their humour would affect their symptoms.[37] The distinctions between melancholy as a humour and as a disease were not always clear, as some writers felt that one whose humours were dominated by melancholy could easily become subject to the disease of melancholy as well. One aspect of the disease was the dreams, but these would also be formed by the character of the person, so that if an ambitious man became melancholy, "he straightaway dreams that he is a king, an emperor, a monarch." The dreams of people suffering from melancholy could be very disturbing, and Burton frequently described them as "fearful." Laurentius stated that men suffering from melancholy suffer greatly from insomnia, and when they do finally sleep, they are "assailed with a thousand vain visions, and hideous bugbears."[38] Thomas Nashe described the disease of melancholy as "the mother of dreams, and of all terrors of the night whatsoever."[39] Some argued that melancholic vapors came from a disordered spleen and their fumes troubled the brain and caused troublesome dreams.[40] According to Pierre de Loyer, people with this disease frequently dreamed they were being strangled or choked but when they tried to call out for help, "their voice for the time is suppressed and taken away."[41] To present another common point of view of the time, Hill, however, states in his book on dreams that if one dreams that one cannot speak it means poverty is in that person's future.

Richard Saunders argued that the same dream could have different meanings depending on which humour dominated the body. For example, "To dream that one hath much money" and was counting it was a bad dream for someone who was sanguine as it meant they were to be deceived, but it meant good news for melancholic, and was "indifferent" to those who were choleric or phlegmatic. To dream of being in church was positive for the sanguine or choleric, but meant ill for the phlegmatic or melancholic. Perhaps most striking was the difference in meaning depending on one's humour if one dreamed that one's beard was shaved off. "To the sanguine it is melancholy and affliction; to the melancholy good, to the choleric madness, and to the phlegmatic indifferent." Another example Saunders provided of how one's humour determined the meaning of the dream had to do with religion and arguments over its import. If one dreamed that one was in a dispute over religion and one was of a sanguine humor, it was an "ill dream." Saunders added, "That happened to a friend of mine." The man dreamed he was "disputing with an ill physiognomy and cruel countenance." Soon after, that man in his waking life was arrested. Given that Saunders's book was published in 1653, one can imagine that, during the political and religious upsets of the time, dreaming about religious arguments could easily be seen as prognosticating ill fortune. To a person of choleric disposition, it would also mean "contempt and prejudice." To a melancholic, it would signal honor. A related dream—that of worshipping in church—would mean joy for those who were either sanguine or choleric, but it would suggest bad tidings for the phlegmatic and melancholic. Apparently in premodern times, just as today, people dreamed that they were naked in the middle of a public place, but the meaning for the dream appears quite different. Saunders explains that, while it is bad fortune for a sanguine to dream that he is "stark naked" in a church, for the melancholic it is very good.[42] While today such a dream causes people to feel embarrassment and anxiety as they dream, we might wish we could know why this presaged good tidings for the melancholic. According to a medieval dream book it meant "sorrow and great lamentation."[43] At least, someone with a melancholy disposition might be cheered with the discovery that this dream was positive, particularly given the gloomy nature of most of their dreams. Melancholy and nightmares seemed to be intertwined.

Another book that discussed dreams was Thomas Walkington's *The Opticke Glasse*. Walkington received his B.A. and M.A. from Cambridge, went to Oxford for his B.D., and finally returned to Cambridge for his D.D. in 1616. Before he went on to Oxford (probably about 1607), Walkington wrote a book intended to promote both physical and mental health so that his readers would "be more able not only to live but to live well." We might see *The Opticke Glasse* as the early modern equivalent to one of today's ubiquitous self-help books. John Popplestone and Marion White McPherson suggest that Walkington deliberately provided translations of Latin and Greek quotations for an audience who were informed but who might lack a complete classical education. Walkington was one of the last authors to use Galen as his model.[44] In his chapter on dreams, Walkington argued that there are three kinds of dreams: fatal, vain, and natural. Fatal dreams continued the tradition of being prophetic, though Walkington felt that they might be symbolic and have to be interpreted. Walkington provided many examples: Dreaming of gold meant good luck but dreaming of a hare signified death. Vain dreams were simply "when a man imagines he doth such things in his sleep, which he did the day before." But Walkington warned that if one does not do the action as well in dreams as had happened in life, then this foretells "some perturbation of body." Walkington considered that the most significant dreams are those that are "natural," that is, ones that "arise from our complexions."[45]

Bright's *A Treatise on Melancholie* also described a characteristic of a melancholic nature to be "given to fearful and terrible dreams," but his view on dreams as a way to know the future is far more sophisticated than most others of the same time period. He argues that "sleep is a kind of separation of the soul from the body for a time," since in deep sleep there is "no power at all to see, hear, smell, taste or feel," dreams are a way for the soul to communicate, "to make evident unto us. . . . [in] dreams we see with our souls." The soul, Bright contends, can see "past as present," but can also observe "future things sometimes. . . . If any man think it much to advance the mind so high, let him remember from whom it proceeded, and the manner how it was created, and the most excellent estate and thereof before the fall." Bright implies that, since God created the soul, then the soul can convey what God wants that individual to know.[46]

DREAMS ARE DECEIVING

While many early modern books on dream interpretation were based on humoural theory as well as on dreams as prognostication, some texts in the early modern period were convinced that believing in dreams' ability to foretell the future was simply foolish superstition. Perhaps Saunders's chapter on dreams was a hastily put together compilation since, despite the later pages on dream interpretation, especially based on the different humours, he begins his discussion by stating that "there is nothing true in matter of dreams, for all that Artemidorus, Cardan, Niphius, etc., have written thereof . . . wherein as they have deceived others, so they have deceived themselves."[47]

Cardin and Artemidorus were also dismissed by Nashe, whom "I thank God I had never the plodding patience to read, for if they be no better than some of them I have perused, every weather-wise old wife might write better." Nashe was convinced that it was foolish superstition to believe that, if someone dreamed he had a nosebleed, it meant that "some of his kinsfolk is dead." A Cambridge-educated writer and playwright, Nashe was well known for his witty but scurrilous pamphlets; however, he also wrote about dreams in his book about apparitions, *The Terrors of the Night*. As a son of a clergyman, Nashe felt that he had been exposed to superstition in his childhood. "I have heard aged mumbling grandmothers as they sat warming their knees over a coal scratch . . . and they would bid young folks beware on what day they trimmed their nails, tell what luck every one should have by the day of the week he was born on; show how many years a man should live by the number of wrinkles on his forehead. . . . When I was a little child I was a great auditor of theirs."[48] Nashe had moved to London to make a living as a writer in 1588; by 1592, he enjoyed the patronage of Ferdinando Stanley, Lord Strange, who aided a number of writers including Nashe's friend Christopher Marlowe. In 1593, Nashe stayed with Robert Cotton at his home Conington Manor, Huntingdonshire where Nashe wrote an early version of *The Terrors of the Night*—a text that he revised and expanded for its publication in late 1594. Significantly, it was also at Conington Manor where, nearly a decade later, Ben Jonson would have his dream about his son. Charles Nicholl suggests that the twenty-two-year-old Cotton was ill and suffering from melancholy after the death of his father, and Nashe's visit was intended in part to cheer him up.[49] *Terrors of the Night*, however, is not a cheerful read. The text deals frequently with the dangers of melancholy. While Nashe does not completely rule out apparitions, he warns how easily they can, instead, be the products of one's own mind.

Nashe is utterly convinced that only fools or charlatans predict the future from dreams. "This is my definitive verdict: that one may as well by the smoke that comes out of a kitchen guess what meat is there upon a spit, as by paraphrasing on smoky dreams portend of future events." Nashe discusses the causes of dreams as physiological and psychological, suggesting that dreams are based on thoughts and experiences that happened over the course of the day, especially ones that were not thoroughly scrutinized. "A dream is nothing else but a bubbling scum or froth of the fancy, which the day hath left undigested; or an after feast made of the fragments of idle imaginations." Nashe also wished to convince his readers that, even in sleep, an individual remained somewhat aware of one's surroundings—an awareness that similarly could influence dreams.

> As for example, if in the dead of the night there be any rumbling, knocking, or disturbance near us, we straight dream of wars, or of thunder. If a dog howls, we suppose we are transported into hell, where we hear the complaint of damned ghosts. . . . If we be troubled with too many clothes, then we suppose the night mare rides us.

Heavy meals soon before bed, or diseases could also cause bad dreams. "He that is inclining to a burning fever shall dream of frays, lightning and thunder, of skirmishing with the devil, and a hundred such like. He that is spiced with the gout or the dropsy, frequently dreams of fetters and manacles."[50]

In what might sound strikingly modern, Nashe proposed that nightmares were the result of guilty feelings on the part of the dreamer. Feeling guilt over one's sins during the day, especially the terrible sins of treason and murder will cause terrible dreams at night.

> Dreams to none are so fearful, as to those whose accusing private guilt expects mischief every hour for their merit. . . . In the day time we torment our thoughts and imaginations with sundry cares and devices; all the nighttime they quake and tremble after the terror of their late suffering, and still continue thinking of the perplexities they have endured. To nothing more aptly can I compare the working of our brains after we have unyoked and gone to bed, than to the glimmering and dazzling of a man's eyes when he comes newly out of the bright sun, into the dark shadow.

But Nashe has a foot in both worlds, the medieval as well as the modern. While he dismisses dreams as prognostication, he does not doubt that the devil is keeping track of people's sins in order to use dreams as a method for causing despair. Devils can manipulate dreams in a number of ways to gain control over the souls of humankind. "It will be demanded why in the likeness of one's father or mother, or kinsfolk, he oftentimes presents himself unto us? No other reason can be given of it but this, that in those shapes which he supposes most familiar unto us, and that we are inclined to with a natural kind of love, we will sooner harken to him than otherwise."[51]

DISCOVER OURSELVES THROUGH OUR DREAMS

In the next century, Owen Fellthem took the more modern, rationalist perspective expressed by Nashe and elaborated on it even further. In his very popular *Resolves diuine, morall, politicall,* Fellthem stressed the importance of taking the time to think seriously about one's dreams. The first edition of

Resolves was published in 1623; the greatly expanded second edition was published five years later during the year that Fellthem became the steward for an estate at Great Billing in Northamptonshire—an estate owned by Barnabas O'Brien—a younger brother of the Irish fifth Earl of Thomond. Felltham held this position as steward for the rest of his life, but he also continued to write poetry as well as other texts. *Resolves* itself was so successful that it went through six more editions during Felltham's lifetime. In the text, he argued that one should analyze one's own dreams as a "notable means" of "discovering" one's own nature, since "in sleep, we have the naked and natural thoughts of our souls." Felltham warns that we can understand both our vices and our virtues by observing our dreams. He tells his English readers that "among the Indians, when their Kings went to sleep, to pray, with piping acclamations, that they might have happy dreams; and withal, consult well for their subjects benefit." Felltham adds that a wise man who thinks seriously about his dreams is "wiser for his sleeping." Felltham readily admits, however, that not all dreams are significant but that all should be examined thoughtfully and with caution. Just as we ought not to dismiss them with contempt nor should we necessarily trust what they tell us. "The best use we can make of dreams, is observation, and by that, our own correction or encouragement. For it is not doubtable, but that the mind is working in the dullest depths of sleep." Felltham suggests the great importance of dreams "to preserve health or amend the life," proclaiming that "I doubt not . . . dreams may, to a wise observer, be of special benefit." In the mid-seventeenth century, John Evans was so impressed by Felltham that he copied what he had to say about dreams into his commonplace book.[52]

For Nashe, a terror of the night was a nightmare, and much was written in this period to define nightmares more precisely and to outline what to do about them. Just as the belief in witchcraft and magic was embedded in the culture, so too was the idea of how demons were created. As was mentioned in the previous chapter, the belief was that a succubus, which was a demon or evil spirit in female form, would have carnal intercourse with men while they slept, and then this spirit would transform into an incubus in order to deposit the gathered "seed" into women while they slept. The belief in these spirits may well have originated as an explanation for nightmares that had a sexual component, since in the Middle Ages the existence of such demonic spirits was widely accepted. More specifically, some called the nightmare the experience of feeling in sleep as if one were being pressed down by someone on top, and many believed that a female spirit or monster would land upon a sleeping person and cause him to feel as if he were suffocating. In 1561, John Hollybush produced an English translation of a German book on health care titled, *A most excellent and perfecte homish apothecarye or homely physik booke, for all the grefes and diseases of the bodye,* which provided a particularly succinct definition of this kind of nightmare. "The disease called Incubus that is the Mare which is a sickness or fantasy oppressing a man in his sleep." Reginald Scot describes "the mare" as a goblin who was thought to come to children in the middle of the night and sit on their chests.[53] As we saw in the previous chapter, King James I, despite his belief in witches, was convinced of the natural quality of dreams and did not believe that nightmares were caused by demons who had come to seduce or frighten the dreamer. In Widdowes's translation of Wilhem Scribonius's text, a nightmare is described as "seeming of being choked or strangled by one keeping upon him: fear following this compression."[54]

The physician, religious philosopher, and author Sir Thomas Browne also devoted considerable thought to dreams, including nightmares. He once wrote that if he were able to remember his dreams faithfully, then he would have studied dreams to the exclusion of all else. For Browne, dreams were, in part, a communication with God as well as part contemplations of astrological influences.[55] Browne discussed a variety of interpretations regarding how and why people dream even as he sought to provide explanations that would help individuals understand their dreams. He discussed such topics in many of his works, including his most famous *Religio Medici,* as well as *Pseudodoxia Epidemica, Plaints in Scripture, A Letter to a Friend upon occasion of the Death of His Intimate Friend,* and the specific work, *On Dreams.* Browne claimed that "I am happy in a dream, and as content to enjoy a happiness in a fancy, as others in a more apparent truth and reality." He gave as an example that he might be unhappy if he is far away from a friend "but my friendly dreams in night requite me, and make me think I am within his arms. I thank God for my happy dreams, as I do for my good rest." For Browne, dreams could also be, as Reid Barbour points out, an "elevated performance" to enjoy: "comedy played extempore for a private audience of one in the theater of his bed." Browne was also convinced that the dream world allowed, quite literally, for dramatic kinds of self-expression. "I am no way facetious, nor disposed for the mirth and gaiety of company, yet in one dream I can compose a whole comedy, behold the action, apprehend the jests, and laugh my self awake at the conceits thereof." But Browne urged his readers to exercise caution in that dream world, since "The day supplies us with truths: the night with fictions and falsehoods. . . . to add unto the delusion of dreams, the fantastical objects seem greater than they are; . . . it may prove more easy to dream of giants than pigmies."[56] Philip Goodwin also described dreams as staged dramas, but he perceived this as far more dangerous, suggesting that "A man's bed and head [could] be Satan's stage, upon which he brings strange disguised persons to play their parts, whereupon follows such effects as do defile both head and bed."[57]

Browne believed there were some ways one could control the nature of one's dreams. In addition to being concerned about what one eats (especially at dinner), Browne argued that "virtuous thoughts of the day lay up good treasures for the night; whereby the impressions of imaginary forms arise into sober similitudes." In addition, Browne, like some other writers on dreams, was convinced that there were distinct varieties. "That there are demoniacal dreams we have little reason to doubt." The Devil "by the delusion of dreams, and the discovery of things to come in sleep, above the prescience of our waked senses" more ability to influence people while asleep than awake. Browne also argued for divine dreams. "If there be guardian spirits, they . . . may sometimes order our dreams: and many strange hints, instigations, or discourses, which are so amazing unto us, may arise from such foundations." Despite his assertion of the reality of divine dreams, Browne strongly warned against believing dreams that can foretell the future, stressing that "he that should order his affairs by dreams, or make the night a rule unto the day, might be ridiculously deluded." Yet this does not make dreams lack meaning. "However dreams may be fallacious concerning outward events, yet may they be truly significant at home; and whereby we may more sensibly understand ourselves." Dreams, claimed Browne, "intimately tell us ourselves." Dreams can serve as windows into the self because, as Browne indicated, one's fundamental character remains relatively stable in waking as in sleeping: Someone who is brave or generous in life will be so in dreams, just as someone who is cowardly or selfish will dream of cowardly or selfish actions. "Persons of radical integrity will not easily be perverted in their dreams, nor noble minds do pitiful things in sleep." To support this idea, Browne provided a series of examples that includes the steady and fearless Martin Luther as well as the Roman general Crassus, who was known for his avarice, treachery, and ambition. "Luther was not like to fear a spirit in the night, when such an apparition would not terrify him in the day. . . . . Crassus would have hardly been bountiful in a dream, whose fist was so close awake." But while one can be in a sinful state in dreams, one should not be blamed for the sins so committed.

> Dionysius was absurdly tyrannical to kill a man for dreaming that he had killed him; and really to take away his life, who had but fantastically taken away his. Lamia was ridiculously unjust to sue a young man for a reward, who had confessed that pleasure from her in a dream which she had denied unto his awaking sense: conceiving that she had merited somewhat from his fantastical fruition and shadow of herself.

Browne, who had read widely as he studied medicine at Oxford, Montpellier, Padua, and Leiden, well knew a range of theories about dreams. As we saw in the previous chapter, fellow medical doctor Richard Haydock had agreed with the authorities who claimed that not every person dreams and that dreams were not necessary for good health. But the theory that some people did not dream at all also reflected a belief in the superiority of people who did. The 1556 edition of *A Summary of the Antiquities and Wonders of the World . . . Out of the Sixteen First Books of . . . Pliny,* for example, describes a certain group of people who do not dream. This text, which includes many fabulous stories of the peoples of Africa, claimed that "in Libya which is at the end of the Ethiopes, there are people differing from the common order of others, they have among them no names and they curse the sun for his great heat, by the which they are all black saving their teeth and a little the palm of their hands, and they never dream."[58] Browne dismissed this idea as impossible while also demonstrating his belief in the unreliability of early night dreams when he stated "that some have never dreamed, is as improbable as that some have never laughed . . . that men dream not in some countries, with many more, are unto me sick men's dreams; . . . and visions before midnight."

How to Avoid a Nightmare

Browne and others had argued for a variety of reasons that bad dreams could be the result of disruptive foods, personal biology, or spiritual forces. If people were in dispute over what caused bad dreams, they also espoused different theories about how to combat them. For example, some believed in the power of gemstones. Robert Burton suggested that wearing either a ruby or coral around one's neck could "repress troublesome dreams."[59] Various lapidaries offered advice concerning what gems could help or hurt one's dreams. Some claimed that diamonds helped a person avoid nightmares. One lapidary noted that "if a man wear it," then the diamond would give him strength and protect him from poison, but it would also keep "him from dreaming in his sleep," whether bad or good. For women diamonds could be more dangerous. According to Thomas Nicols, in his *Arcula Gemmea, or, A Cabinet of Jewels,* a man could use a diamond to ascertain the fidelity of his wife, but it had to be a "true diamond," that was put on the head of a sleeping woman. "If she be faithful to her husband," she will turn to embrace him, "but if she be an adulteress" she will "turn away from him."[60]

If one was concerned about sad dreams, then chalcedony, also known as sardonyx, was the stone to wear. An amethyst was particularly helpful in keeping one from becoming inebriated if one was drinking, but it could also cause exciting dreams.[61] (Certainly, wearing an amethyst was easier and more pleasant than some other early modern suggestions for avoiding getting drunk, such as eating the roasted lungs of a goat.[62]) Crystal was especially valuable because it could preserve its wearers from the terrors of the night. Wearing onyx, on the other hand, could cause someone to have bad dreams. Almost as magical as these cures was one presented by Edward Topsell, who told his readers that "men are delivered from the spirits of the night, called Incubi and Succubi, or else Nightmares," if they would eat the tongue or gallbladder of a dragon boiled in wine.[63] Only slightly less extravagant was the recipe in a commonplace book that suggested if one took mink's blood and rubbed it on one's temple "and so go to your bed and you shall see marvelous things in your sleep." The book also informs us that if one wants to have exciting dreams of wild beasts, one only has to put an ape's heart under one's pillow, a recipe that may have come from the 1615 text, *The Secrets of Alexis,* which gives the same advice.[64]

In the early modern period, many of the people who realized that being aware of what they ate and drank would have more impact on their dream life than the gemstones they wore had less spectacular cures than Topsell or some early modern recipes. In *Terrors of the Night,* Nashe warned that "any meat that in the day time we eat against our stomachs, begets a dismal dream."[65] Browne also discussed how food could influence dreams for good or ill: "some food makes turbulent, some gives quiet, dreams. Cato, who doted upon cabbage, might find the crude effects thereof in his sleep; wherein the Egyptians might find some advantage by their superstitious abstinence of onions."[66] People were cautioned not to eat too late at night, especially heavy meals. A number of books on dreams also discussed what specific foods could cause bad dreams. For example, heavy meats such as boar, rabbit, venison, and beef could cause disturbing dreams as could water fowl, such as duck and goose. It was not only meat but a number of vegetables too; including gourds, cucumbers, melons, beans, peas, cabbage, garlic, onions, and leeks.[67] Those concerned about their dreams were advised to avoid chestnuts. *The Haven of Health,* which went through seven editions, warned that "coleworts engender melancholy humors, and ill dreams, and that they hurt the stomach, nourish little, dull the sight." The author Thomas Cogan was especially concerned that these "qualities be very noisome to students," making one wonder if students were being fed a great deal of cabbage in the early modern period.[68]

Despite the wearing of amethysts, alcohol could be problematic as well. The 1568 book by William Turner on wine drinking warned that "new wine . . . is hard of digestion and breeds heavy dreams."[69] Some were convinced that the newly popular use of tobacco could lead to ill dreams as well. Henry Butts suggested that the way Native Americans used tobacco in religious matters led to strange drug-induced dreaming. He described how when Indian priests used tobacco "consulting in matters of importance," it caused them to behave as if they had fallen into drunkenness, and later they would "give answers according to the phantasms and visions, which appeared to them in their sleep."[70] Interestingly, soon before his death, Forman dreamed that a dead friend "was come from the sea and brought me more tobacco."[71] Beliefs about how food and drink (or abstinence from them) could influence dreams echoes back to much earlier claims. In the third century, Tertullian suggested that sobriety and fasting could help one dream.[72] Burton also talked about the "strange accidents [that] proceed from fasting; dreams, superstition, contempt of torments, desire of death, prophecies, paradoxes, madness; fasting naturally prepares men to these things."[73] In the early modern period, people argued that some foods could also promote agreeable dreams. Burton suggested that the herb hippoglossa, commonly called horsetongue, could be distilled into water and would "procure pleasant dreams"[74] if taken before going to bed. Aniseed and saffron were definitely helpful in causing someone to "dream very acceptable things."[75] A number of dream practitioners also realized that medications made from plants could be of use. The juice of poplar leaves "is not only the provocation of sound sleep, but it causes also delightful and facetious dreams." In the early modern period, "facetious" meant "polished and agreeable, urbane" or "witty, humorous, amusing." Poplar leaves were only one of a number of remedies. More in the way of a spell was the use of the leaves of the bay tree:

The tree "will make you believe that if you put his leaves under your pillow, you shall be sure to have true dreams."[76]

Culpeper, the seventeenth-century physician and astrologer, was particularly concerned with using plants and herbs to cure problems of sleeplessness and then of dreams. Culpeper's maternal grandfather, the Puritan minister William Attersole, had wanted his grandson to follow in his footsteps, and with that goal in mind, Culpeper matriculated at Cambridge in 1632 at the age of sixteen. But Culpeper was not really interested in theology. As his contemporary biographer W. Ryves pointed out, from the time he was about ten, Nicholas had been interested in astrology. Culpeper left Cambridge without a degree and studied with several apothecaries before eventually establishing his own practice. It was just as well that Culpeper did not pursue a career in the Church as he later wrote of his religious beliefs: "All the religion I know is Jesus Christ and him crucified, and the indwelling of the spirit of God in me."[77] Similar to the practice of a number of apothecaries of his day, Culpeper not only dispensed remedies but also diagnosed illness and prescribed medication. The College of Physicians disliked losing clients to less expensive competitors, and in December of 1642, Culpeper was tried for witchcraft but fortunately acquitted. The following year, he fought on the side of Parliament and was seriously wounded.

Perceived as a radical in many of his beliefs, Culpeper believed ardently in helping sick people who were poor and powerless. He decided to help not only his expanding number of clients but others as well, by translating medical works from Latin and writing his own books that could be easily understood. With the lack of censorship at the end of the 1640s, Culpeper was able to publish *A Physciall Directory, or A Translation of the London Dispensatory*. This was not simply a translation of the College of Physicians' *Latin Pharmacopoeia, known as the "London Dispensatory."* Culpeper also defined terms and explained clearly and simply how to make the medicines, turning the book into a "handbook of medical self-help," as Patrick Curry puts it. There were certainly some who were highly critical of what Culpeper was attempting to do. One contemporary pamphlet described him as "This man indeed is the Vicar of St. Fools, yet contradicts physicians and the schools."[78] Culpeper published a number of other works on astrology and medicine, but the most significant was *The English Physitian, or, An astrologo-physical discourse on the vulgar herbs of this nation, being a compleat method of physick, whereby a man may preserve his body in health, or cure himself, being sick* (1652). Unfortunately, Culpeper was not able to preserve his own body in health or cure himself; he died in January 1654 at only thirty-eight.

Culpeper was particularly scornful of the idea of seductive demons and blamed the medieval Church for its continued popularity.

The night-mare was supposed by the ancients not to be any real disorder of the body, but to be an effect, or sensation, derived from carnal contact in the night with some evil spirit or daemon during the hours of sleep. . . . Absurd as was this doctrine, whole volumes have been written upon it; and in former days it opened a large field for priestcraft. . . . How many reasons have we to be thankful for the lights of the gospel dispensed in our own tongue, and for the illuminations of the present era!

Culpeper had a far more developed physiological description of the nightmare. "In this disease, the patient, in time of sleep, imagines he feels an uncommon oppression or weight about his breast or stomach, which he can by no means shake off." Sometimes such a dream will cause someone to groan or cry out, but more frequently as part of the dream, when he attempts to speak, he cannot. Often movement as well as speech is frozen. "Sometimes he imagines himself engaged with an enemy, and in danger of being killed, attempts to run away, but finds he cannot. Sometimes he fancies himself in a house that is on fire, or that he is in danger of being drowned in a river." Culpeper also described a common nightmare. "He often thinks he is falling over a precipice, and the dread of being dashed to pieces suddenly awakes him." Culpeper did not even mention supernatural causes, but he was dismissive of some medical theories. "This disorder has been supposed to proceed from too much blood; from a stagnation of blood in the brain, lungs, etc. But it is rather a nervous affection, and arises chiefly from indigestion. Hence we find that persons of weak nerves, who lead a sedentary life . . . are most commonly afflicted with the night-mare." Culpeper warned that "nothing tends more to produce it than heavy suppers, especially when eaten later, or the patient goes to bed soon after."[79]

Culpeper was especially concerned about melancholics who suffered from disturbing dreams. One suggestion he made was to make the seeds and roots of the peony into a syrup and take it at bedtime. Another remedy he suggested was to take the polypody, or fern, that grows on an oak tree: "The distilled water, both from the roots and leaves, . . . if taken for several days together; as also against melancholy, or fearful or troublesome sleeps or dreams." If someone was worried because of the lustful dreams that were occurring, the seeds of the salad herb purslain provided the solution.[80] William Turner also suggested peony seeds in his herbal, but he suggested drinking them in mead or wine as "a good remedy against the strangling of the nightmare."[81] Culpeper, however, was, for the most part, against using alcohol as a way to deal with bad dreams. "Some say a dram of brandy taken at bed-time will prevent" nightmares, but he called this "a bad custom, and, in time, loses its effect." His recommendation instead sounds both sensible and modern, arguing for "the use of food of easy digestion, cheerfulness, exercise through the day, and a light supper taken early, than to accustom himself to drams." His final advice, however, is far less appealing: "persons who are young, and full of blood, if troubled with the nightmare, ought to take a purge frequently."[82]

Certainly nightmares appeared to be common, given the amount of advice written about them. But as well as all the advice on how to avoid certain disturbing types of dreams, there was also advice on how to have dreams that some might perceive as an invitation to a nightmare. We will probably not take seriously the recipe given in the 1615 pamphlet, *The Secrets of Alexis,* which informs its readers that if one wishes to see "marvelous things,"? including "all kinds of beasts, as lions, bears, wolves, apes, tigers, and other such like," one has only to procure the heart of an ape and place it under one's pillow before one goes to sleep.[83] For some, dreaming of someone who died was a nightmare, and in Herefordshire, if someone visited a house where a dead body lay, they were expected to look at it and touch it, "in order that he or she may not dream of it afterwards."[84]

DREAMING OF THE DEAD

Some people actually wanted a spell so that they might dream of someone who had died. While some lapidaries warned against wearing onyx because it could cause bad dreams, one also offered that if someone has the "desire to speak with his friend that is dead," he should put the onyx under the pillow: This will lead to "conference with him in his sleep."[85] Browne attempted to comfort those who were frightened of dreaming of the dead, arguing that it was not strange that one "should sometimes dream of the dead," and doing so takes nothing away from the living. Browne thought there was nothing wrong even if we "dream that we are dead" ourselves.[86] For some, to dream of someone who had died brought great comfort. William Laud was fifty-seven when, in January 1627, he "dreamed that my mother, long since dead stood by my bed and looked pleasantly upon me, and that I was glad to see her with so merry an aspect."[87] Eight-year-old Simond d'Ewes's dreams of his much beloved grandmother came far sooner after her death, and they were a great comfort to him, especially since he had not been with her to say goodbye. "As soon as I heard of her death, I mourned most bitterly for her in the daytime, and was often revived in the night by continual dreams of her being alive, and of my conversing again with her." These dreams were so intense, D'Ewes recounted, "as if I had but then begun to love her."[88]

Losing a dearly beloved wife could cause deep emotional pain. Ashmole's dream about his wife, as discussed earlier, appears nightmarish. Kenelm Digby, the natural philosopher and oldest son of Sir Everard Digby (who was executed for his involvement in the Gunpowder Plot) also had a nightmare after the death of his wife. Venetia Digby died suddenly on 1 May 1633. Theirs had been an intense love affair. Childhood friends, they had met again in 1619 and fell in love. He was sixteen and she, three years older. Attempting to break up their relationship, his mother had sent him on a Grand Tour of the continent. In an effort to avoid being drawn into an affair with the middle-aged French Queen-mother Marie de Medici, Kenelm had allowed people to believe that he was dead. Actually, he had settled in Florence where he stayed for the next two years. He wrote to Venetia to assure her that he was safely alive, but the first letter never arrived, and his mother managed to suppress the others. Venetia, meanwhile living alone in London, was grief-stricken by the news that Digby had died. Extremely beautiful, she was pursued by several aristocrats, perhaps having an affair with one or more of them. Digby saw Venetia when he returned to Court in late 1623, but each doubted the other. Since Venetia had received no letters, she thought she had lost his affections, and the gossip surrounding Venetia made Digby wary. After a horseback ride together in the summer of 1624, however, the two were more in love than ever, and despite his mother's and her father's objections, the two secretly married. Venetia suffered several miscarriages and the infant death of one son, but three other boys survived. Despite his passion for his wife, Kenelm had several affairs, which tinged his intense grief with guilt when she died suddenly, probably of a cerebral hemorrhage, after only eight years of marriage. Kenelm became convinced that her death was his punishment for foolishly following his passions. Six weeks after her death, he wrote to his brother about his overwhelming sadness: "I have in my wife lost half of my self and indeed the better half." Though it was mid-June and the nights thus the shortest of the year, he wrote that

> these nights appear so longsome and so tedious to me while my corroding thoughts do banish sleep from my distempered head. . . . a storm of torturing thoughts that will not let me be one minute at quiet. And if after some hours I chance through weariness to slumber, I dream of that Angel that is so deep imprinted in my soul as it can take impression of nothing else. . . . I waken in a fright, and peradventure all bedewed with tears.[89]

After her death, a number of the poets of the artistic circle around Digby wrote poems for him about Venetia. One such poet was Owen Fellthem. One wonders if perhaps Digby spoke with Fellthem about his dreams concerning his dead wife, and if Fellthem could have provided comfort about them.

Bulstrode Whitelocke did find comfort when he dreamed about his much-loved second wife right after her death. Whitelocke was a lawyer and participant in the civil wars. He served as a member of Parliament in the late 1620s and expressed his opposition to ship money in 1635. Elected to Parliament in November 1640, Whitelocke reluctantly chaired the committee to prepare the impeachment of Thomas Wentworth, Earl of Strafford, and drafted the bill ensuring that the Long Parliament could not be dissolved without the committee's consent. He greatly desired a compromise between king and Parliament and spoke in Commons against the king's trial, expressing a willingness to hazard all rather than go against his conscience. Whitelock's first wife had had serious emotional problems and starved herself to death at the age of twenty-five, leaving him with a young son. Like Digby, Whitelocke eloped with his second wife, Frances Willoughby. Not only had he fallen in love with her the first time they met, but his motherless three-year-old son adored her as well. Whitelocke wrote in his diary that he loved her for "her birth, her beauty, her disposition, her wisdom, her cheerfulness . . . her incomparable love of her husband and desire to please him." He and Frances were married for fourteen years and had nine children. Writing in the third person in his diary as was his wont, he proclaimed May 16, 1649, "The saddest day of Whitelocke's life" because this was the day "when his dear wife died." Unlike the dreams of some others who had lost much-loved wives, Whitelocke's dream brought him great comfort. As he lay in bed the night that she died, "he saw a perfect apparition of his wife standing at his bed side, dressed as usually, at which he was not frightened but delighted with it, and so she appeared to him several times but spoke nothing to him, only looked cheerfully upon him."[90] Whitelocke seemed to accept that it was indeed his wife who appeared to him, and this belief was not unusual. For example, Lewes Lavater believed that ghosts could inhabit not only the visible world but also the world of dreams and that God allowed ghosts to communicate with the living through dreams.[91]

CONJECTORS AND ASTROLOGERS

Though both Digby and Whitelocke wrote about dreams pertaining to their dead wives, as far as we know they never consulted anyone professionally about them; there were, however, astrologers—many of them also medical practitioners—who not only noted their own dreams but also interpreted dreams as part of their practice. Saunders referred to someone who professionally interprets dreams a "conjector."[92] It was not the safest profession. From its beginnings, the Christian hierarchy had spoken out against professional dream interpreters, and an early Church Council had required five years of penance for anyone who had consulted with one. As Jacques le Goff points out, throughout the Middle Ages people probably continued to seek dream interpretation from sorcerers, cunning men and women, and witches, but they had to be clandestine about it.[93] While it was more acceptable in the early modern period, those who practiced magic including dream interpretation could easily be accused of witchcraft. Culpeper, Dee, and Forman all had to deal with such accusations. In the early modern period, astrology was both "natural" (used for such things as the calculation of fixing the dates of holy days and the predictions of tides and eclipses) and "judicial" (the art of understanding the influence of stars and planets upon human affairs). Dee, Forman, and Ashmole were among the judicial astrologers who recorded their own dreams, took them seriously, and interpreted the dreams of others.

Dee, whose dream about the philosophers' stone was discussed earlier in the chapter, studied at Cambridge and on the continent. Dee disliked being known as a conjuror and presented himself as a mathematician and antiquarian as well as an astrologer. He did well in the reign of Edward VI, being granted an annual pension of 100 crowns, and entered the service of first William Herbert, Earl of Pembroke, and later John Dudley, Duke of Northumberland, serving as tutor for his son John and possibly some of the other boys. When Mary became queen, and the Dudleys fell from power, Dee's fortunes changed; he taught mathematics in London for a while. In May 1555, the Privy Council ordered the arrest of Dee for calculating the nativities of Mary, her husband Philip, and her sister, the Princess Elizabeth. Later the charges of conjuring and witchcraft were added. The charges were dropped, and in August, Dee was released into the custody of Edmund

Bonner, bishop of London so that the bishop might examine Dee on his religious beliefs. Dee obviously satisfied Bonner because he continued in the bishop's household as his chaplain. Robert Dudley helped Dee establish himself when Elizabeth became queen, and sought from Dee to indicate the most propitious day for the queen's coronation. While the Bonner connection may have made Protestant enemies for Dee, he had the good will of William Cecil. About 1565, Dee settled close to Elizabeth's royal residence at Richmond in Mortlake, Surrey, where he began the practice of alchemy. Dee's magical practice included a distorting mirror, and Elizabeth viewed herself in it in 1575. He was highly regarded enough at court that he offered reassurance about the 1577 comet and, more importantly, at the discovery of an image of Elizabeth found in Lincoln's Inn Fields with a pin stuck through its breast. At this time in his life, he also began his attempts at *skrying,* that is, seeing and conversing with spirits. Since he was not successful himself, he employed a series of mediums, the most famous of which was the probable con artist, Edward Kelley. Leaving Mortlake in 1583, Dee traveled on the continent with Kelley for some years. When he returned in 1589, he found his library at Mortlake had been looted and partially destroyed.

A number of people came to consult Dee professionally, and at least some, about their dreams. In 1581, Harry Prince "came to me at Mortlake, told me of his dreams, often repeated." But Dee was more concerned with his own dreams and those of his wife Jane. He was pleased that six months into the marriage in August 1578, she had dreamed that all her rings were broken, hoping that "perhaps she is about to have as many children as there are rings." That the rings were broken does not appear to have given Dee pause. Perhaps it should have; Jane had numerous children, but only Arthur and Katherine lived to adulthood. Despite a dream Jane had in December 1579 where an angel informed her of her pregnancy and ordered that the son be named Zacharias, there are no notes about a pregnancy in Dee's diary in 1580.

Some of Dee's own dreams were disturbing. People he knew, such as Cecil and Sir Francis Walsingham, appeared in his dreams. In one of the strangest, one that he had in November 1582, he "dreamed that I was dead, and afterward my bowels were taken out I walked and talked with diverse, and among other with the L. Treasurer who was come to my house to burn my books when I was dead: and thought he looked sourly on me." Seven years later in August of 1589, Dee had another nightmare that concerned the loss of his books. "In the night following, my terrible dream that Mr. Kelly would by force bereave me of my books etc." While Dee did not record the time of night in 1582, in 1589 he wrote that this dream had occurred "toward daybreak," a time we know that a dream was perceived more likely to be true. Edward Kelley was quite well known and many were suspicious of him. In the 1594 *Terrors of the Night,* Nashe mocked those he referred to as "famous conjurers," suggesting they are dangerous con men. Charles Nicholl argues that Nashe was probably referring to Kelley but also to Forman, the professional astrologer and dream interpreter who was consulted in the aftermath of the Gunpowder Plot.[94]

Forman had been interested in dreams since he was a boy, and when he composed his autobiography many years later, he claimed that he had had a series of dreams "every night continually for three or four years space." While the dreams were frightening, they also showed Simon triumphantly over-coming his difficulties. He dreamed that "mighty mountains and hills [had] come rolling against him," but he was always able to go up on top and over them. He dreamed of "great waters like to drown him, boiling and raging as though they would swallow him up," but he was always able to overpass them.[95] We should also remember that, as Sir Thomas Browne pointed out, "fantastical objects seem greater than they are; . . . it may prove more easy to dream of giants than pigmies. . . . A little water makes a sea; a small puff of wind a tempest."[96] Forman did have mountains and ocean tempests to over-come. His father's death soon after his eleventh birthday meant that the schooling he so desired soon came to a halt. Three years later, he apprenticed himself to a hosier and a grocer on a ten-year contract with the agreement that for the first three years he would be allowed to attend the town free school. His master reneged, however, and even confiscated his Latin books to keep him from studying in the evenings. Forman broke off the apprenticeship five years later in 1572 and spent the rest of that decade studying and working as a schoolmaster. Much of his education in astronomy, physic, magic, philosophy, and surgery had to be self-taught. By the 1580s he was practicing medicine and was periodically imprisoned, at least in part because of having been found in possession of books on magic. He pursued alchemy and judicial astrology and began attempting to call angels and spirits. In 1592, he moved to London and established what became a thriving practice in astrological medicine, which again led to confrontations with the College of Physicians and occasional imprisonment. But people continued to come to "Dr." Forman; while most of his consultations were about illness, many were for advice on a wide range of other topics. A dream Forman had as an adult in the mid-1590s echoes these childhood dreams and also depicts a Forman who not only overcomes danger and adversity but helps others to do so as well. Forman dreamed that he was in a place of great danger "where many boys and maids were like to die and I too." Suddenly, as he alighted on a plum tree, he realized that he could fly. After refreshing himself with a num-ber of red plums, Forman flew back to his companions and assured them that they, too, could fly if they would make the attempt. As their enemy approached, Forman made them all hold hands. While some flew much higher and better than others, they all managed to fly to a house where they rested on the roof before flying over fields, hedges, and water. Finally they went "up into a wild down, a desolate place on the side of a hill, and there we rested."[97] Forman was convinced that this dream was a hopeful omen.

Forman believed that dreams were a way for him to have prophetical visions and to acquire alchemical knowledge. He would mark the dreams in the treatises that he read, and he carefully recorded his own dreams, being convinced that each dream was in some way connected to what would hap-pen the day after. As we read his dream notations, we see that his dreams expressed anxieties and hopes about his professional life as well as his personal one. His efforts to learn magic invaded his dreams. In one, he dreamed "that Dr. Blague had lent him many books of magic." In another, "I dreamt I did see in a glass when I did call and that I did hear also, and that it was the first time that ever I did hear or see and I was answered directly of all things."[98] In a dream similar to Dee's but more positive, Forman dreamed that he was dead, but at his own wake he was given his books. Other dreams of his own death were more unpleasant, such as the one in which he had died and been washed and laid out in his coffin and heard those around him say that he was dead and they should bury him.[99]

When Forman had moved to London in 1592, he met and became deeply and tumultuously involved with a married recusant, Avisa Allen. Their relationship lasted intermittently until her death in June 1597. Just as Digby was both obsessed with Venetia and unfaithful to her, Avisa appears to have had a deep emotional hold on Forman though he continued to "halek" as he put it in diary, many, many women. Just as Dee recorded his wife's dreams, Forman recorded Avisa's, at least the ones that had to do with him. Forman was convinced that the boy to whom she gave birth in late June 1596 and who died only two weeks later was his. Avisa's health was not good after her pregnancy and in November of that year Forman dreamed that the ailing Avisa was wrapped in a white sheet and laid on the bed next to him, "but she was exceeding cold like one dead." Forman's medical and astrological practice continued to thrive with aristocrats among his clients. He also continued his conflicts with the College of Physicians, and he continued to record his dreams. After Forman died in 1611, his papers were given to his friend Richard Napier, another medical astrologer.

Napier also listened to the dreams of his clients. One was Elizabeth Banebery, who consulted Napier three times in 1618. He recorded that "she suffered mental disturbances" after childbirth. Three days later, she had a "frightful dream," which left her "well in health, but much troubled in mind." She could not sleep well, fought with her husband, and "her milk was suddenly dried up." Elizabeth became so distraught that she was "tempted to kill herself." She saw Napier three times between January and March of 1618 but was still "much troubled in mind" in the words of Napier in his final report.[100]

The self-taught Forman, along with Dee, gained the esteem of the next generation of respected professional astrologers and dream keepers such as Lilly and Ashmole, who were the closest of friends despite being on opposite sides of the Civil War. Ashmole did research on Dee and contemplated writing his biography. Browne obtained some of Dee's books and manuscripts from Dee's son Arthur, an old friend of Browne's, and sent them to Ashmole. Lilly wrote positively about Forman. In certain ways Lilly's background echoed Forman's. A very bright child of parents of yeoman stock, at the age of eleven he was sent off to grammar school where an eminent Puritan school master, John Brinsley, instructed him in grammar, rhetoric, Latin, and Greek. Lilly, too, was very concerned about dreams, especially in his youth. Lilly wrote in later life that in 1618 when he was "in the sixteenth year of my age I was exceedingly troubled in my dreams concerning my salvation and damnation, and also concerning the safety and destruction of the souls of my father and mother; in the nights I frequently wept, prayed and mourned, for fear my sins might offend God."[101]

Lilly's mother died the following year. When Lilly was eighteen, he had to leave school because of his father's poverty and therefore could not attend university. He soon obtained a position in London in the household of a salt merchant Gilbert Wright. Some months after Wright's death in 1627, Lilly secretly married his widow, Ellen, a woman considerably older than himself. It was apparently a happy marriage, and upon her death six years later, he inherited nearly £1000. Lilly diligently studied astrology and by the mid-1640s had nearly 2000 clients a year and was earning a good income.

In December 1646, the royalist Jonas Moore introduced Lilly to his friend Ashmole, the beginning of a strong friendship between Lilly and Ashmole that lasted all their lives. Soon after they met, Ashmole dreamed about Lilly. As we know, by the middle of the 1640s, the young widower Ashmole had begun to consider remarrying. At the beginning of January he had proposed to a Mrs. March, who told him she loved him and would be delighted to marry him but she had already agreed to marry Mr. Lollier if he met certain conditions. Ashmole dreamed that his new friend Lilly assured him he would get Mrs. March to marry him "by his art," which probably meant magic.[102] This dream was not prophetic; in the end Mrs. March did not marry either Lollier or Ashmole. In November of 1649, Lilly clearly demonstrated how much he valued his friendship with Ashmole. Ashmole's friend George Wharton had been arrested in March 1648 because he authored the openly Royalist pamphlet, "Prognostic Notes." Ashmole had been afraid for Wharton's life, but Wharton had managed to escape. He was rearrested on 21 November 1649 and was sentenced to death. Lilly and Wharton had never gotten along, but Wharton was a valued friend of Ashmole. When Ashmole approached Lilly for help, he managed to use his influence so that Wharton would be freed on the condition he would no longer write anything critical of Parliament or the State of England.[103]

Ashmole shared many of his dreams with Lilly, who wrote that Ashmole had "sometimes very slight dreams signifying nothing at all." But when the times were right according to his astrological signs "I conceive his dreams may signify some truth, and chiefly may concern things of old. . . . I should and do rather conceive, that his dreams do rather concern honors, preferment, fame, glory, estimation, friendship, arts and sciences, office, grandeur, writings, books, laws, ordinances." Lilly, himself a committed astrologer, believed that Ashmole's sign was "so strong in the nativity he has a restless fancy, and therefore dreams of sublime and high matters, of things almost impossible, and for the most part of such matters as concern learning and high mysteries."[104]

Ashmole recorded his dreams for a number of years. He also professionally interpreted dreams and recorded in his diary several times that clients had sent for him so they could tell him their dreams.[105] His own dreams were often vivid and disturbing. Ashmole's mother died in early July 1646, but he did not learn of her death until the end of the month. In early October she came to Ashmole in a dream and told him that "she died for mere wait, and that I would not send to her which I excused saying I could get no messenger to go to her after I came from Worcester." Ashmole also dreamed of danger to himself and the deaths of people he knew and cared about who were still alive. On 1 March 1647, he dreamed that "this night I lay at Mr. Hook's and dreamed I had poisoned myself with eating poison in with butter that a young man had given me." In May he dreamed disturbingly of his friend, "that Jonas Moore was dead and died suddenly which I much lamented." That same month, he dreamed that a whole family named Kirk died. Of course, 1647 was a very difficult time for royalists and may have led to some of the distressing dreams Ashmole had.[106] Ashmole's dreams, as well as Forman's, reflected not only the issues of their personal and professional lives but also the larger political cultural issues of early modern England. We will come back to them throughout the book.

De la Pryme was another young man in the seventeenth century who became interested in understanding the supernatural and dreamed disturbingly of someone he had cared about who died. In 1690 when he was nineteen, he began his studies at Cambridge University. He and Humphrey Bohun, his best friend at Cambridge, pursued their studies of magic, but the intense ideas may have been too much for Bohun, who committed suicide at the beginning of December 1692. A month later, de la Pryme dreamed vividly of his dead friend. "I dreamed last night that methought as I was walking I overtook my old friend Mr. Bohun, but he seemed to be melancholy, and as we were walking, 'Oh, Abraham!' says he . . . 'I could never have imagined that my father would have taken my death so ill, or else I would never have done the act.'" As Abraham wrote later, he noted how the Bohun in his dream "had the exact gate that he used in his life-time, flinging out an elbow as he walked, and shaking his head when he spoke." Edmund Bohun was indeed deeply troubled by the death of his oldest child, and a week after the dream Abraham received "a very kind though a very severe letter" from him. De la Pryme recorded in his diary that "he persuaded me exceedingly to desist from all magical studies, and lays a company of most black sins to my charge, which (he said) I committed by daring to search in such forbidden things."[107] De la Pryme gave up magic for the study of botany; he also became very interested in folklore and later in 1693 recorded in his diary the story by which this chapter began.

CHAPTER 3

RELIGION AND WITCHCRAFT

As we saw in the previous chapter, dreams were powerful in the belief systems of early modern English people. One of the areas where dreams had the most powerful resonances had to do with religious belief and practice. Dreams allowed many in early modern England not only to see devils, angels, and even Christ himself but also to experience heaven and hell while still on earth. In the sixteenth century, England underwent a time of tumultuous change in terms of what those in power deemed to be acceptable religious practice. After decades of persecuting heretics, Henry VIII broke with the Catholic Church and assumed his role as Supreme Head of the Church—an act that prompted both Catholics and Protestants to be wary for the rest of his reign. A particularly vivid example that worried many individuals occurred on 30 July 1540, when all on the same day, Henry had Thomas Barnes, William Jerome, and Thomas Gerrard burnt for heresy under the Six Articles and then had Thomas Abel, Richard Fetherstone, and Edward Powell hanged for treason for denying the royal supremacy. While the Reformation was pushed forward in the reign of Edward, it was violently renounced by Mary, who brought England's Church back into its allegiance to Rome. John Foxe's *Actes and Monuments* vividly described the bravery of Protestants and the horrific deaths they suffered. After Mary's death in November 1558, England again became Protestant, though Elizabeth attempted a settlement that would be acceptable to as many of the English as possible—more Protestant in its theology and more reminiscent of Catholicism in its ceremony.

Many passionate reformers who had fled England under Mary returned at the beginning of Elizabeth's reign determined to purge all Catholic remnants from the English church and, more importantly, to convince the English emotionally that it would be a true tragedy for Catholicism to be the state religion ever again. In the first decade of Elizabeth's reign, the queen hoped that Catholicism would eventually die away peacefully on its own. But a series of events caused that hope to crumble a decade after she became queen: In

1568, Mary Stuart fled to England; the Northern rebellion took place the next year; Elizabeth was excommunicated in 1570; and there were a number of attempts to assassinate the queen and restore England to its obedience to Rome. While no one was executed for being Catholic until 1574, there then began to be a number of such deaths, but Elizabeth and her government would claim these executions were for treason not religion. Catholic martyrologies played effectively to their intended audience much the same as Foxe's descriptions of martyrdom did to his. Both Foxe and Catholic martyrologies used dreams to make the depiction more emotionally powerful as well as to show how God favored the martyr.

Conflicts among Puritans, Catholics, and Anglicans continued in the reigns of the early Stuarts in part leading to the civil war and the execution of the king. The other sides of the strong religious convictions were the deep belief in witchcraft and the fear it engendered. As religious, social, and political conflicts escalated, so too did the vivid feelings of cultural anxiety expressed both in actual dreams and in the use of them as metaphor. Dreams were described and created to express a view or to try to influence how people reacted.

Dreams could have very powerful resonances, particularly, as we have seen when they are attributed to those who died for their religious beliefs. A number of post–Reformation writers, however, tried to develop criteria by which someone could tell if the dream came from the devil, from God and the angels, or simply from severe indigestion. Some Protestants were convinced that dreams ought to be ignored altogether because believing in them only brought problems. Thomas Cranmer, archbishop of Canterbury in the reigns of Henry VIII and Edward VI, though he did own a book on predictions and prognostications, argued that it were best if people paid no attention to their dreams because such night visions "deceived, destroyed, and [have] overthrown many good men."[1] (figure 3.1) Thomas Newton, a Church of England clergyman who was a writer and translator, translated Andre Gerhard's *The true tryall and examination of a mans owne self,* which argued that it was contrary to the first commandment to attempt to procure anything "either good or bad" through "unlawful means, or superstitious and damnable helps." Among the "damnable helps" were "demanding questions and answers of the dead" or "dealing with damned spirits;" and also mentioned were "dreams."[2] Some Catholics were equally hostile to dreams and also used the first commandment as the rationale. The English Catholic priest Laurence Vaux fled the country soon after Elizabeth's accession and settled in Louvain, where he established a school for the children of English exiles. He lectured his students that the first commandment forbade "all idolatry and . . . magic, divination, superstitions, observations, and all wicked worshipping." He made sure that they understood that "interpreters of dreams and such like" were "prohibited by the law of God."[3]

One reason Cranmer might have so warned against dreams was the strong belief in this period that the devil and his demons could cause people to have false dreams that might lead them greatly astray. The devil could also tempt

THOMAS CRANMER, ARCHBISHOP OF CANTERBURY.

OB. 1556.

FROM THE ORIGINAL OF 'GERBIER'S FLECCES' IN

THE BRITISH MUSEUM.

J & F. TALLIS, LONDON & NEW YORK.

Figure 3.1 Thomas Cranmer.

Private collection.

those weak in faith to practice witchcraft, leading to dreams that could be
equally dangerous, deceiving, and destructive. Just as religious texts warned
of the dangers of demons invading dreams, so too was it strongly believed
that witches could both communicate with the devil through dreams and cast
spells that caused their victims to have dreadful nightmares. Some women
and men who practiced witchcraft apparently believed their experiences took
place in some alternate reality while their bodies were at home asleep.[4]

Some Protestants believed in the importance of dreams. A prayer published by Richard Day to be said when one was "going into bed" begs God that "we may not be absent from thee, not even in sleep: that such dreams may keep our beds and bodies pure and undefiled."[5] A number of Protestant authors, however, decried the belief in dreams as foolish, superstitious, or dangerous. Foxe, in his compendium of martyrs, often mocked dreams as being "monkish fables," adding that "of such prodigious fantasies our monkish histories be full: and not only our histories of England, but also the heathen histories of the Gentiles be stuffed with such kind of dreams of much like effect."[6] While Foxe might have been scornful of dreams, he treated them with great seriousness when they were the dreams of future martyrs.

Dreams in Foxe's Martyrology

Foxe also treated some Catholic dreams seriously as well. A telling example is his discussion of how the Dominican order was begun. Foxe described how a Spanish churchman, Dominicke, who had been laboring for ten years preaching against the Albigensians and any others perceived as heretics by Rome, begged Pope Innocent III to have his order of preaching friars confirmed. For a long time Pope Innocent refused. The pope changed his mind after he had a dream that "the church of Laterane was ready to fall. Which when he beheld, fearing and much sorrowing thereat, comes in this Dominic: who with his shoulders under propped the church, and so preserved the building thereof from falling." Foxe then explained that "this dream may seem to be verified, for that friars have been always the chief pillars and upholders of the pope's church." This, Foxe argued, was the beginning of the "Wolfish order of the Dominics." His reason for calling them "wolfish" also involved a recounting of a dream, "for that his mother when she was great with this Dominic, dreamed that she had in her womb a wolf, which had a burning torch in his mouth, which dream, the preachers of that order do greatly advance, and expound it to their orders' glory." But Foxe stated that, however they explain the dream, a wolf is "but a wolf, and this . . . a wolfish order."[7]

Despite Foxe's disdain of some dreams, in his depictions of the martyrdom of the faithful, he narrated some truly prophetic dreams of brave men and women. William Hunter was only nineteen when he was burned as a heretic on 26 March 1555. The night before his death, Hunter had a dream. Foxe was careful to tell his readers that it occurred at two o'clock in the morning—and his readers would well know that dreams after midnight were far more likely to be true. Hunter dreamed "that he was at the place where the stake was . . . where he should be burned." He also dreamed "that he met with his father as he went to the stake, and also that there was a Priest at the stake, which went about to have him recant." The next morning the sheriff came to take Hunter. The sheriff's son came too and embraced the condemned man, telling him, "William, be not afraid." Hunter answered, "I thank God I am not afraid." And "then the Sheriff's son could speak no more to him for weeping." Foxe wanted his readers to know that Hunter was such a fine young man that he was loved even by the son of the man leading him to his execution. As Hunter was being walked to the stake, he "met with his father according to his dream, and he spoke to his son, weeping and saying, God be with thee son." Hunter responded, "God be with you father, and be of a good comfort, for I hope we shall meet again when we shall be merry." His father agreed but was so upset that he left before his son's execution. "So William went to the place where the stake stood, even according to his dream." Hunter prayed, " 'Son of God, shine upon me,' and immediately the sun in the element shone out of a dark cloud . . . whereat the people mused, because it was so dark a little time afore." The priest was so upset that this phenomenon was swaying the observers that he turned to Hunter and said, "look how thou burnest here, so shall thou burn in hell." Hunter's response was also aimed at the audience: " 'thou lyest, thou false prophet: away thou false prophet, away.' Then was there a gentleman which said, I pray God have mercy upon his soul. The people said: Amen, Amen." The fire was made, but Hunter stated that he was not afraid and called out, " 'Lord, Lord, Lord, receive my spirit,' and casting down his head again into the smothering smoke, he yielded up his life for the truth, sealing it with his blood, to the praise of God."[8]

Foxe's portrayal of William Hunter's martyrdom showed a brave man of deep belief. That he foresaw his martyrdom in his dream the night before makes it all the more powerful a statement of true faith to the readers. John Bradford also had a dream about his martyrdom only a few nights before his death. In 1547, when Bradford was about thirty-seven, he went through a conversion experience, sold off a number of his valuable items to distribute funds among the poor and needy, and dedicated himself to the study of the Bible. He went on to study at Cambridge, where he received his M.A. in 1549, and then became a fellow of Pembroke College. The following year Nicholas Ridley, bishop of London, ordained him and gave him a preaching license. By the end of 1551, he was appointed one of six chaplains to Edward VI, demonstrating that he was regarded as one of the significant Protestant preachers. When Mary became queen, Bradford was charged with preaching seditious sermons and imprisoned in the Tower; in March 1554, he was moved to the King's bench prison at Southwark, where he stayed for the next ten months. As one of the leaders among the prisoners, he was allowed to preach and administer the sacraments to the other prisoners charged with heresy. He also read, wrote, and especially prayed, extensively.

In January 1555, Bradford was examined three times at Winchester and proclaimed a heretic. He was moved to another prison where he was no longer allowed to preach or interact with others. In attempts to force him to recant, he was subjected to numerous examinations and debates throughout that spring. It was clear that he was important enough to make it worth the while for authorities to try to get him to recant. It was however, to no avail, and on June 30, he was sent back to Newgate and dispatched to Smithfield to be burned the following day.[9] Right before he was sent back to Newgate, Bradford was "sore troubled diverse times in his sleep by dreams, how the chain for his burning was brought to the Counter gate, and how the next day being Sunday, he should be had to Newgate, and on the Monday after burned in Smithfield." These dreams disturbed him so much that, about three o'clock in the morning, he woke his cellmate "and told him his unquiet sleep, and what he was troubled with all. Then after a little talk, Mister Bradford rose out of the bed, and gave himself to his old exercise of reading and prayer, as always he had used before." He felt so much better that he was in his "accustomed manner" all the next day, when he learned that indeed he was being sent to Newgate and to his death.[10] His dream had accurately predicted the end of his life and had given him the time to meet the news of his death with dignity.

In Ispwich in 1556, Agnes Potten, the wife of Robert Potten, along with the wife of Michael Trunchield, stated that they believed that "the Sacrament was the memorial only of *CHRIST'S* death and passion," and, Foxe stated, for that they were burned. He expressed how impressed he was that "so simple women" had such constancy and "so manfully stood to the confession and testimony of Gods word and verity." Just as Hunter and Bradford dreamed about their coming deaths, so too had Potten dreamed about her impending martyrdom. She "saw a bright burning fire, right up as a pole, and on the side of the fire she thought there stood a number of Q. Mary's friends looking on." As she was asleep "she seemed to muse with her self whether her fire should burn so bright or no." Foxe told his readers that "indeed her suffering was not far unlike to her dream." But Foxe also asserted that the dreamer was the braver of the two women, who were always together in prison and would be burned together: "the one which was Michael's wife seemed to be nothing so ardent and zealous as Potten's wife was"[11] (Figure 3.2).

John Rough, the minister of the underground London congregation, had dreamed about his deacon Cutbert Symson. He was the head of a family who dreamed as well. One night around the same time as the arrest of Cutbert, Rough and his wife had their two-year-old daughter, Rachel, in bed with them. She suddenly awoke in the middle of the night and, according to Foxe, cried out, "alas, alas, my father is gone, my father is gone." They turned on the light to convince Rachel that her father was still there. When she came to herself, Rachel threw herself into her father's arms, telling him "now I will hold you, that you go not away." The family finally got back to sleep, and Rough's wife then dreamed that a member of their congregation, James Merings's wife, Margaret, was "going down the street with a bloody banner in her hand, and a fire pan on her head." The blood on the banner symbolized the deaths of so many true Christians, while the pan demonstrated Margaret's role in her family economy. In the dream, Rough's wife suddenly "arising to go see her, she thought she stumbled on a great Hog, and had a mighty fall there by." The shock of the fall wakened her, and she said, "I am never able to rise again."[12] In terms of rising with pleasure to be with her family, it was true that soon she would never rise again. These dreams were significant, Foxe implied, because soon after this night, Rough was arrested. When Margaret Mearing brought Rough a clean shirt in prison, she, too, was arrested, and the two were burned together.

Figure 3.1 Martyrdom of Agnes Potten.

John Foxe, Actes and Monuments
by permission of Love Library, University of Nebraska.

CATHOLIC MARTYRS ALSO DREAM

Catholic martyrologists also used dreams to demonstrate that those who died had been shown by God that they were heroes who should meet death with serenity. In a narration (of perhaps overly obvious symbolism), John Bodey is described as coming to terms with his death because of a dream. Bodey was born in 1549; he studied at the University of Oxford and became a fellow of New College in 1568. In 1576, he was expelled from Oxford, along with seven other fellows, because of his outspoken advocacy of Catholicism. Bodey left England to study at Douay College and returned to England two years later. He was arrested in 1580 for denying the royal supremacy and maintaining the supremacy of the pope, or, as the English authorities called this figure, the bishop of Rome. Bodey was kept in prison for three years before he was executed in Andover. The night before his death, "as trustworthy Catholics relate," Bodey dreamed that there were "two bulls attacking him very furiously, but without at all hurting him, at which he was much astonished." The next day, two hangmen came from London to execute Bodey. As he walked with them he asked them their names, "and as they one after the other answered that they were called Bull." Bodey remembered his dream and called forth: "Blessed be God; you are then those two bulls who gave me such trouble last night in my dream, and yet did me no harm." According to witnesses, as a result of his understanding of the meaning of his dream, he was able to "then joyfully composed himself for death." When Bodey's mother heard of his death, she "made a great Feast to her neighbors, as her son's marriage day, rejoicing of his martyrdom."[13]

BIBLICAL DREAMS AND EARLY MODERN DREAMERS

Of course, one enormous change that came with the Protestant reformation was the emphasis on reading the Bible as the word of God and the importance of having the Bible available in the vernacular. Thus people could read of Biblical dreams such as those of Daniel, Abraham, Jacob, and Joseph. The seventeenth-century Protestant minister and writer Philip Goodwin, in his *The mystery of dreames, historically discoursed,* told his readers that they should pray for good sleep and for good dreams. He suggested that one way to help that happen was to take the Bible to bed and read it until one fell asleep. " 'Tis to good dreams a good help." Goodwin's book is particularly significant to this chapter as it is entirely devoted to religion and dreams. While arguing that "Before the times of Moses or any of the prophets in the Old Testament . . . God in dreams declared his mind," he also maintained that, though less frequent, God could come in dreams in Goodwin's age as well, since from the time of the Apostles "God sometimes sent in dreams of deep concern as various and very good authors" attested. Even in the Old Testament, dreams were often described as an authentic method of receiving divine communication and were also a way for a prophet to learn the truth, though some early modern scholars believed that dreams were inferior to the revelations received directly from God while someone was awake. Goodwin, however, argued that God sent visions when prophets were awake and dreams when they were asleep. He did not present one as superior to the other, in fact arguing that dreams were "the prime and principal manner in which God was wont to reveal his will and to speak his mind." He went on to explain that "in sleep God revealed divine truths to [the Prophets] which they taught to others in their waking times."[14]

While the content of divine messages was usually presented clearly and with no ambiguity, this was not always the case in dreams. In the stories of both Daniel and Joseph, the skills of experts or professional interpreters were necessary to understand the dreams. When Joseph was imprisoned because of the false accusation of Potiphar's wife, it was his ability to interpret dreams that brought him to the Pharaoh's notice and saved his life.[15] The Old Testament Joseph was particularly popular in early modern texts. Goodwin, for example, described him as a "Captain-Dreamer" because of his "sublime and divine knowledge" and his "marvelous insight for the interpreting of dreams." But even Joseph could not completely trust his dreams. "Joseph dreamed of his preferment but never dreamed of his imprisonment."[16]

William Patten was a minor chaplain who in 1547 accompanied the English army that Edward Seymour, Duke of Somerset, led into Scotland for the "rough wooing" of Mary Stuart as a bride for young Edward VI. Patten published an account of the experience the following year. He had read widely about the meaning of dreams. When describing a dream of the Duke of Somerset, he put it within the context of Joseph as a dream interpreter, "That if for example like to this I should rehearse to you out of the Old Testament, how the seven plentiful years, and the seven years of famine in Egypt were plainly signified afore to Pharaoh by his dreams." Patten also assured his readers that ancient philosophers as well as "holy scripture" prove that "sometimes in dreams we be warned of things to come."[17]

Somerset's dream had clearly upset him, and the Duke could not get it out of his mind. As he was "walking upon the rampart of the town walls, on the side toward Scotland," he met up with Patten and told him that a few nights before he had dreamed that "he was come back again to the Court, where the king's Majesty did heartily welcome him home, and every estate else." One might think this a very positive dream, but it was actually one that caused Somerset acute anxiety, as he "thought he had done nothing at all in this voyage." Still in the dream, Somerset had considered the "great costs, and the great travail of the great men and soldiers, and all to have been done in vain, the very care and shamefaced abashment of the thing did waken him out of his dream."[18]

Patten reported the dream to first show Somerset's regard toward his king and all the men he led. But he also used the dream as an example of how interpreting dreams sometimes requires one to read them as opposites, a belief held for many centuries. Referring his readers back to the dream book of Artemidorus, Patten argued that some dreams are "allegorical . . . and sometime one contrary is meant by another." Writing once the invasion was over, Patten claimed Somerset's dream was indeed one that could be understood only as an opposite: "Of which sort of dreams, this of my lord's grace was, that showed he had done nothing, and signified (as we may now behold) he should do so much." Before leaving the topic, Patten again turned to religious belief; he informed his readers that, while he discussed this, he wanted to have "no man so much to note and esteem dreams, as to think there are none vain, but all significant," as that is not only superstitious but "against the mind of God uttered in the old law." Patten would also not want anyone "to think we can at no time be warned by them, a thing also both of too much incredulity, and against the promise of God."[19]

In some ways, Patten was correct that the dream should be read as an opposite, and that the invasion was a success because the Scots suffered a bitter defeat at the battle of Pinkie in September 1547. It did not, however, lead to a marriage between Edward and Mary. Mary Stuart's mother, Mary of Guise, feared that she would lose her daughter by force to the English; therefore, she decided to send Mary to France to be raised and eventually to marry Francis, the eldest son of Henry II and Catherine de Medici and heir to the French throne. Somerset's anxiety dreams may well have been telling: Only a few years later, he lost his position and soon after his life. The sickly boy king Edward died at the age of fifteen in 1553, before he could marry anyone. After the failed coup to put Lady Jane Grey on the throne and after Henry VIII's eldest daughter Mary was universally recognized as queen, England was restored to its obedience to the pope. In this reign as well, dreams continued to hold great consequence.

In the reign of Mary I, the Protestant minister Bradford, who had dreamed significantly just before his death, used the example of Joseph and his dreams in a letter to Erkinald Rawlins, letting him know that he would not be disgraced if he took his family and fled England to avoid persecution. Bradford himself was writing from prison when he told Rawlins, "As God told Joseph in a dream by an angel, that he should fly: so if ye feel such infirmity in your selves, as should turn to God's dishonor, and your own destruction withall: know that at this present, I am as God's angel, to admonish you to take time while ye have it." In a marginal note, Foxe informed his readers that "This Erkinald and his wife following this counsel did fly both beyond sea."[20]

Certainly Old Testament dreams made their way into the sermons preached in early modern England, and thus they had their own impact on the dreams of the people. In the seventeenth century, Arise Evans described significant dreams that he had experienced over the course of several decades. In 1633, he dreamed that a voice came to him stating, "Get thee to the root," which Evans understood as meaning "the Lord God Almighty." This led him soon after to the Black-Friars Church to hear a sermon whose subject was Jacob wrestling with the angel of God, which moved Evans enough for him to describe the topic. When he returned home, he read his Bible and went to bed. After he had fallen asleep, the voice came to him again and commanded him to read the Bible more closely and he would learn what he needed to do. This dream and subsequent Bible reading directly led to Evans's travels and public preaching of visions. Times were not always pleasant, such as when his family imprisoned him, fearing he was mad.[21]

We do not know more of the sermon that so greatly influenced Evans other than that the topic was Jacob. We know much more about a sermon preached by the outspoken radical John Everard, who was described by William Penn as a "great spiritual separatist" and who was one of the dominant preachers influencing London separatism in the 1630s.[22] "The Mystery, or Life, and Marrow of the Scriptures" was printed, and we can see specifically what Everard had to say about Jacob's dream. Everard speaks movingly of how Jacob has to leave his father's house and forsake all of his kindred and friends, fearing he will never see them again. He was filled with sad thoughts as he walked, and at nightfall, finding no lodging, he lay down in an open field resting his head upon a heap of stones. Yet when he fell asleep he "dreamed such a dream as never was dreamed on a pillow of down." Jacob dreamed that "he saw a ladder reach from earth to heaven, and God himself stood at the top of the ladder, and the angels of God were ascending and descending on it." God said to him, "Jacob, I will be with thee, I will provide for thee; take no thought, I will be thy God, thou shall want for nothing." This dream was deeply important to Jacob; it was "that which comforted Jacob in all his journey, that whatever he met withal, or wheresoever he was, he still had recourse to what his vision taught him." For Protestants in troubled times in the sixteenth and seventeenth centuries, this dream would also have brought much comfort. As Goodwin put it, Jacob during his travels "had only a pillow of stones, yet he slept sweetly and dreamt comfortably."[23]

Though there were far fewer dreams mentioned in the New Testament, there were some powerful ones, particularly in the gospel of Matthew, and of course these dreams are all to do with the life—and death—of Jesus Christ. Because of her dream, Pilate's wife attempted to convince her husband that he should avoid any connection with causing the death of Jesus, "that just man." While she did not relate the dream with any specificity, it clearly disturbed her. In his 1620 sermon on the nature of conscience, Anthony Cade used the example of Pilate's wife and quoted in part from Matt 27:19. "Pilate's wife, by revelation, as she thought, from heaven, willing her husband by a messenger: Have you nothing to do with that just man, for whom I have suffered many things in my dreams." This sermon was originally preached before Sir Henry Hobart, the Lord Chief Justice of the Common Pleas, and Sir Edward Bromley, one of the barons of the Exchequer, at the assizes at Leicester. It was then published with a second edition the following year.[24] Goodwin also considered the dream important, and while he condemned Pilate he praised his wife. "Pilate's wife, who in her dream sorely suffered . . . Though Pilate was stupid about the state of Christ, yet his wife had such a dream, as made impressions and moved compassions in Christ's innocent case."[25] Henry Howard argued that it was Pilate's wife's distress "by reason of her musing and revolving in the day time (as some gather) with her self, how grievously the plagues of God would light upon her husband and her house, for giving sentence against that holy Lamb," that she was so "tormented in her sleep." Howard acknowledged that "I am not ignorant that others derive this dream of Pilate's Wife, from an inspiration of God . . . yet (for mine own part) I choose rather to arraign her at the bar of nature in this case, by light whereof she discovered the sincerity of Christ."[26]

While we know only that Pilate's wife "suffered many things" in her dream, we do not know the exact nature of that dream; however, the dreams of another Joseph, husband to the Virgin Mary, are clearly elucidated in Mathew and have enormous significance. Joseph, also described as a "just" man, had to decide how to deal with the pregnancy of the woman he intended to marry. Not wanting to make a public example of her, he was considering putting her away "privily," when, in Dr. John Webster's seventeenth-century paraphrase of Matthew, "the Angel of the Lord appeared unto Joseph in a dream" as a "blessed and clear apparition, though in a dream in his sleep." The angel "bade him to take unto him Mary his wife."[27] Goodwin's version does not have God use an angel as an intermediary; God himself "appeared to him in a dream saying, Joseph thou son of David, fear not to take to thee Mary thy wife, for she shall bring forth a Son . . . Thou shalt call his name Jesus, for he shall save his people from their sins." This was not the only dream sent to Joseph from God. "Likewise by the appearing of an angel unto him in a dream, he was warned to take the child, and his mother, and to flee into Egypt, and also again was commanded by an angel, after the death of Herod, that appeared in a dream, and bade him to take the young child and his mother, and go into the land of Israel." As Goodwin put it, "God by dreams preserves" the infant Jesus.[28]

These examples from early modern writings suggest how people could believe both in the truth and power of dreams and in the idea that dreams came from God and his angels. There was also the possibility that the dreams might be false, and the book of Deuteronomy stated that someone who told of dreams that encouraged apostasy ought to be put to death. Goodwin wrote about how Martin Luther found "many fanatic spirits . . . who boasting of their Dreams sought to seduce him." While Goodwin praised the Old Testament Joseph for his skill in interpreting dreams, he also assured his readers that while God shall send "good Dreams in these latter times," he could also "make Dreams terrible." He used the biblical examples of "Thus Daniel had dreadful Dreams and visions about the Desolations of Jerusalem and the Jews, and their bloody persecutions by the Tyranny of Antiochus and others," while "the great horror which fell upon Abraham's heart in his sleep. . . . it might signify such sad Events as afterward himself and his Seed suffered."[29] Goodwin also quotes Job, who said, "Then thou scarest me with Dreams." David, because of his righteous fear of the Lord, wanted to arm himself against bad dreams and would repeat, "I have remembered thy Name O Lord in the night." Yet it is not necessarily true that God's dreams feel good and that the Devil's are upsetting. "Some divine Dreams do disturb sleep, and may molest the mind, and interrupt men's rest. . . . Yet be it so, 'tis better in sleep to be somewhat troubled with molesting Dreams from God, than sinfully tickled with enticing and seducing Dreams from the Devil." There was a way others, at least, could tell if someone's dreams came from God or not: Goodwin asserted that false dreams would cause men to become arrogant and cruel, but God's dreams would not. Yet we can certainly doubt that anyone who had become arrogant because of what he dreamed would have the self-knowledge to admit it.

Goodwin also wanted his readers to know how dreams were often obscure and how difficult it was to comprehend their real meaning. Just as we have dreams "in the dark night, [they are] so of a dark nature: so veiled and covered as they commonly require an Interpreter." Understanding the true nature of the dream, Goodwin explained, was critical since "A Dream is a close covered Dish brought in by night for the Soul to feed on; And is it not suitable for a man, after to uncover the Dish, to see and know upon what Meat he hath eaten? That he may not like Isaac, abide beguiled with Kid for Venison." Goodwin would know that his readers would be well familiar with the story of Jacob fooling his father Isaac into thinking he was Esau and thus underhandedly gaining his blessing.[30]

Demons Visit Dreamers

Goodwin emphasized the great importance of dreams and told his readers that the Apostles advised Christians that they "ought, as in other things to differ from others, so in their sleep: others so sleep as therein they have a multitude of Dreams of diverse vanities, but let our bodies sleep, the fear of God possessing our souls." He also believed that Christians had to exercise great caution because it was equally possible to have demonic visitation as it was a divine message in one's dreams. He was especially concerned because he believed that the dreams men examined with most care were the ones that would "dispose them to action." But such dreams might be ambiguous, and using a dream as a reason to act might be dangerous and lead to one's destruction. Such dreams might be deluding, which Goodwin termed "intellectual," or they might be defiling, which he labeled as "sensual." It would be easy for the Devil to send deluding and defiling dreams since "he that can appear as a roaring Lion, to affright a waking Christian: cannot he present himself as an enticing Damsel, to affect a sleeping man, and affect these filthy Dreams?"[31]

On the other hand, if the dream were divinely inspired, then acting on it would be a duty, and not obeying it a sin. But sometimes, clearly, it would be difficult to know, and Goodwin explained how some people were convinced that God had spoken to them in their dreams even when that was not the case. "The last Instance I heard related, was of a Woman in a neighboring Town, who dreamed that God one night said to her, 'Come out from among them, and be ye separate.'" The woman woke up, thought about the dream, and then went back to sleep where the same thing happened. This time upon waking she was convinced that God had sent the dream twice to demonstrate its veracity. From that day onward she obeyed the dream and "ever after forsook all public Ordinances," which Goodwin believed to be a terrible sin, and as punishment she died soon after. So that his readers would take the story to heart, he added, "Her own sister, who received this same from her mouth, is yet alive to witness it."[32]

Even knowing that a dream was demonic would not allow someone to simply dismiss it. "Defilement in Dreams does not fasten upon the body barely," Thomas Cooper explained, "but settles upon the soul also. And this adds much to the mischief of such filthy Dreams, that the soul or mind, man's most precious part is by this means polluted." He also argued that Satan used the weaknesses of someone when he placed "devilish Dreams . . . in the brain" since he made them "answerable to our desires."[33] Nor could people always blame the devil for sinful dreams, since such dreams might well be "the products of man's own evil heart, which is always evil, but may be worst in the night." There is much more opportunity for good influence during the day "by reading, hearing, seeing; by means of others' company, counsel, examples, exercises; other good words and works, a wicked man may have many good thoughts moving in his mind." But at night while asleep "when he hath no such helps, his thoughts may be most notoriously naught. . . . with men many times that wickedness which breaks out in the day, was formed and framed in the night." Though no one would know about the actions of the dreamer in the dream but the dreamer himself, such dreams could lead to terrible secret guilt, and, Goodwin suggested, such "sinful dreams" could be even more serious than the sins committed by people awake and in their daily life.

For whatever casts under filth, brings under guilt. . . . Filthy Dreams that defile, though these effects are secret and unseen, yet that makes them never the less but the worse: The outward sins of waking men lay blots and blows upon them in the eye of the world, but these inward sins of sleeping men lay blows and blots upon them in the sight of God who sees in secret.

Because Goodwin was convinced that a person is open to these dreams as a result of daytime thoughts, he maintained that the guilt is—and should be—all the stronger. "A man that hath no body with him in his bed, may in the sleeping time of the night, be adulterously naught by the filthy Dreams of his mind: and commonly those filthinesses that a man's mind is fixed upon in the day when awake, will visit him in the night, find him out, and fasten upon him in his sleep." But even the best, most virtuous people, "God's Saints" are subject in sleep to defiling dreams. "There are no persons Satan seeks more to make them sinful, than God's Saints. That there are no seasons when Satan seeks more to make them sinful, than in nights. . . . When the servants of God are asleep in their beds, [Satan] surprises them by putting sinful thoughts in their minds." Not only, warned Goodwin, do such dreams take "our minds off from good, but take good out of our minds."[34]

Some English Protestants became fascinated with the story of the Italian Francis Spira, whose dreams were disturbed by devils. Spira was a very successful lawyer in the town of Cittadella, which was under the jurisdiction of Venice. When Luther's ideas became known in Italy in the 1540s, Spira began to read about them; he converted and began to teach Luther's gospel. He was so successful at converting not only his family but others in the circle, that in 1548 he was brought before the Inquisition. In fear of his life, he recanted and was forced to go to the public square to repeat his recantation before two thousand people. Spira was so distraught that he could not sleep the night before his public recantation. Overwhelmed with shame and fear, he attempted to kill himself. About eight weeks after his recantation, he starved himself to death. Almost immediately, Spira's story was told all over Europe. One of those who had been with him at his death, Matteo Gribaldi, wrote about Spira, and his text was translated into English about 1550. Foxe published two letters that mentioned Spira. Both letter-writers referred to the story in a way that made it clear that they expected their correspondents to know the Spira story already. In the letter Lady Jane Grey wrote to Mr. Harding, who had been her father's chaplain (but who had converted to Catholicism when Mary became queen), Lady Jane expressed how appalled she was by this behavior. "Remember . . . the lamentable case of Spira of late, whose case (me think) should be yet so green in your remembrance, that being a thing of our time, you should fear the like inconvenience seeing you are fallen into the like offence." Foxe also published a letter from Bradford to Lord Russell, where he told him to "remember Lot's wife which looked back. Remember Francis Spira."[35]

Spira's story was also popularized in Thomas Beard's 1597 translation of Jean de Chassanion's *Theatre of Gods Judgements,* which went through another four editions by the middle of the seventeenth century, and Nathaniel Bacon's *Relation of the fearfull estate of Francis Spira, in the yeare, 1548,* that circulated for some years in manuscript before being published in 1638, and which also went through many editions. There was also the 1581 play, *Conflict of Conscience* by Nathiel Woodes. Goodwin wrote that the recantation put Spira into "such a despairing condition, that he was filled with the horrors of Hell, not only in his wake-full times, but in his sleeping Dreams." Goodwin narrated how Spira told someone who had come to comfort him that "no sooner in the Night can I snatch a little sleep, but I see therein, the Devils come flocking into my chamber, and gathering all about my bed, and terrifying me with dismal noises."[36] Spira's dreams sound not so different from those that plagued John Bunyan as a boy in the 1630s. He had "fearful dreams" and in his sleep would see "the apprehensions of devils, and wicked spirits, who still, as I then thought, labored to draw me away with them." As an adult, Bunyan read about Spira when he was dealing with his own spiritual despair. He found "that dreadful story of that miserable mortal . . . was to my troubled spirit as salt, when rubbed into a fresh wound."[37]

ANGELS ALSO VISIT DREAMS

The Widdowes' translation of Scribonius's book on *Naturall Philosophy* told about the importance of angels as messengers from God. Angels help people celebrate God's glory. They also watch over the world and protect people. They enable people to understand God's will, putting good ideas into people's minds, and helping them resist ill spirits. Scribonius was arguing that angels have a wide swath of duties. To do them, they sometimes appear in "true and real bodies" but more often in "dreams and visions."[38]

Many in the early modern period were convinced that angels could help good Christians dream well and in fact take care of them in their dreams. Thomas Hill's dream book tells the reader that "to see and talk with an Angel, declare[s] a happiness to follow." Goodwin assured his readers that "God sends Angels from Heaven in the night and sets them about men's Bed when asleep; as to prevent Satan in Dreams that be bad, so to convey himself in Dreams very good. By bad Dreams would Devils break in, but are beat off by Angels."[39] Scribonius asserted that an angel's purpose was to "watch over the world, to preserve us, to declare and do God's will, to put good motions into our minds, to resist ill spirits." Writing in the middle of the seventeenth century, Joseph Hall suggested that if someone had an illness "which the physicians it seems could not cure" and in a dream "receive the prescript of the remedy of his disease," then, Hall argued, "whence can this be but the suggestion of spirits?"[40]

ROBERT ASHLEY'S MYSTERIOUS DREAM VISITORS

The French Protestant theologian and pastor Moise Amyraut, in a book translated into English, argued that while some dreams sent to humans were straightforward, others were "Symbolical and Mysterious."[41] Robert Ashley, who never managed to achieve the public or university career for which he had striven, kept a private journal that recorded a number of his dreams. On several occasions, Ashley dreamed about angels as well as bad spirits, and some were indeed mysterious.[42] In 1595 when Ashley was about thirty, he had a very disturbing dream in which "the image of a certain woman showed herself." She was coming into his house "swinging a bosom full of fury," and she "prophesied me doom and disappeared. I was trembling in all limbs because of the horrible sight." Once Ashley woke up, he "implored God so that he in his great mercy would avert all impending evil and sad cases animated by a bad spirit and turn it into good." At the time of this dream, Ashley was attempting to create a public career for himself, and the anxiety over it may have led to the dream. His prayers appeared to at least help avert some of Ashley's doom, though apparently not all.

While still young, Ashley had discovered his love of theatre and reading, delighting in such adventure stories as Guy of Warwick and Arthur and the Knights of the Round Table. He was also talented in the study of foreign languages and became fluent in French at a young age. He played leading roles in school plays performed at Wilton before the Earl of Pembroke. He went on to Oxford and received his B.A. in 1582 and his M.A. in 1587. Though he studied mathematics, he also loved to read medieval romances and became proficient in several foreign languages. The same year he received his M.A., he was delighted to be chosen as Lord of Misrule for the Christmas festivities. Instead of the Oxford career he desired, his older brother Anthony insisted he move to London to study law. At the Middle Temple, he was again chosen as Lord of Misrule, a role he clearly enjoyed. But Robert quarreled with Anthony and abandoned his studies to travel on the Continent. Later, he entered into the service of Sir Thomas Puckering, but he continued to translate and publish. Due to his poverty, however, he yielded to Anthony's pressure and resumed his residence in the Middle Temple, being called to the bar in 1595. Ashley could not seem to attract patronage, despite his authorship of his only original work, a comprehensive, beautifully produced essay on honor, dedicated to Sir Thomas Egerton. By the end of the decade Ashley had abandoned hope for a public career and had a small legal practice. He spent most of his time acquiring and reading books, and though he thought seriously of marriage, he died a bachelor.

At the age of forty-four, Ashley felt very unhappy with what he had accomplished. As a result, he had trouble sleeping. When he finally did sleep and thus dream, however, unlike the dream he had recorded earlier, this one in 1609 was especially comforting. "I remember well when I was besieged by the sharper stimuli of the flesh." This was so disturbing to Ashley that he got "out of bed and having fallen on my knees fervently implored God in my bedchamber, so that he would succor me against so many evils which were tormenting me miserably." After this prayer, Ashley hoped that, once he went back to bed, he would be able to sleep quietly until the next morning. The dream that followed provided more than quiet. In his dream, "the angelic form of a certain beautiful woman" came to him and "ordered me to be of good cheer. In this way she refreshed me sufficiently, built hope and trust in better things." Ashley was delighted with this dream and felt it was deeply significant. "Then I woke up full of joy having seen and contemplated such good things of my guardian angel and dedicated and lived out exultingly and triumphantly my days for God." Ashley had one other highly significant dream—this one in 1622—when he was fifty-seven. He noted that the dream occurred on June 17, at the time when the moon was in Aquarius. It was a morning dream, which we know many people at the time thought were the most significant. "After dawn I saw in my dream a certain august form of a man or woman who trod under her feet like a victor a golden and fire spewing serpent or dragon which was inscribed with beautiful letters ALCHIMIA."

DREAMS OF CHRIST AND HEAVEN

For some people, it was not angels who came to them in their sleep, but Christ himself. In 1591, Simon Forman recorded in his diary that "I saw appearing in the clouds of heaven a man ten times bigger and greater then any other man, with a marvelous great face" and high forehead. He had a chestnut colored beard and was dressed in purple. "Round about him shined a marvelous great light and brightness, much brighter then the sun." Forman was convinced that "when I saw him me thought that it was Christ himself."[43]

Christ also appeared in the dreams of children. The Puritan minister Ralph Josselin kept a diary where he recorded not only some of his own dreams but those of his wife and children as well. Josselin cared deeply about his children, especially his three eldest, Mary, Tom, and Jane. Josselin was deeply pained at the death of his oldest child Mary in 1650, when she was only eight.[44] Perhaps it is not surprising, being raised in a minister's household, that his children recounted to him their dreams of Christ, heaven, and the beloved dead. On 2 March 1651, Josselin's daughter Jane, then five years old, told him that she "dreamed that Jesus Christ was in our church, and went up into my pulpit, and that he stayed a while, and then he came down, and came into bed to her. She said to him, 'why doest thou come to me,' and he answered her, 'to sleep a little with thee,' and he laid down and slept, and again she dreamed that Jesus Christ told her that he should come and reign upon the earth ten thousand years." Three years later on 8 December 1654, soon before his eleventh birthday, son Tom told his father of "his wonderful dream." In the dream, Tom was listening to his father preach, when Jesus, clad in a white robe, came into the pulpit and hugged Josselin. Christ then went to Tom "put his inkhorn in his pocket, and carried him into the churchyard, and asked him, what he would have." Tom replied that all he wanted was Christ's blessing. Christ not only gave the boy his blessing but he also said that he would take the boy and others up to heaven with him. Jesus, Tom, and the rest "passed through over a mountain and over the sea, and then over the land," but when they could no longer see Christ they "fell a praying." The devil then appeared, "but presently Jesus Christ came, and drove him away and bid him get him behind his back." Jesus took them to heaven where everyone was "singing melodiously and praying all in white." Christ said that he must take everyone back to earth, but by then Tom had found his sister Mary, and she "would not let him come away." Tom saw Jesus "sit at the Father's right hand, which was wonderful then while in heaven, he thought there was terrible thunder, but he was not afraid." After that, Christ told Tom he must return to earth. Josselin was deeply impressed by his son's dream, and he was also possibly comforted that Tom had seen his dead sister in heaven. He gave his son texts to read that were similar to his dream and commented in his diary that "the Lord do my child good by such things."[45]

The girl known only as "E.R." was far more distraught when she dreamed of Jesus Christ. She grew up in a household that took religion so seriously that when she was eleven she became convinced that she was damned. As a result, she considered suicide. She felt she had done some mischief and told her parents it was her sister, not her. They believed her and punished her sister. After three months, she became ill and her conscience troubled her greatly that, she wrote when an adult, "for that sin committed against God, and my Sister, as that I saw nothing but desperation, and feared that the horrors of Hell-fire would seize" her.

E.R. cried out to her parents that she was damned, tore her pillow, and ate some of its feathers. After her parents sent for a doctor, who helped her, they then asked two ministers to talk with her. E.R. told them that she believed in God, but she also believed that God "would damn me" because she had "lost the love of God." The ministers assured her that "Christ died for sinners," but E.R. replied that "Christ never died for such a one as I was, neither could his mercy save me." The ministers tried to assure the child that "Christ was a Christ of tenderness, that I was a beloved Christian, a dear Christian, and Christ was a preparing comfort for me." Yet all these assurances did not comfort E.R. "I told them that I saw nothing but Death, and Hell, and confusion of body and soul . . . I was a going into Hell, for the Devil with his chains was ready to throw me into the utter pit of darkness."

For the next four months, E.R. would get some comfort before again succumbing to utter despair. One night, she recalled, after "having taken no rest a long time, I fell into a slumber; and in my sleep there did appear unto me a little child in white, with an apple in one hand, and a white wand in the other." Though only a child, this boy was able to carry E.R., and he brought her "into a place where I did see much terror of fire, and shrieking, and a great deep ditch where was nothing to hold by, yet there I must go over that burning lake." E.R. was greatly afraid, but the child "took the white wand and laid it over the Ditch, and bade me to tread upon it, and fear not." E.R. was still too afraid, but then the child came to her, "and took me by the hand and trundled his apple on the wand, which bowled over very level." E.R. recognized that the child was sent from God, and the two of them together crossed over the fiery lake. On the other side by the shore, E.R. cried, "my Lord, my God, and my Savior, am I in Hell, or am I redeemed out of Hell?"

Before there was an answer, E.R. awoke. When she told her friends about the dream, they convinced her she was indeed saved. "They told me, that it was Jesus Christ that had appeared in the shape of a Child and that he had overcome Death, and Hell for me." E.R. cried out, "Blessed be Jesus Christ for evermore." E.R. became resolved that she would become a member of the Church.[46]

In the mid-seventeenth century, Sarah Wight had a very powerful dream that moved her so deeply that she not only wrote it down almost immediately but also related it to her mother and to their maid, Hanna Guy, as well. She wrote in early July 1647 that "on Saturday-night last, I was in Dream, in great terror, and so quaked, that the bed did shake under me. I so wept, that my face was wet, when I awoke." In her dream, Sarah found herself "violently hurried down a very steep hill." There were swine and horses, "red and white, and black, and some other color," which were running down as well. The further down she went, the darker it became, and "I could see no bottom of it." Sarah felt completely overcome, and, weeping, she cried out, "Lord help, I perish, I perish; I am not able, I am not able to go down it." In the midst of her feelings of terror and despair, Sarah heard a voice tell her, "I am able to carry thee upon Eagles' wings." Then a man appeared, "but the Glory of him was so great, I cannot express it," and he took Sarah in his arms and carried her to the bottom of the hill. He told Sarah that the horses were "all thy spiritual enemies; and I have trampled them under thy feet." The man picked up Sarah and carried her back to the top of the hill. He told her: "I could have carried thee at first to the top, and not to the bottom: but thus I did, that thou may prize the mercy the more, in delivering thee from the lowermost hell: and that thou may prize Heaven the more." He went on to tell her, "I have gone before thee, and have made crooked places straight before thee . . . I have done it for thee." Sarah awoke in tears. She knew that she had been in the arms of Christ himself.[47]

Dreaming that one was in the arms of Christ might well suggest being in heaven. Jesus told Sarah in her dream that her experience at the bottom of the hill—hell—allowed her to prize heaven—the top of the hill—all the more. Hill's dream book argued that if one dreamed that one would "fly to heaven," it meant many travels. If one dreamed that one was sitting in heaven, Hill assured readers, then it (perhaps obviously) meant happiness. But some who dreamed of heaven were not necessarily happy at all; some of these individuals were even more assured than Sarah Wight that they had seen heaven—and hell—in their dreams, and they still feared damnation as well as hoped for salvation.

The early seventeenth-century Puritan artisan Nehemiah Wallington suffered two years of what his biographer Paul Seaver has referred to as a mental breakdown. When Wallington was about twenty years old, he doubted his salvation and considered suicide. When he did attempt it, however, his efforts may not have been completely serious because he also feared the disgrace his family would face if he succeeded. When he recovered in 1620, he set up shop as a turner, fashioning objects of wood or metal on a lathe, and within a year, he married Grace Rampaigne, the sister of a minister. Wallington's family life proved tragic: Four of his five children died in childhood. From the time he was in his teens, Wallington had kept a record of his religious experiences. At first he related his sins, but the year of his marriage, he started anew with a book of God's mercies that he kept for nearly two decades. Wallington read widely and wrote often. He was not a successful businessman, and he often found it difficult to balance his life in the world, his life as a Christian, and his concerns with the world to come. Often these concerns expressed themselves in his dreams.

Wallington recorded in his notebook that one night "I dreamed I was dead, and the day of Judgment was come." Wallington found himself standing between heaven and hell, "but whither I should go I knew not." He saw that heaven "was a glorious place . . . a very spacious large room, and there sat in the midst of it our Saviour Jesus Christ." Sitting with Jesus were "all the saints that ever was." When Wallington looked to his left, however, he saw hell, "a large deformed place, only a kind of burning there, and the damned spirits facing one another." As Wallington stood there in his dream, he hoped that he might go to heaven, even as he "thought I should not." For Wallington, the dream was the opportunity for a second chance; while still in the dream and fearing hell, he wished "that I would I were on the earth again, I would love better than ever I have done."[48]

Elias Ashmole also dreamed of heaven, but though he came close, it was not accessible to him. In a morning dream he had in June 1646, Ashmole "was near paradise which seemed to be toward the North pole/and the four springs issued out of a hill upon which was a chapel erected to our Lady Mary/but I could not be come nearer but four or five miles because of the cold and frost."[49]

In 1555, just before his death, M. Philpot wrote to a friend of his (who, like him, was imprisoned for heresy) to tell him of a very powerful dream he had experienced. "Being in the midst of my sweet rest," he saw "a great beautiful City all of the color of Azure and white, four square in a marvelous beautiful composition in the midst of the sky, the sight whereof so inwardly comforted me that I am not able to express the consolation I had thereof." Philpot was convinced that this was no ordinary dream: "This dream I think not to have come of the illusion of the senses, because it brought with it so much spiritual joy, and I take it to be of the working of God's spirit."[50]

WOMEN DREAM OF CHRIST

There were a number of other dreams of Christ and heaven, and Christ appeared in a range of different presentations within the dreams of medieval and early modern English women. How Christ was described tells us about not only the individual women but others aspects of religious belief and culture. In some cases, Christ appeared in the guise of a beautiful man. Margery Brunham's experience as a visionary in the final years of the fourteenth century began after she married John Kempe at about the age of twenty. She soon became pregnant with what would be the first of her fourteen children. According to Margery's famous biography (which she dictated in the 1430s and which is virtually our only source for her experience), Margery became severely ill for about eight months after the birth of her child. The event that finally restored Margery's wits, after this bout of what sounds like postpartum depression, occurred when Christ appeared to her dressed in glorious purple silk and sat at the end of her bed, asking her why she had deserted him.[51] Margery believed that Christ had truly come to her in her waking state, though she was in bed at the time, but we might wonder if it were a dream. We might also note how gorgeously Christ was dressed and how it appears that Margery found him to be very attractive. Other women's dreams of Christ also sometimes devote substantial description to his apparel and appearance.

In the late seventeenth century, Jane Lead founded a group called the Philadelphian Society. Anne Bathurst was also one of the founders of the group, according to another member Richard Roach. Members of the group met in the household of Jane Lead and Francis Lee daily except for Sunday, when they met in Bathurst's household, which was where the first public and open meetings of the group were held, though Roach described Bathurst's frail health and her aversion to the noise of the world. Still, Bathurst met with a small group of people daily to inquire about the spirit of God and to work in gaining mystical insight. Because this group had such close bonds, it is perhaps not surprising that Bathurst apparently died not long after Lead. Sylvia Bowerbank makes this assumption because soon after Jane died, Roach dreamed that she appeared to him in the form of a small heavenly globe and told him that "upon the death of Mrs. Bathurst it being needful somebody should strike into her Place for the Support of the Meeting . . . and no other Appearing willing to undertake, it must be my Province and Lot."[52]

Bathurst dreamed often of Christ, and Christ was no less beautiful to her than to Kempe; Christ came to her "in a figure like a Man, in clearness and color like a Jasper Stone, with his legs of white beryl-stone: which did greatly ravish me, yet one day I should be like Him." Indeed, Bathurst described some of her dreams about Jesus in what Patricia Crawford describes as "sexual and ecstatic." For example, in September 1679 she wrote of how much she longed for night to come so that she could again dream about Christ, "yet I might lie in his Arms as I had done the night before. . . . God has touched me with fire from his Lips, a pledge of his love . . . O Jesus . . . thou hast ravished me . . . O the sweetness and full Satisfaction." In another dream "I saw Jesus in the appearance of a Man, all surrounded by a most glorious Light. . . . I appeared as a spark of Light, and according to my desire I sometimes mounted up to see Jesus; and then ascended again to Paradise."[53]

For Katharine Canval Evans, when Christ brought her comfort he was in the guise of a servant. Katharine began her life as a member of the Church of England, became a Baptist, later claimed she was an Independent, and then, in her mid-thirties (about 1654), she and her husband became Quakers. Soon after, she traveled to the Isle of Man to work as a missionary. After she was banished from that island, she went on to Ireland, where she was imprisoned for four days. She next came to the attention of the authorities in May 1657 when she was arrested and publicly whipped in the market square in Salisbury. Not daunted, she also preached to hostile crowds in Portsmouth and Warminster. At the end of that year, she became convinced that God wanted her to go to Alexandria with Sarah Cheevers, who experienced, independently, the same inspiration. It took some time to organize their journey, and in December of 1658, they arrived in Malta where they were interrogated by the Inquisition and promptly arrested. Soon after their arrival, God appeared to Katharine in a dream and "showed me, that round about us, and above and beneath us, there were many magicians of Egypt." Then the Lord told her, "The Devil hath desired to winnow you as wheat; but pray that your faith fail not." Hearing the voice of God caused Katharine to wake with "much trembling and amazement." While in Malta, Katherine and Sarah were first kept under house arrest in the house of the English counsel, but the next April, they were moved to the Inquisition prison in Birgu. Eventually released in 1662, they returned to England, and there, Katharine had another dream. She saw "a large room, and a great wood fire in the chimney; and I saw the eternal Son of God sitting in a chair by the fire, in the form of a servant." She also saw a lovely baby boy sitting in a hollow chair by the fire. All he was wearing was a fine linen shirt and he clearly enjoyed the closeness of the fire. Katharine was afraid that the child would get burned and started to pick him up, but "he that sat in the chair bade me let it alone." She then "saw another heavenly angel of God's presence standing a little ways off." After she looked at the angel, "he that sat in the chair, bade me take up the child, and it had no harm." Katharine then woke up. This dream might be thought to have a range of different meanings. Katharine's own interpretation says a great deal about her beliefs and sense of self. She immediately "called to my friend Sarah, and bid her she should not fear, for the heavenly host of God's presence did follow us."[54]

Dorothy Emett did not see Christ at all, but only heard him. In the mid-seventeenth century, she heard John Owen, an independent minister preach. She was "much cast down" when he asked her if she believed in Christ, asking him what "should I do to believe?" That night she lay in bed very troubled, "until in my sleep one night came to me a voice, (I thought) that said, I am the Fountain of living water: and when I awaked, I was much refreshed, for I had a great thirsting after Christ."[55]

Mary Penington had two vivid dreams about Christ many years apart, and to her he was a lovely youth, dressed very simply. Mary was born in 1625 in Kent, the only child of Sir John and Anne Proud. Sir John was serving under the Prince of Orange in Holland when he was killed, and his wife died soon afterward. At the time, Mary was only three. We do not know who took care of Mary for the next few years, but when she was eight or nine, she joined the household of Sir Edward Partridge. Also living in the household was Sir Edward's widowed sister Katherine Springett and her three children, William, Herbert, and Catherine. Mary was an intelligent, well-educated child who took her religious beliefs very seriously. When she was about twelve, she decided that there was a great difference between *saying* prayers and actually praying. People in Sir Edward Partridge's household simply read prayers out of books, but Mary did not believe this was true prayer and begged God to tell her what prayer really was. She began to write prayers of her own. Soon after, she heard a Puritan minister preach, and she was deeply moved. "I felt that was true prayer."[56] Her guardian, who was a member of the Church of England, was very upset by Mary's behavior and warned her that she was jeopardizing any chance of a good marriage because no gentleman would want someone like Mary for a wife. Sir Edward was certainly wrong. Mary had grown up with the Springett children. The eldest, William, was about three or four years older than she was. When he returned home after receiving his Cambridge education, Sir William and Mary wed in 1642; he was twenty or twenty-one and she not yet eighteen. William and Mary loved each other, and he shared her attraction to Puritan ideology. As a result, they refused to have their son John baptized. William was a colonel in the Parliamentarian army. When there were dangerous uprisings in Kent, Mary moved to London. She was heavily pregnant with her second child when she went to visit her husband after he and his men had successfully besieged Arundel Castle. Sir William was seriously ill and died of spotted fever in 1644. Their marriage had lasted only two years. Shortly afterward Mary gave birth to her daughter, whom she named Gulielma Maria Springett, after her baby's parents. Mary also refused to have her daughter baptized.[57]

Widowed before she was even twenty-one, Mary soon suffered another loss when her infant son John died. The next years were very difficult for her. She went to hear ministers from a number of different sects, but none satisfied her. Mary began to try to forget her sorrows with a life of pleasure, but "in the midst of all this my heart was constantly sad, and pained beyond expression." Sometime in the early 1650s, after an especially intense "indulgence in such follies," Mary decided to go to the country for a few days with only her daughter and her maid. She relates that she "was in great trouble and anguish. . . . restless [and] distressed."

One night Mary went to bed "very disconsolately and sad." She dreamed that she "saw a book of hieroglyphics of religion, of things to come in the church." In her dream, Mary took no delight in the book. Turning away from it "greatly oppressed," she left the house and went into a field, where she cried out, "Lord, suffer me no more to fall in with any wrong, but show me the truth." The sky opened, and a "bright light, like fire, fell upon my hand." Mary was so frightened that she awoke from her dream. She continued to question, and over the next weeks, she felt very unsettled. "My mind being thus almost continually exercised, I dreamed that I was sitting alone, retired and sad." In the dream she heard a loud, confusing noise: Some of it sounded as if people were very upset, while others were joyful and triumphant. As she listened, she realized that the tumult was because Christ had come. She continued to stay by herself in the room, and finally became silent. Then someone came in and told her, "Christ is come indeed, and is in the next room, and with him is the bride the Lamb's wife." Mary felt her heart leap in her body. She began to get up, "but something within me stopped me, and bade me not to be hasty, but patiently, coolly, softly, and soberly, go into the next room, which I did, and stood just within the entrance of a spacious hall, trembling and rejoicing, but dared not go near to Him." There were many people in the room, and Mary stood at a great distance from Christ: He was at the upper end of the hall, but she could see him clearly, and he was "a fresh lovely youth, clad in gray cloth very plain and neat," with an expression that was "sweet, affable, courteous." What impressed Mary the most was that, as Christ went around talking with those assembled, he embraced "several poor, old simple people, whose appearance was very contemptible and mean, without wisdom or beauty." Mary figured out that while he looked so young, he had great insight and discretion because he saw "hidden worth in those people, who to me seem so mean, so unlovely, and simple." Finally he bade Mary to come near him, and while she was glad, she was also trembling and had a feeling of dread. Then she heard a voice say, "The Lamb's wife is also come." There was a "beautiful young woman, slender, modest, and grave, in plain garments, becoming and graceful. Her image was fully answering his, as a brother and sister." Finally, seeing the two together, Mary felt great joy, and with that feeling of joy over the coming of Christ, Mary awoke.[58]

For Mary, this dream was one of such great significance, that it is one of only three that she wrote about in her autobiography. Her searching continued, and she was "wearied in seeking and not finding" when she became acquainted with Isaac Penington, the son of a wealthy London merchant who was active in the parliamentary cause. Mary found her "love was drawn to him," as he also "refused to be comforted by any appearance of religion" until he was convinced that was what God truly meant for him. From the time Isaac was young, he had felt drawn to God, and he read widely and went to hear many sermons. But Isaac was afraid of being drawn into others' perhaps faulty interpretation of Scripture, so he continued to pray and wait for God to point him in the right direction. After studying at Cambridge between 1648 and 1656, Isaac Penington published widely as he moved from Puritanism, through advanced Spiritualism, to serious engagement with the Ranters, to finally being on the threshold of acceptance of the Quaker beliefs.[59] Mary and Isaac married in 1654, and they continued their searching together. Their interest in the Quakers began when, one day after they had been married for about two years, Mary and Isaac were walking in the park and met a man who "frequented the Quakers' meetings." Through him they met others of the same persuasion, and Mary became convinced "that they came in the power and authority of the Lord, to visit us." At the time that Mary had had the dream years before, she had "not heard of the Quakers or their habit," but now she vividly remembered this dream, and it seemed to her that Christ and his bride had been clad as Quakers.[60] Becoming Quakers was not easy for the Peningtons. They were the highest status of any to join the Quakers in their tumultuous first decade. The couple lost money and land, but they "endured, patiently, despisings, reproaches, cruel mockings, and scornings, from relations, acquaintances, and neighbors." People called them "fools, mad, and bewitched." Mary and Isaac found themselves being "stoned, abused, and imprisoned . . . at several towns and meetings where we went." But for all of that, they knew they had found the way they should worship God.

Several decades after the first dream when Mary had beheld Christ, she had another dream. By this time, her daughter Gulielma was grown and had married William Penn. Mary went to visit them in the summer of 1676 and had a vivid dream that she then recorded. Mary dreamed that she was in an upper room in the house with two other people, but once awake she could not remember who her companions were. She looked out the window and saw a very black, dismal sky, and she called her companions to come over and see it as well. They agreed that "it was very dreadful," but just then the sky suddenly cleared, and in it began to appear "a very bright head, breast, and arms, the complete upper part of a man, very beautiful (like pictures I have seen to represent an angel form), holding in his hand a long, green bough; not so green as a laurel, but of a sea, or willow-green color, resembling a palm." Mary and the others went from dismay to elation. The angel raised the palm over his head, "which to us was such a signification of good, that both by voice and action we made acclamations of joy." In the dream, Mary was so excited she could not even talk, but uttered sounds like "oh! oh! ah! ah!" She and others spread their hands out and ran about the room. "After a little while there appeared lower in the element, nearer the earth, in an oval, transparent glass, a man and a woman (not in resemblance, but real persons)." Mary found both of them to be the loveliest and most caring people that she had even seen. "The man wore a greater majesty and sweetness than I ever saw . . . his hair was brown, his eyes black and sparkling, his complexion ruddy; piercing dominion in his countenance, splendid with affability, great gentleness, and kindness." The woman looked very much like the man, resembling him "in features and complexion; but appeared tender and bashful, yet quick-sighted." Mary and her companions just looked at the "heavenly forms" for a while, then "in a sense of their majesty and dominion, did reverence to them, falling on our faces in a solemn, not in a disturbed, confused manner, crying glory! glory! glory! glory! glory! at which the man ascended, but the woman came down to us, and spoke to us with great gravity and sweetness."

While Mary could not remember the exact words once she woke up, "the purport of them was, that we should not be formal, nor fall out." After delivering the message to Mary and her companions, the woman disappeared. Mary and the others looked at one and another seriously. Mary said: "This is a vision, to signify to us some great matter and glorious appearance; more glorious than the Quakers at their first coming forth. I added, that I had a distinct vision and sight of such state in a dream, before ever I heard of a Quaker; but it was in a more simple, plain manner than this." In this dream, Mary remembered her previous dream. She told the others that in that one she "saw Christ like a fresh, sweet, innocent youth, clad in light gray, neat, but plain; and so, likewise, was the bride, the Lamb's wife, in the same manner; but under this plain appearance, there was deep wisdom and discernment." In the dream, Mary pondered how Christ and his bride differed between this dream and the other one, as "his countenance and garb are altered: in the former was united to sweetness, majesty; in the latter, to plainness and neatness is joined resplendence." As Mary finished saying this, she awoke from the dream.[61] In her second dream, Mary experienced a memory of her first. The meaning Mary Penington had found in her life was bracketed by these two important dreams of her savior.

MARTYRS, WITCHES, AND DREAMERS

We know that Thomas Cranmer was suspicious of dreams; so too was he suspicious of magic. One section of the 1548 Articles of Visitation for the province of Canterbury asked investigators, "Whether you know any that use charms, sorcery, enchantments, witchcraft, soothsaying, or any like craft invented by the Devil."[62] The devil invaded people's dreams and caused them to fear damnation; he was also said to invade dreams of witches in order to convince them to give him their souls in return for power. Some suspected witches were treated in a way that parallels and echoes the treatment of those perceived as religious heretics of one sort or another. Mobs' reactions to Katherine Evans and Sarah Cheevers were reminiscent of the treatment of poor women thought to be witches. In the late seventeenth century, the Puritan Richard Baxter compared Quakers with witches.[63] Mary Penington described how people shouted abuse at her and husband Isaac, how they threw stones at them, and how they were also imprisoned. Sometimes their dreams reflect the confluence of religious martyrs and those accused of witchcraft.

MOTHER SAMUEL AND LADY CROMWELL

One of the methods that someone could use to overcome a spell by a witch was to cut off some of the suspected person's hair and burn it. In 1589, five young sisters of the Throckmorton family in the town of Warboys were acting bizarrely. They claimed their behavior was the result of having been bewitched by one of their poorest neighbors, Alice Samuel. We know about this case because of the pamphlet *The Most strange and admirable discoverie of the three Witches of Warboys,* written in 1593, the year Alice, her husband John, and her daughter Agnes were all executed as witches. The Throckmorton girls' outrageous behavior continued for a long time, and more and more people in the area heard of the family's trouble. In September of the next year, Lady Cromwell came from Ramsay, two miles away, to the Throckmorton household to sympathize with them on their troubles. Her husband, Sir Henry, was the wealthiest landowner in the area. Lady Cromwell insisted that Mother Samuel be sent for, and the old woman came because her husband John was one of Sir Henry's tenants and she feared the consequences if she refused. Once Mother Samuel was in the house, stated the author of the pamphlet, "the children grew to be worse than they were before, which caused the greater sorrow." Lady Cromwell "took mother Samuel aside, and charged her deeply with this Witchcraft," and, suggested Francis Hutchinson, who wrote about the case a century later, Lady Cromwell called her "Witch, and abused her."[64] Mother Samuel stoutly claimed that she had done nothing to harm the children. Lady Cromwell suddenly tore off Mother Samuel's cap, cut off a lock of the woman's hair, and gave it to Mrs. Throckmorton, instructing her to cast it in the fire as a charm. Cutting off hair and burning it was considered a way to counter a witch's evil spell. As we shall see, this visit had dreadful consequences for Mother Samuel and, at least by contemporary reckoning, for Lady Cromwell as well.[65]

Not everyone in this period believed that burning the hair of a witch was a successful method of curing someone who was bewitched. Writing a guide to juries in the early seventeenth century, Richard Bernard suggested that he knew not "what effect it may have" to heal someone bewitched by "burn[ing] something of the Witches." But he added, "this I am sure of, that when the Lady Cromwell made some hair of Mother Samuels to be cut off, and . . . burnt, the children of Master Throckmorton were not the better, and the Lady was bewitched soon after."[66]

Half a century earlier, only a night or two after the Protestant minister Rough had dreamed about his curate Symson being arrested, he "had another dream in his sleep concerning his own trouble." In his dream, guards came and arrested him as well and "carried him self forcibly to the Bishop." At the bishop's residence, the bishop "plucked off his beard, and cast it into the fire, saying these words: Now I may say I have had a piece of a heretic burnt in my house." Rough's dream ties the experiences of accused heretics and witches that much closer together.

While we know nothing more about the bishop in Rough's dream, we do know more about Lady Cromwell's dream. After Lady Cromwell had attempted to get Mother Samuel to confess and after she had cut off a lock of the woman's hair to burn, Mother Samuel had muttered something. Later it was said to be: "Madame why do you use me thus? I never did you any harm as yet." Those last words, if indeed said, were a threat and "were afterwards remembered." According to the 1593 pamphlet, the very same night of that confrontation, Lady Cromwell returned home and "suffered many things in her dream concerning Mother Samuel." Lady Cromwell shared her bed with her daughter-in-law, who testified that Lady Cromwell "was very strangely tormented in her sleep by a cat (as she imagined) which Mother Samuel had sent unto her, which cat offered to pluck off all the skin and flesh from her arms and body." Lady Cromwell was "struggling and striving" to defend herself against the demonic cat Mother Samuel had sent against her while she slept. She also made such a "mournful noise" that her daughter-in-law woke her up. Lady Cromwell told her that in her dream she had been beseeching the cat and Mother Samuel to leave her alone and thanked her daughter-in-law for ending the dream. But she was so afraid that she could not sleep again that night or even have quiet rest. "Not long after," Lady

Cromwell "fell very strangely sick." Fifteen months later she was dead. The dream that was alleged to have led to her death was part of the evidence used to prove that Mother Samuel was a witch who had used a dream to harm Lady Cromwell.[67] Bernard suggested that once witches had cast a spell, they could not lift it, and his example was: "The three Witches of Warboyse, would have unwitched the Lady Cromwell, but could not."[68] Perhaps it was Lady Cromwell's fear of being bewitched that led to her dream and her eventual death. Robert Burton argued that many people had such fear that they "cannot sleep for witches and fascinations."[69] John Brinsley believed that "those who ne'er Dream of Witches, or ever regard them, are hardly at any time tormented or hurt by them." On the other hand, "such as are afraid of them . . . have commonly some mischief done, as the Reward of their fears and jealousies." Francis Hutchinson was even more judgmental about Lady Cromwell, arguing that if she "dreamt of Mother Samuel and a Cat, and fell into Fits," it "was very likely she would after such an ill Day's Work. . . . And if her Death was really occasioned by the Fits that began then, I can only count it a just Consequence of her own Sin, and Folly, and Superstition."[70] The Warboys case was very well known in the years that followed, and not only because of the pamphlet. Lady Cromwell's husband seized the Samuel's meager estate and used it to endow a yearly antiwitchcraft sermon in honor of his wife. Sixty years later, Henry More wrote that the memory of the case "is still kept fresh by an Anniversary sermon preached at Huntington by some of the Fellows of Queens College in Cambridge."[71]

WITCHES DREAM OF DEMONS

The Pendle Forest witches' trials in Lancashire were among the most significant in early modern England. Elizabeth Southerns, also known as Old Demdike, had been a witch for many years when she gave her confession in 1612. She explained how she had become a witch: She had been begging and was returning home when she met "a spirit or Devil in the shape of a Boy" who called himself Tibb. Demdike "was contented to give her Soul to the said Spirit." One Sunday morning about six years later, "this Examinate having a little Child upon her knee, and she being in slumber, the said Spirit appeared unto her in the likeness of a brown Dog, forcing himself to her knee." Being asleep made Old Demdike vulnerable, as did the fact that she was "without any apparel saving her Smock." The child with her was vulnerable, too. The creature, just as a child would, came to Old Demdike for nourishment, attempting to get blood from under her left arm. Old Demdike woke up, deeply worried about her child. She called, "Jesus, Jesus, save my Child." But, Thomas Potts added, while she could ask Jesus' help for her child, she could not ask Jesus to "save her self." Though the dog disappeared, "after which, this Examinate was almost stark mad for the space of eight weeks."[72] Dreams, devils, and witchcraft lead to madness in this narrative, serving as a dire warning of what could happen if one gave one's soul to the devil, and thus allowed demons to invade one's dreams.

THE EARL OF DERBY'S DREAM AND HIS DEATH

While Lady Cromwell died fifteen months after her dream that was supposedly caused by witchcraft, Ferdinando Stanley became very ill the night after he had a dream, and he died less than two weeks later.[73] Ferdinando, Lord Strange, the oldest surviving son of Henry Stanley, Earl of Derby, was, during his teenaged years, a squire in the household of Elizabeth I, to whom he was related because his mother was a descendent of Henry VIII's younger sister Mary. Elizabeth was apparently very fond of Ferdinando, though she generally distrusted her Tudor relatives since they also had claims to the throne. In 1579 or 1580, when Ferdinando was about twenty-one, he married Alice Spencer; it was a very happy union and the couple had three daughters. As his father's heir, he held a number of administrative appointments, but he was also known for his passion for poetry and drama. In addition to composing poetry himself, he patronized a company of players who by 1592 performed often at court and were perceived as the leading company in England. It was the company in which the young Shakespeare was an actor and playwright. While still at court, Ferdinando was one of the knights who tilted before the queen in 1590. At court during Christmas the following year, his company was strikingly successful, presenting six plays before the queen as opposed to only one from each of the other companies.

When his father died in the fall of 1593, Ferdinando became earl. The Dowager Countess of Derby and her two sons were English-born heirs to the throne of whose legitimacy there was no question.[74] While Ferdinando was a regular communicant of the Church of England, a number of his followers were Catholic. At the same time, some foreign Catholics apparently were plotting that he should claim the throne as his inheritance because of his mother's line. Through his younger brother William, Ferdinando was also on the edge of a group of alchemists and magicians, such as John Dee and Edward Kelley. At the time of his father's death, encouragement for him to claim the throne was afoot. At this time, an Englishman named Richard Hesketh was already on his way from the Continent to bring Ferdinando a letter that, at least according to the official version presented by the English authorities, was asking him to rebel and assume England's throne. Christopher Devlin argues that Heskin did not know the contents of the letter he was carrying and that he was "a carefully chosen dupe" who "had connections both with occult circles in Prague and with Catholic exiles." Devlin suggests that the letter may have been a plant to keep the Stanleys in their place with the expectation that the letter would be suppressed and then produced later by the government. Ferdinando, however, as Devlin points out, had "imagination, intellect, and decision." Instead of keeping quiet about the message, he responded by turning Hesketh in to the authorities, who had him executed two months later. The plot did play on Elizabeth's fear, and for a while she distrusted Ferdinando. Devlin argues that both Robert Devereux, Earl of Essex and Robert Cecil (two men who gravely distrusted each other) both worried about Ferdinando's position, and the "Hesketh Plot and its sequel . . . was a determined and successful campaign to eliminate him as a political factor."[75]

What role Ferdinando might have played either in politics or in patronage of the arts cannot be known, however. Less than seven months after he became earl, he became desperately ill after a day of hunting on 5 April 1594. According to John Stow, the night before Ferdinando became ill, "he dreamed that his lady was most dangerously sick to death, and in his sleep being sore troubled therewith, he wept, suddenly cried out, started from his bed, called for help, sought about the chamber betwixt sleep and waking."[76] Once he was fully awake, he found that his wife was fine, and he was comforted. His dream of her illness, however, presaged his own. He began to vomit, and this continued for the next several days, with physicians unable to do anything to help him. He died on April 16. The death of such a potentially significant man who was only in his middle thirties and who was apparently healthy made people very suspicious. Though his physicians attested that he died from overexercise, they had also given him antidotes for poison. A commission was immediately set up to investigate the death, and a week later Sir George Carey reported to Robert Cecil that there was "greater presumptions that the Earl of Derby was bewitched than poisoned."[77] Stow publicized that conjecture in his 1600 edition of *Annals of England*. Writing after the Gunpowder Plot, Camden, however, argued that it was the Jesuits who had poisoned the Earl of Derby because of his refusal to join the Catholic plots. Devlin suggests that Ferdinando may have suffered from "a burst appendix resulting in acute peritonitis." Whatever was the actual cause of Ferdinando Stanley's death, his dream just before his fatal illness was perceived as critical.

DREAMING WITCHCRAFT

Just as dreams and religion were intertwined in much of the cultural belief systems in early modern England, so too were dreams and witchcraft. In the early eighteenth century, Francis Hutchinson argued that, when witches confessed, they spoke about all they had done through magic, "either these Things are real, or else they are Dreams." He asked those who prosecute witches if "Dreams and Representations, tell me what Reason you have for hanging and burning poor People, for dreaming they do that which you are such they do not do." If indeed there was any truth to the confessions, Hutchinson wanted to know why those who believed strongly enough about the power of witches that they would be willing to put them to death were also so selective about what supernatural events they would accept, since they "deny the Tales of the Golden Legend, and yet receive these?"[78]

One of the traditional arguments made by such scholars as Brian Levack about the difference between English witchcraft accusations and those on the Continent was that there was no torture in England as there was in places such as France and Germany. Diane Purkiss is even more absolute when she states that torture "was absent from the scene of English witchcraft."[79] It is certainly true that the horrific, explicit torture on the Continent was not allowed in England, but accused witches were treated terribly in England as well. As Christina Hole points out, though torture was illegal in England, "some of the tolerated forms of ill-treatment seem to have been almost as dreadful."[80] Hutchinson pointed out that it was sanctioned for witches to be examined after many hours of sleep deprivation. "It hath been said by the Witch-finders, in their own Justification, that because our English Law does not allow Tortures," they instead "made use of this keeping them awake . . . and walking of them betwixt two till they have not been able to stand for Weariness, which is both a great Torture, and exceedingly disorders the Understanding."[81] Apparently some accused of witchcraft were kept awake and on their feet standing or walking for as much as ninety-six hours straight, which certainly could cause hallucinations and disorder understanding. For someone writing in the early eighteenth century, Hutchinson showed a rare understanding of the subtle ways torture could be inflicted, a point well argued in the modern period by Gail Kern Paster. When Purkiss takes Paster and other such critics to task for calling this torture, she claims that "they miss the historical point." I think it is Purkiss, whose scholarship is usually highly insightful, who is misjudging both the historical period and the insidious means of torture.[82]

There were other reasons to keep the suspected witch awake: The dreams of the supposed witches could be very dangerous as well. Richard Boulton was one of those who supported the practice of sleep deprivation. Writing to refute Hutchinson, Boulton explained that it "was to prevent their couching down; for indeed when they be suffered so to couch, immediately come their Familiars into the Room, and scare the Watchers, and hearten on the Witch." H. R. Ellis Davidson points out that in Icelandic sagas there were many examples of witches acquiring significant knowledge while asleep.[83]

Reginald Scot, however, was convinced that when old women confessed of magical crimes, they were actually suffering from melancholy and mistook their dreams of Satan, visits to the underworld, murder, and mayhem to be reality, when in fact they "lie at home fast asleep." Certainly, some ingredients in the recipes for witches' ointments would cause hallucinations, especially the feeling of flying, as well as deep sleep. Joseph Granvil, however, maintained that such arguments as Scot's played right into Satan's hands, since Satan wanted everyone to believe "that the stories of Witches, Apparitions, and indeed everything that brings tidings of another world, are but melancholic Dreams." G. R. Quaife points out that "The inability to separate the dream from waking reality is the critical factor in the accumulation of witch lore." One can clearly see the confluence of belief in the connections of witchcraft and dreaming. In the latter part of the seventeenth century Richard Bovet wrote that "there are diverse other General names for students of this Infernal Art" besides "witch," and then he described it as "Dreamer."[84]

CHAPTER 4

SEXUALITY, POWER, AND DREAMS
OF A NEW DYNASTY

Those in the Tudor period looked back to the previous century and reign of Henry VI and remembered times of a long minority and then a king, when he came of age, unable to rule effectively. The problems of Henry VI's reign led to the disastrous end of a long, debilitating war with France and a country wracked by struggles over who would be the next king—Lancaster or York. The latter part of the fifteenth century was also a time when passion and sexuality intermingled with quests for control, and the desires for power played out not only in the politics of the time but in reputed dreams as well. The Tudor dynasty was born of passion and a struggle for power, and some dreams were central to the establishment of the Tudor line. Once the Tudors ruled England, further dreams challenged the monarchs. When the fifteenth-century history was dramatized in the next century, dreams were used to express the difficulties of the remembered time. Issues of religion and witchcraft, as discussed in the previous chapter, continued to interplay with questions of power and sexuality.

THE CONFLICTING DREAMS OF THE DUKE AND
DUCHESS OF GLOUCESTER

When Henry V died in 1422, his son was still an infant. Henry V's youngest brother, Humphrey, Duke of Gloucester, became the Lord Protector, though there were continual struggles for power. In 1423, Humphrey married Jacqueline of Hainault, who two years earlier had fled from her husband, John, Duke of Brabant, whom she refused to acknowledge as her legal spouse, and had taken asylum in England. Humphrey hoped to help her recover lands from her uncle and estranged husband. In October 1424, he and Jacqueline went abroad with a small army, securing Hainault by mid-December. But John of Brabant, with the aid of Philip, Duke of Burgundy, began to retake Hainault, and Gloucester left Jacqueline in Hainault to return to England; Jacqueline, left on her own, was forced to surrender to the Duke of Burgundy. Meanwhile in 1428, the Pope declared Jacqueline's marriage to the now-deceased John of Brabant valid, and Humphrey would have had to remarry Jacqueline if he wanted to continue his Flemish claims. Instead, he took advantage of his freedom and married Eleanor Cobham, his mistress, or as John Stow described her, "his wanton paramour."[1] Humphrey's problems with other nobles continued, including most severely with his older brother John, Duke of Bedford, regent in France. At various times, John returned from Paris, where the English were losing control of France, to London. He was upset that Humphrey and his supporters had been unable to finance more support for the French wars.

Henry VI's attainment of his majority in 1436 did nothing to make Humphrey's position more secure. He was the heir presumptive to Henry VI once John Duke of Bedford died, and no one could ever forget the possibility of his succession. Certainly his wife Eleanor never forgot, and from early 1440 she began to consult astrologers about the likelihood of Henry VI's death. Roger Bolingbroke "was examined before the King's Council, where he confessed that he wrought the said Necromancy at the stirring and procurement of the said Dame Eleanor, to know what should befall of her, and to what estate she should come, whereupon she was cited to appear before Henry Chicheley, Archbishop of Canterbury . . . to answer to certain articles . . . of Necromancy, witchcraft, sorcery, heresy, and treason."[2] Eleanor was found guilty of treasonable necromancy; for her public penance, she was required to walk barefoot through London carrying a taper that she finally took to St. Paul's and placed on the high altar. Eleanor and Humphrey were also forced to divorce, and she was imprisoned for the rest of her life. Though he was not implicated, Humphrey was discredited and gained his nephew's distrust, forcing him into retirement. In 1447, Humphrey's public opposition to the French led his enemies at court to decide to charge him with treason. His death soon after his arrest was probably due to a stroke, but many of the English were convinced that he was murdered. After his death, he became known as the "Good Duke," a term used not only in the fifteenth century but in the sixteenth as well.

Christopher Devlin suggests that in *Henry VI, Part 2* "Shakespeare depicts Humphrey as being pulled down by a temporary and iniquitous alliance between York and his Lancastrian rivals. This is a Shakespearean invention."[3] It does, however, mirror the brief coalitions between the Earl of Essex and Robert Cecil, usually at odds with each other, to get rid of rivals, such as the Earl of Derby. In this play, the Lord Protector Humphrey, Duke of Gloucester, is a principal—and principled—advisor to his nephew, the young king; he is also the only one of the lords who is completely loyal. The play opens with Henry overjoyed at meeting his new French wife, Margaret of Anjou. But Gloucester is deeply concerned that the marriage treaty gave Anjou and Maine back to France in return for Margaret. These were the lands for which Henry V and English knights had fought so hard. Gloucester tells the king and other lords that with such a policy England will soon lose all of its holdings in France. After Gloucester departs, a group of lords gets together to plot his overthrow.

The next scene is a domestic one; it is morning at the home of Gloucester and his wife. Eleanor notes how sad her husband seems and attempts to cheer him with thoughts of triumphs if they should someday be king and queen.

> Why doth the great Duke Humphrey knit his brows,
> As frowning at the favors of the world? (1.2.3-4)[4]
>
> . . . .
>
> We'll both together lift our heads to heaven
> And never more abase our sight so low. (1.2.14-15)

This does not cheer Humphrey, however.

> O Nell, sweet Nell, if thou dost love thy lord,
> Banish the canker of ambitious thoughts! (1.2.17-18)

Humphrey does not welcome any suggestion that he might become king as a result of something happening to "my king and nephew, virtuous Henry" (1.2.20). He adds that "My troublesome dream this night doth make me sad" (1.2.22). Eleanor asks Humphrey to tell her his dream, promising that she will then "requite it/With sweet rehearsal of my morning's dream," to cheer him (1.2.23-24). Humphrey's dream is indeed troublesome:

> Methought this staff, mine office badge in court,
> Was broke in twain—by whom, I have forgot,
> But, as I think, it was by the Cardinal—
> And on the pieces of the broken wand
> Were placed the heads of Edmund, Duke of Somerset,
> And William de la Pole, first duke of Suffolk.
> This was my dream. What it doth bode, God knows. (1.2.25-30)

Humphrey's dream in the play is like one a person might actually have; he is upset that his staff, the object that symbolizes his office as Lord Protector, is broken. As so often happens when trying to recapture a dream, he cannot remember just who did it, though it may have been the Cardinal—who has been his enemy "from back to the beginning of *1 Henry VI* in play time," as Nicholas Grene puts it.[5] The dream is violent, with the heads of Somerset and Suffolk placed on each broken piece. It is also ominous and foretells ill for a number of the characters. Eleanor has not listened attentively to her husband, who has already warned her not to be too ambitious. She responds to his grim dream by narrating her own, which she found delightful:

> Methought I sat in seat of majesty
> In the cathedral church of Westminster,

And in that chair where kings and queens are crowned,
Where Henry and Dame Margaret kneeled to me
And on my head did set the diadem. (1.2.36-40)

As Robert Presson suggests, Eleanor's narration of her dream "vividly delineates" her character.[6] Gloucester is appalled by his wife's dream, and particularly by the glee with which she describes it:

Presumptuous dame, ill-nurtured Eleanor,
Art thou not second woman in the realm,
And the Protector's wife, beloved of him?
Hast thou not worldly pleasure at command
Above the reach or compass of thy thought?
And wilt thou still be hammering treachery,
To tumble down thy husband and thyself
From top of honor to disgrace's feet? (1.2.42-49)

Eleanor is angered in turn.

What, what, my lord! Are you so choleric
With Eleanor for telling but her dream?
Next time I'll keep my dreams unto myself,
And not be checked. (1.2.50-54)

Gloucester wishes to get along well with his wife, the woman the actual Henry had married for love: "Nay, be not angry; I am pleased again" (1.2.55). He might have been much less pleased had he known what Eleanor would do as soon as he left. She plots to employ a witch and conjuror who can summon spirits who will tell her the future of the king's reign—and potentially of her and her husband's rise to power. Prefiguring Lady Macbeth,[7] she says to herself:

While Gloucester bears this base and humble mind.
Were I a man, a duke, and next of blood,
I would remove these tedious stumbling blocks
And smooth my way upon their headless necks. (1.2.62-65)

When the duchess has the witch and conjuror summon a spirit, the replies are typically cryptic and ambiguous. Before Eleanor can ask for more information, lords enter and arrest her for participating in witchcraft. Eleanor was entrapped by her own ambition. Gloucester is with the king and lords when news comes that Eleanor has been arrested. Devastated, Gloucester starts to leave, but the king stops him:

Stay, Humphrey, Duke of Gloucester. Ere thou go,

Give up thy staff. (2.3.22-23)

With so many other ambitious, self-interested nobles eager to take power, the staff "will soon be broken between them," argues Grene, "so that the dream-image of the staff destroyed is premonitory not just of the fall of Gloucester but of the very principle of law that he represents."[8]

Whereas Humphrey's dream is prophetic, the opposite of Eleanor's dream comes true, despite the fact that it was a morning dream. As some in the early modern period believed, dreams could indeed reveal opposites. When Eleanor is tried before the king and his lords, she is stripped of her titles and is referred to as "Eleanor Cobham," her maiden name. She is ordered to do penance by being led through the streets of London and then is banished to the Isle of Man for perpetual imprisonment. In the next scene, we see Gloucester unhappily observing Eleanor wrapped in a sheet walking barefoot through the streets carrying a taper. When she sees him, she calls out:

Trust thou that e'er I'll look upon the world,

Or count them happy that enjoy the sun?

No, dark shall be my light and night my day;

To think upon my pomp shall be my hell. (2.4.39-42)

Instead of walking in triumph to the throne in Westminster as she had done in her dream, Eleanor is miserably walking through the streets in penance the last time the audience sees her.

Later, Gloucester is arrested but is murdered before he can come to trial, and Somerset and Suffolk are two who helped bring about his fall. Their heads upon the pieces of his staff (that Gloucester had seen in his dream) are later actually shown to the audience. While neither is killed onstage, their heads do appear subsequently: Suffolk's lover, Queen Margaret, in anguish cradles his head in Act IV, and Somerset's head is the trophy of the new Duke of Gloucester—and future Richard III—in the opening scene of *3 Henry VI.*

Eleanor Cobham as dreamer was portrayed not only in Shakespeare's play but in other works as well. She narrates her dream in the 1578 additions to *The Mirror for Magistrates,* which was composed in the mid-Tudor period and first published in 1559. That work consisted of nineteen tragic monologues of historical persons describing their rise and fall, written in verse by a variety of authors including William Baldwin and George Ferrers. The book was very popular, and expanded editions appeared in 1563, 1578, and 1587. Before the 1559 edition, there had been an earlier attempt to publish parts of it in 1555, but it had been suppressed. The verse stories in the *Mirror* were a continuation of the fifteenth-century poet John Lydgate's *The Fall of Princes,* which Lydgate began around 1431 at the request of Humphrey, Duke of Gloucester; it was completed at the end of that decade. Over a century later, both Humphrey and his Duchess Eleanor describe their tragic ends in the expansion of the book based on Lydgate's work. Eleanor narrates her life after she has been convicted of consulting with witches and wizards, and her dreams of the royal places she had experienced while she was Duchess of Gloucester.

> Farewell Greenwich my Place of delight,
> Where I was wont to see the Crystal streams,
> Of royal Thames most pleasant to my sight
> And farewell Kent, right famous in all realms
> A thousand times I mind you in my dreams
> And when I wake most grief it is to me
> That never more again I shall, see you.

Even worse than the dreams that remind her of the loss of her luxurious life are those that fill her with guilt over how her actions placed her beloved husband Humphrey in such danger.

> In the night time when I should take my rest
> I weep, I wail, I wet my bed with tears
> And when dead sleep my spirits hath opprest
> Troubled with dreams, I fantasy vain fears
> Mine husbands voice then ringeth at mine ears
> Crying for help, O save me from the death
> These villains here do seek to stop my breath.[9]

LORD RIVERS'S NIGHTMARE

Eleanor's dreams were not the only ones described in *The Mirror for Magistrates*. Before the addition of hers in 1578, dreams were part of the stories of the lives (and deaths) of both Anthony Woodville, Lord Rivers, and William, Lord Hastings—stories that were newly included in the 1563 edition. When Shakespeare wrote his first series of history plays, these dream passages provided him with a way to describe Richard, Duke of Gloucester's evil machinations to become king. Anthony Woodville, Lord Rivers, was the brother of Edward IV's widowed queen, Elizabeth, and was known as a highly educated and religious man. Like Gloucester, he was also an uncle of the new King Edward V. In 1483, both uncles wished to rule for the minor king, though Richard's plans in the end went much further. Edward IV's unexpected death at the age of forty led to a serious power struggle, leaving Richard as victor and Woodville dead.

In the long poem in *The Mirror*, Lord Rivers narrates that he was sleeping soundly when "suddenly my servants sore afraid awaked me." They told him, "My Lord we are betrayed." When Lord Rivers heard this, he remembered "this fearful dream" he had just had when he was awakened.

I saw a river stopped with storms of wind

Where through a Swan, a Bull and Boar did pass.

Fraunchyng the fish and fry, with teeth of brass

Richard's emblem was the boar, and in the dream the boar with his brass teeth was fraunching—devouring—the fish. As Lord Rivers's dream continued, "The river dried up save a little stream, which at the last did water all the realm." At first, the dreaming Woodville "thought this stream did drown the cruel boar." But not only did the boar survive, it also killed the bull and swan. The dream continued with Woodville also seeing "an ugly toad" that was crawling toward him. Before Woodville could find out "what became of her, or what of me, My sudden waking would not let me see."[10] *In the Pleasant Art of the Interpretation of Dreams,* Thomas Hill informed his readers that for someone "to see: or behold himself in the water, doth pronounce death to him which sees the dream, or else to some most near or familiar friend to him." But it would have special meaning for Woodville as Lord Rivers. It could represent the terrible fate awaiting him, as the authors of *Mirror for Magistrates* are certainly hinting. The dying river could represent Woodville's death, though the fact that even though it was drying up it watered the entire realm suggests that Rivers wanted to take care of the entire kingdom, whose fate will also be troubled with Richard as king. Lord Rivers apparently assumed that he and Gloucester were on good terms, which made him vulnerable when Gloucester moved against him, and he was executed by the duke in June 1483.

The Duke of Clarence Dreams of Death

While Shakespeare does not use Lord Rivers's dream, he does give the character George, Duke of Clarence a dream right before his death. Although the chronicles describe a number of dreams in the history of Richard III, none of them mentions that Clarence dreamed. There is quite a scholarly debate about what sources Shakespeare used to create Clarence's powerful and haunting dream. Emrys Jones argues that Shakespeare was influenced by both Thomas Kyd's *The Spanish Tragedy* and Vergil's *Aeneas,* but that the most significant reason that Shakespeare gave Clarence the dream was to balance Richard III's own dream the night before his fatal battle. "He gave Clarence a dream so as to match Richard's own on the eve of Bosworth. Indeed he seems to have transferred to Clarence Holinshed's account of Richard's frightening dream on his last night alive."[11]

I believe that Jones is correct about the various influences he mentions and particularly the value of having the dream of Clarence in Act One as a counterpoint to Richard's dream in Act Five. But even more intriguing is Geoffrey Bullough's argument that the representation of Lord Rivers's dream in *The Mirror for Magistrates* was the basis for Shakespeare in his depiction of the Duke of Clarence's dream in Shakespeare's *Richard III.* Early in the play, Richard feigns great dismay when he meets his brother, George, Duke of

Clarence on the street being taken as a prisoner to the Tower. Clarence explains that the reason he has been arrested is that their brother King Edward "harkens after prophecies and dreams" (1.1.54). While Richard consoles Clarence, in fact he has orchestrated a plot to murder his brother, as we know from Richard's soliloquy at the very beginning of the play. "Plots have I laid, inductions dangerous,/By drunken prophecies, libels, and dreams" (1.1.32-33). While Richard has manipulated the meanings of others' dreams, Clarence's own dream while in the Tower, like Woodville's, is about water and the foretelling of death. Clarence tells the Keeper of the Tower:

> O, I have passed a miserable night,
> So full of fearful dreams, of ugly sights,
> . . . .
> So full of dismal terror was the time! (1.4.3-4, 7)

At the Keeper's request, Clarence tells him his dream, explaining that in it, he "had broken from the Tower/And was embarked to cross to Burgundy" (1.4.9-10). Unlike Woodville's dream, where Richard was represented by the boar, in Clarence's dream Richard himself is present.

> And in my company my brother Gloucester,
> Who from my cabin tempted me to walk
> Upon the hatches. Thence we looked toward England
> And cited up a thousand heavy times,
> During the wars of York and Lancaster,
> That had befall'n us. (1.4.11-16)

As Gloucester and Clarence walked,

> Methought that Gloucester stumbled, and in falling
> Struck me, that thought to stay him, overboard
> Into the tumbling billows of the main.
> O Lord, methought what pain it was to drown! (1.4.18-21)

The dream went on even after Clarence's death, and here is a strong classical influence as Clarence saw the ghosts of those he injured. They shrieked at him: "Clarence is come—false, fleeting, perjured Clarence" (1.4.55). When Clarence is narrating the dream to the sympathetic keeper, he ascribes Gloucester's shoving him overboard to his death as an accident—he stumbled—but the audience would know this was a prescient dream. The dream suggests that, though Clarence refused to recognize consciously that Richard would bring about his death instead of his rescue, on some level he understood his brother's guile. Clarence cannot escape this tragic fact when the assassins inform him that not only would his brother Richard of

Gloucester not reward them for rescuing him (which would be the natural brotherly response), but they were indeed sent by him. Though the actual Duke of Clarence was executed, the London mobs scathingly described his death as being drowned in a butt of malmsey, a sweet wine, which was no doubt a comment on the duke's widely known drinking habits. In Shakespeare's play, the character of Clarence does learn the pain of drowning, as his murderer stabs him and then dumps him into the barrel of wine: "Take that, and that, if all this will not do/I'll drown you in the malmsey butt within" (1.4.273).

Lord Hastings Dismisses a Dream

Dreams continued to be an integral part of the narration of Richard's story in both early modern chronicle histories and history plays. While Shakespeare may have transformed Lord Rivers's dream into that of the Duke of Clarence, both chronicles and Shakespeare's play depict a warning dream that Thomas, Lord Stanley had about William, Lord Hastings. Thomas More presented it in his history of Richard III, calling it a "marvelous case," as does Richard Baker, who describes the death of Hastings as demonstrating "how inevitable the blows of Destiny are."[12] Hastings had been Edward IV's chamberlain and had been very close to the king; unlike many royal favorites, Hastings was both successful and well liked. After Edward's death, Hastings was deeply concerned that the Woodvilles, especially Dowager Queen Elizabeth's brother Lord Rivers, would seize power, and he vehemently supported the appointment of Richard, Duke of Gloucester, as Lord Protector. Gloucester and Hastings had worked well together during Edward's reign, but there is no evidence that they had conspired together against the Woodvilles after Edward's death. Because of Hastings's decisiveness, Gloucester was recognized as the Lord Protector as soon as he arrived in London in the beginning of May. Throughout May and into early June, Gloucester and Hastings were on good terms, though of course Hastings was far less close to Gloucester than he had been to Edward. But while Hastings had supported Gloucester as Lord Protector, he was appalled at the idea that Richard would supplant Edward's son and become king himself, and when he made that clear, his fate was sealed. By the middle of June, Gloucester had Hastings summarily executed. One way to explain such a dreadfully swift fall is to have Hastings refuse to listen to a warning dream that could have saved his life.

Holinshed's *Chronicles* narrates that the night before Richard suddenly charged Hastings as a traitor, Lord Stanley had such a "fearful" dream that he got out of bed and sent a secret messenger to Hastings at midnight. In the dream, a boar had gored both Stanley and Hastings; they both received head wounds that bled terribly around their shoulders. Stanley easily recognized that the boar represented Richard, and "this Dream made so fearful an impression in his heart, that he was thoroughly determined no longer to tarry." The messenger told Hastings that Lord Stanley wanted him to go with him, "to ride so far yet the same night that they should both be out of danger," before it turned day. Hastings's response—"Good Lord! leans your Master so much to such trifles, to put such faith in Dreams . . . Go back there fore to thy Master and commend me to him, and pray him to be merry, and have no fear"—would immediately alert an early modern reader that Hastings's remaining time on earth would be numbered in hours not days, since scoffing at warning dreams always seemed to portend the dream would come true.[13] Shakespeare retells Stanley's dream and Hastings's response in *Richard III,* but he makes much less of this one than he did of Clarence's. Hastings, quite displeased when the messenger rouses him in the middle of the night, asks: "Cannot my Lord Stanley sleep these tedious nights?" (3.2.6). The messenger explains that Stanley sent him to tell Hastings that his lord "dreamt the boar had razed off his helm." Stanley wants to know if Hastings will take horse with him "to shun the danger that his soul divines" (3.2.18). Hastings does not take the dream seriously:

> Tell him his fears are shallow, without instance:
> And for his dreams, I wonder he's so simple
> To trust the mockery of unquiet slumbers. (3.2.25-27)

Hastings tells the messenger to

> Go, bid thy master rise and come to me,
> And we will both together to the Tower,
> Where he shall see the boar will use us kindly. (3.2.31-33)

Hastings's mistrust in the ability of dreams to foretell the future and his trust that Richard, Duke of Gloucester will deal with him justly, lead to the sudden, horrible attack on Hastings two scenes later. Richard abruptly turns on Hastings:

> Thou art a traitor.
> Off with his head! Now, by Saint Paul I swear,
> I will not dine until I see the same. (3.4.75-77)

Hastings recognizes too late that he should have listened when he was told about Stanley's dream and that he should have taken Stanley's advice to flee.

> Woe, woe for England! Not a whit for me,
> For I, too fond, might have prevented this.
> Stanley did dream the boar did raze our helms,
> And I did scorn it and disdain to fly. (3.4.80-83)

Lord Stanley's dream and Lord Hastings's fate intertwined within belief and attitudes about dreams. They balance the bookending of dreams of Clarence at the beginning of the play and Richard's own at the end.

Richard III Sleeps and Dreams

Of all of Shakespeare's plays, *Richard III* is one of the most shot through with references to sleep, lack of sleep, and dreams. Early in the play, Richard sleeps well, though he claims he does not when it suits his needs, and he is not troubled by his dreams if he does have any. While he tells Lady Anne (wooing her over the corpse of her father-in-law, the saintly Henry VI) that it was her beauty "that did haunt me in my sleep to undertake the death of all the world," we know this is all a cynical ruse to trick Anne into marrying him (1.2.125-126).

Later in Act One, Queen Margaret curses the Yorks, saving her most savage one for Richard.

> No sleep close up that deadly eye of thine,
>
> Unless it be while some tormenting dream
>
> Affrights thee with a hell of ugly devils! (1.3.125-27)

Margaret's curse does not take effect immediately. When Richard enters in the scene in which he orders the execution of Hastings, he blithely states, "I have been long a sleeper" (3.4.23). But once he has achieved the throne, his sleep is far more bothered, as is that of his now-wife Anne.

> For never yet one hour in his bed
>
> Did I enjoy the golden dew of sleep,
>
> But with his timorous dreams was still awaked. (4.1.82-84)

As a precursor to Macbeth who also feels anxiety about a boy (Banquo's son) who might claim his newly won throne, King Richard is sleepless over thoughts of his nephews, whose claims to the throne are far more legitimate than his own. As he explains to Tyrrell, whom he has hired to murder these boys, they are

> Foes to my rest and my sweet sleep's disturbers
>
> Are they that I would have thee deal upon—
>
> Tyrrel, I mean those bastards in the Tower. (4.2.73-75)

Much earlier than Shakespeare, in *The History of King Richard III*, More described a Richard whose sleep and dreams were greatly disturbed once the boys had been dispatched. More claims that his information comes from eyewitness accounts: "I have heard by credible report of such as were secret with his chamberers." Richard would take "ill rest a night, . . . sore wearied with care and watch, rather slumbered than slept, troubled with fearful dreams, suddenly sometimes started up, leaped out of his bed and ran about the chamber." More's Richard performs terrible deeds but is not without a conscience; rather he is greatly troubled, "his restless heart continually tossed and tumbled with the tedious impression and stormy remembrance of his abominable deed."[14] His deeds are punished by restless sleep and terrible dreams. More's depiction is taken up in the next century by Richard Baker in his *Chronicle*, as he vehemently presents Richard's troubled sleep and dreams as God's retribution for the terrible murder of his innocent nephews.

> And now see the Divine Revenge upon the Actors of this execrable Murder. . . .
> King Richard himself, after this abominable fact done, never had a quiet mind,
> troubled with fearful Dreams; and would sometimes in the night start out of his
> bed, and run about the Chamber in great fright, as if all the Furies of Hell were
> hanging about him.[15]

As Richard's brief reign rushes toward its dramatic end, Richard's dreams only get more frightening and disturbing. Holinshed's *Chronicles* describes the rumors of how terrifying Richard's dreams were on the last night of his life. "The Fame went that he had the same night a dreadful and terrible dream: for it seemed to him, being asleep, that he did see diverse images like terrible devils, which pulled and haled him, not suffering him to take any quiet or rest . . . But I think this was no dream but a . . . prick of his sinful conscience."[16] Richard's dreams were so dreadful that it made it difficult for him, the next morning, to concentrate sufficiently on his speech to rally his troops before battle. According to Baker, "King Richard, to encourage his Soldiers, made a solemn speech to them." But his soldiers did not feel loyalty to their king, and worse, how could he "raise alacrity in others, who had none in himself?" He was lethargic because of the "fearful Dream he had the night before, (wherein it seemed to him, he saw diverse Images like devils, which pulled and haled him, not suffering him to take any rest or quiet) so damped his spirits, that . . . he could not choose but have a presaging fear."[17]

In Shakespeare's play, the tents of both Richard III and Henry Tudor, Earl of Richmond are presented on stage. As each character dreams, the ghosts of Richard's victims—Prince Edward, his wife Anne's first husband; Henry VI; Lord Rivers, Lord Grey, and Sir Thomas Vaughan; Lord Hastings; his nephews Edward and Richard, the Princes in the Tower; his wife Anne; and the Duke of Buckingham—haunt Richard's dreams and bring encouragement to Richmond in his. The impact of these dreams on Richard is tremendous. As Marjorie Garber points out, "When Richard himself becomes the dreamer, the recipient of omens and supernatural warnings," he loses his "rationalist posture . . . [and] the terrifying world of dream overwhelms him."[18] Some of the apparitions mention very specifically that they are coming to Richard as part of his dream. These characters are the ones who, when alive, had the closest relationship to Richard. His nephews, the princes tell him:

> Dream on thy cousins smothered in the Tower.
> Let us be lead within thy bosom, Richard,
> And weigh thee down to ruin, shame, and death! (5.3.151-53)

Anne is also deliberately invading her husband's dream:

> Richard, thy wife, that wretched Anne thy wife,
>
> That never slept a quiet hour with thee,
>
> Now fills thy sleep with perturbations. (5.3.159-61)

Richard's final dreams are the culmination of a play—and a history—filled with problematic sleep and troubled dreams as the dynasty of the Plantagenets comes to an end.

Margaret Beaufort Dreams of Marriage

While Richard's life ended with dreams, Henry VII's life, according to his mother, came into being because of one. Henry Tudor's claim to the English throne came through the maternal line, but it was rather problematic: Margaret Beaufort, born in 1443, was the great-granddaughter of John of Gaunt, Duke of Lancaster (fourth son of Edward III), and she was the sole heiress of her family. The Beauforts were, technically, illegitimate children of John and Katherine Swynford because Lancaster did not marry Katherine until 1396, which was after the birth of all their children. In 1407, the children were legitimized by Act of Parliament but with the proviso that this line had no claim to the throne. Margaret's own background was troubled. Her father John Beaufort, Duke of Somerset, was a disgraced war commander who died when Margaret was only a year old; he may have committed suicide. After her father's death, Margaret became the ward of William de la Pole, Earl of Suffolk. When Suffolk's own political situation became perilous in 1450, he attempted to secure the status of his son John by arranging a marriage between him and his ward Margaret. They were six and seven at the time. Since Margaret was below the age of consent, in 1453 Henry VI had the contract dissolved, and he regranted her wardship to his half-brothers Edmund and Jasper Tudor, the children of his mother Katherine of Valois and her Master of the Wardrobe, Owen Tudor. Edmund believed that marrying Margaret would aid him in achieving his political ambitions. They were married in 1455, and in order to secure his right to life interest in her estates, Edmund insisted on not waiting to consummate the marriage despite the extreme youth of his twelve-year-old bride. Margaret immediately became pregnant. Marriage and impending fatherhood did not end up benefiting Edmund; he died when Margaret was only six months pregnant. Even though Margaret successfully gave birth to her son Henry, the early pregnancy may have caused her permanent damage because she never had another child, though she married twice more.

The goal of Margaret's life was to protect her son Henry and, though she was careful not to do it too openly, to support his Lancastrian claim to the English throne. Henry was twenty-eight when he defeated Richard at Bosworth Field in 1485. Margaret did all she could to help her son consolidate his power, and she continued to support him with great dedication throughout his reign. She survived her son, and one of the final acts of her life was to attend the coronation of her grandson Henry VIII and his wife Katherine of Aragon. She died only five days later. John Fisher, bishop of Rochester, was Lady Margaret's friend and confessor, and Margaret confided in Fisher her memory of how she came to marry Edmund Tudor and thus begin the Tudor dynasty. In the sermon Fisher preached the month after Margaret's death in 1509, he shared this story.

While historically, the child Margaret first had an arranged marriage to John de la Pole and later was married to Edmund Tudor, she herself remembered it quite differently, a memory that not only gave her far more autonomy but also stressed the importance of dreams. In his "months mind" sermon of 1509 which was then published by Wynkyn de Worde, Fisher described how a very young Margaret, since "her lineage were right noble" had at the same time the two offers of marriage. She was not even "fully six years old," and Margaret felt "doubtful in her mind what she were best to do." She knew she had to give an answer the following day. The child turned to "an old gentle woman whom she much loved & trusted" and asked for advice. While the woman would not tell Margaret whom she ought to choose, she did suggest that Margaret "commend herself to Saint Nicholas the patron & helper of all true maidens & to beseech him to put in her mind what she were best to do." Fisher narrated how "A marvelous thing the same night as I have heard her tell many a time" occurred. Margaret lay in prayer calling upon Saint Nicholas, "whether sleeping or waking she could not assure." At about three o'clock in the morning, "one appeared unto her arrayed like a bishop & naming unto her Edmund bade take him unto her husband. And so by this mean she did incline her mind unto Edmund the king's brother & earl of Richmond." Fisher then pointed out how momentous this decision was, since as a result, "she was made mother of the king . . . and granddame to our sovereign lord king Henry VIII which now by the grace of God governs the realm."[19]

Michael K. Jones and Malcolm G. Underwood argue for "the authenticity of this remarkable story" because of the great appreciation Margaret demonstrated for Saint Nicholas once her son was king: She strongly supported the Guild for St. Nicholas for poor parish clerks in London. But by authenticity, Jones and Underwood mean this was Margaret's own story, her own memory, not one invented by someone later for political effect. As they point out, however, Margaret's memory distorted the actual event. Margaret the child would not have had the power to decide whom she would marry. These biographers of Margaret argue that what Margaret remembered as a dream was actually the dissolution of her marriage to John de la Pole. Since Margaret was only six years old when her marriage was arranged with de la Pole, she "never understood or recognized the significance of the ceremony." A child marriage was not the same as one past the age of consent, since the child would have the choice of either ratifying or revoking the contract at a later date. Dissent had to be made publicly and before a bishop. The adult Margaret's recounting to John Fisher gives "an insight into the way a young girl might try to make sense of the events around her." Jones and Underwood persuasively argue that a vague memory of a solemn ceremony with someone "arrayed like a bishop," could well be remembered as a dream. "Since a childhood contract need not be permanently binding, Margaret may have genuinely recalled that she was now presented with a real choice." One significance of the event was not that Margaret had a choice, or that Saint Nicholas provided her with the right answer to that choice, but that on this rare occasion, Henry VI actually made a decision himself and enforced his will.[20] Another significance, however, was the believed power of a dream and a dream that came to allow Margaret to understand her life in a way that gave her some sense of autonomy.

Pʀᴇᴛᴇɴᴅᴇʀs Tʜʀᴇᴀᴛᴇɴ ᴛʜᴇ Nᴇᴡ Tᴜᴅᴏʀ Kɪɴɢ

Margaret's remembered dream was her version of what began the Tudor dynasty; once Henry Tudor was king, a dream was the reason why one young man hoped to end it. Though Henry defeated and killed Richard III in 1485, the supporters of the Yorkist claims were not ready to give up. In the spring of 1486 Francis, Lord Lovell, who had been Richard III's chamberlain, and Humphrey Stafford, who had served as under-sheriff of Worcestershire, attempted to stir up rebellions against Henry in Yorkshire, Warwickshire, and Worcestershire. Their attempts failed. Stafford was arrested and executed in July 1486. Lovell escaped and eventually joined the court of Margaret, Dowager Duchess of Burgundy, and sister of Richard III. In 1487, he was joined there by John, Earl of Lincoln, a nephew of Margaret's who had served Henry loyally at the beginning of the reign and headed the inquiry into Stafford's treason; but then Lincoln had begun to fear the new king's reprisals against the Yorkist relations of Richard III. With 2,000 mercenaries supplied by Margaret, Lovell and Lincoln launched an invasion (going via Ireland) in the spring of 1487.

Henry was very concerned about potential Yorkist claimants to the throne. Soon after he became king, he decided to move Edward, Earl of Warwick (the son of Richard III's older brother George, Duke of Clarence) from where he was being kept in Yorkshire to the Tower. The next year rumors spread that Warwick had escaped. In Ireland in late 1486, a young man claimed to be the Earl of Warwick. His name was actually Lambert Simnel, a boy of poor and obscure origins, who had been put forward by the Yorkists. William Simonds, a priest, had found Simnel and trained him for the imposture. Henry paraded the real Warwick through the streets of London, but this did not end the tumult. When the Earl of Lincoln arrived in Ireland, he declared Simnel to be the real Warwick. On 24 May 1487, Simnel was crowned Edward VI in Dublin Cathedral.

That summer, mercenaries, Irish soldiers, and Yorkist supporters invaded England. John Scrope, fifth Baron Scrope of Bolton, and Thomas Scrope, sixth Baron Scrope of Masham, led a company to York and proclaimed the new king, but Henry's supporters held the city. Henry's men met Simnel's supporters at the battle of Stoke near Nottingham, where there was a quick and brutal victory for the Tudor king. Lincoln was killed in battle, Lovell again escaped, and Simnel was captured. With generosity as well as a perverse sense of humor, Henry spared Simnel and put him to work in the royal scullery.[21] But Henry's problems were not over. In December, a plot against him was discovered within his own household.

In 1491, a new pretender emerged, Perkin Warbeck, who claimed to be Richard, Duke of York, younger son of Edward IV. By 1493, a number of significant figures at Henry's court were involved in plots to support Warbeck, leading to a number of arrests and executions. Warbeck gained support from a number of foreign rulers, most notably James IV of Scotland. When people in Cornwall revolted against Henry because of high taxes, rebels turned to Warbeck to lead them. The rebels were defeated, and Warbeck fled to sanctuary in Beaulieu Abbey, Hampshire, leaving only after he received the assurance that his life would be spared. He was ordered to spend the rest of his life in the Tower of London, but after an attempt to escape that may have been set up by an *agent provocateur*, he and the real Earl of Warwick were executed in November 1499. Before Henry made the final decision to execute Warwick, he consulted with his astrologer William Parron, who, though he did not mention Warwick by name, described how hopeless it was for a certain man "not of base birth."

RALPH WULFORD DREAMS OF BECOMING KING

A few months before Warbeck's execution, there was a third pretender, who again claimed to be the real Earl of Warwick. He was the last of the three pretenders to emerge, but the first of them to be executed, even though his imposture did not lead to the uprisings that had occurred to support Simnel or Warbeck. Ralph Wulford, or Wilford, had few supporters, but he received no mercy. Henry, after nearly fifteen years of a rule attacked by rebels, plots, and pretenders and in the midst of attempting a royal marriage between his eldest son and the daughter of the king and queen of Spain, had little inclination for benevolence. What may have upset Henry even more was that in early 1499, obviously feeling he needed more information about what was to come than he was getting from Parron, Henry went to a Welsh priest who was also a fortune-teller. Henry trusted the priest's gift of prophecy because he had "foretold the death of King Edward and the end of King Richard." The king wanted to know what his own future would hold. The priest informed Henry "that his life would be in great danger during the whole year." While Henry told the priest that he could tell no one about this prophecy, the priest could not keep the secret and confided in a friend, who told yet another friend. The friend of the friend was imprisoned, but the priest and the others fled before they could be apprehended. Soon, rumors of the dangers to the king and of the king's fear spread across the court and into the country. The Spanish ambassador informed Ferdinand and Isabella that the king "has aged so much during the last two weeks that he seems to be twenty years older."[22]

It is little wonder that Henry felt so threatened by Wulford. At the time of the imposture, Ralph was about nineteen or twenty years old, four or five years younger than the actual Warwick. He was the son of a cordwainer, or shoemaker, in Bishopsgate, London, and he had been educated by an Augustinian friar Patrick who considered him to be his finest student. Wulford then went on to study as a scholarship student at Cambridge. He later confessed that, while he was there, he often "stirred in his sleep" with dreams informing him that he "should name himself to be the duke of Clarence's son and he should in process obtain such power that he should be a king." Wulford apparently confided his dreams to Patrick, who encouraged him and trained him for the imposture. According to Edward Hall, "They between themselves secretly had taken a crafty deliberation and counseled of their enterprise, and had devised in their foolish wits, how it should be brought to pass."[23]

Wulford was the least successful of the impostors; he also had the most agency, since the idea came from Wulford himself, unlike Simnel and Warbeck, who were approached by others about the impersonations. Not having those more powerful instigate the plot may well have been one reason why Wulford was apprehended so quickly. But some contemporaries saw Patrick as the one pulling the strings. In the *Great Chronicle of London,* Wulford is described as a new "mawmett" who "by sly & covert means essayed to win to him some adherents." A "mawmett" is defined as "a person who is the tool or puppet of another; a man of straw."[24]

Of course, while we cannot know Patrick's motivations in pushing Ralph forward or what specifically he hoped to achieve, his attempts to turn Wulford's dreams into reality were disastrous to them both. In the spring of 1499, Wulford began his impersonation on the borders of Norfolk and Suffolk where he confided to a number of people that he was the real Earl of Warwick and that he had just escaped from the Tower of London with the help of Patrick. From there Patrick took him to Kent—an area that, according to Hall, "in ancient time has not been dull in setting forth of new fantastical fantasies," while Polydore Vergil described it in the same context as "once the breeding ground of revolutions."[25] In Kent, Patrick proclaimed from the pulpit that Wulford was the newly free earl who was ready to return the throne to the Yorkist line. Although Patrick did all he could to incite people to support him, his words generated no mass support: Wulford was apprehended and brought before John de Vere, Earl of Oxford to be examined. When brought before Henry, Wulford soon confessed his true identity. Wulford was tried for having intended "to have made a new Rumor and Insurrection within this land" and was found guilty. This time, there was no sardonic generosity, nor even life imprisonment. Wulford was sentenced to die, and soon after he was hanged on Shrove Tuesday at St. Thomas Watering on the Old Kent Road. As a warning to all, his body was left hanging until Saturday. Friar Patrick, protected by benefit of clergy, was imprisoned for the rest of his life.[26]

SAD AND DANGEROUS DREAMS OF PASSION

While Wulford's dream was focused exclusively on obtaining power, Shakespeare's presentations of Eleanor, Duchess of Gloucester's dreams, Richard's discussion of a dream to woo Anne, and Margaret Beaufort's remembered dream all interconnected power with ideas about marriage or sexuality. There was great concern about the significance of dreams involving lust as well as the terrible dreams that lovers might have. Philip Goodwin warned of the dangers of "Men bewitched, beguiled, befooled, besotted in Dreams" because of the power of Satan, since "he that can appear as a roaring Lion, to affright a waking Christian: cannot he present himself as an enticing Damsel, to affect a sleeping man, and affect these filthy Dreams?" These filthy dreams "defile men's bodies, their hearts and minds pass not free from defilement."[27] Coming from a completely different perspective that emphasized not the devil but physical ailments as influencing dreams, Hobbes also suggested lustful dreams were troubling, explaining that old men "being commonly less healthful and less free from inward pains" were especially subject to such painful dreams as "dreams of lust, or dreams of anger."[28]

People in love or thinking about love could have dreadful, frightening dreams. Thomas Buoni's *Problemes of Beautie and all humane affections,* which was translated into English from Italian and published in 1606, suggested that, because of "those continual passions they are subject unto," lovers "are accustomed to dream of horrible and fearful things." These dreams, in fact, are "monstrous and horrible."[29] Even dreams that were not terrible could cause pain after the dreamer had awakened. In Lording Barry's1607 comedy, *Ram Alley* (published in 1611), it is suggested that when young women dream of sexual pleasure, they are embarrassed and saddened upon waking.

> When maids awak'd from their first sleep
> Deceiv'd with dreams begin to weep.[30]

Thomas Campion's poem, "Sleepe, Angry Beauty," articulates this connection between painful dreams and passion.

> And in her slumber, see shee close-ey'd weepes;
> Dreames often ore than waking passions move.[31]

The connection between danger and sexuality is also implied in some of the charms young women in the period used to find out the identity of their future husbands. For example, in Herefordshire many believed that if a young woman wanted to have a vision of her future husband, then she should, on Halloween night, pluck a sprig of yew from a church yard in which she had never been before and place it under a pillow.[32] Beginning in the early Middle Ages, however, the tradition was different: Halloween was believed to be the night when the souls of the dead returned, and from the fourteenth century onward, the sprig of the yew symbolized sadness.[33]

A DREAM OF THE DEATH OF A QUEEN

The incident that changed the course of English history most thoroughly was Henry VIII's break with the Catholic Church. Both during Henry's lifetime and in the century following, there were reported dreams that depicted the dissolution of Henry VIII's marriage to Katherine of Aragon, his passion for Anne Boleyn, and later her dreadful death. Henry's intense desire for a legitimate male heir led to his attempt to receive an annulment of his marriage to Katherine of Aragon from Pope Clement VII. But the Pope refused to grant the annulment out of fear of Katherine's nephew, Holy Roman Emperor Charles V. Henry's urgency to end his marriage only intensified once he centered on Anne Boleyn who had refused to become his mistress. Henry insisted that he would marry Anne, and she would provide him with the son he craved.

Katherine was a well-beloved queen, and Anne was her highly unpopular supplanter, but for some early English Protestants, Anne was a heroine who had encouraged Henry to break with Rome and reform the Church. Like Katherine, however, whose only surviving child was her daughter Mary, Anne Boleyn had only one child and that, too, was a daughter. In May 1536, less than three years after the birth of Elizabeth, Anne was executed on highly problematic evidence for having committed adultery with five men. If many of the English shed no tears that the "goggle-eyed whore" was dead, some reformers felt great grief.[34]

Alexander Alesius[35] was born in Edinburgh in 1500 and received his B.A. from the University of St Andrews. Originally a devout Catholic, he became critical of the abuses of the Church and had to flee Scotland when he was about thirty. After traveling throughout much of Europe, Alesius settled in Wittenberg. In October 1532, he enrolled in the University there, soon becoming a close friend of Philip Melanchthon. In 1535, Henry VIII and his advisors, concerned that a Catholic alliance against England was brewing, looked to the Protestant Schmalkaldic league for possible support. Alesius traveled to England, bringing copies of some of Melanchthon's writings for the king and Archbishop Thomas Cranmer. Alesius impressed Cranmer and Thomas Cromwell, who felt that Alesius could be helpful in reforming the church in England. After a brief return to Wittenberg, Alesius resettled in England. In 1536, Alesius was living in London; he had developed a close friendship with Cranmer. After being warned by Cranmer, Alesius fled England in 1539 as the political climate became difficult for reformers. Twenty years later on 1 September 1559 (less than a year after Elizabeth ascended the throne), Alesius wrote the new queen a long letter in which he described the dream he had at the time of her mother's death.

Alesius assured Elizabeth that "I take to witness Christ, Who shall judge the quick and the dead, that I am about to speak the truth." On the day that Anne Boleyn was to be executed, between two and three o'clock in the morning while he was in bed, "there was revealed to me (whether I was asleep or awake I know not) the Queen's neck, after her head had been cut off, and this so plainly that I could count the nerves, the veins, and the arteries." Alesius wrote that he had been so "terrified by this dream," that he immediately arose, dressed, and left his lodgings. He crossed the river Thames and went to Lambeth, the residence of Archbishop Cranmer. As Alesius entered the garden, he found Cranmer there walking, and Cranmer asked him why he had come so early, as it was not yet four o'clock. "I answered that I had been horrified in my sleep, and I told him the whole occurrence." Cranmer was so stunned that for a while he stood "in silent wonder." Finally he "broke out into these words, 'Do not you know what is to happen today?'" Alesius told Cranmer that, since the day Anne Boleyn had been taken to the Tower, he had remained at home and had no knowledge of what was going on. "The Archbishop then raised his eyes to heaven and said, 'She who has been the Queen of England upon earth will today become a Queen in heaven.' So great was his grief that he could say nothing more and then he burst into tears." Alesius returned home, deciding that though he had witnessed Anne Boleyn's death in his dream, he would not go to her execution. "I could not become an eye witness of the butchery of such an illustrious lady, and of the exalted personages who were headed along with her."[36] Alesius had not only dreamed of Anne Boleyn's death but had assumed that it would be meaningful years later for her daughter to be told of it.

Whereas Alesius dreamed about Anne's death at the time, during the reign of her daughter, stories were published about Anne's own dreams and how they foretold the great reign of Elizabeth. In 1582, Christopher Ocland published in Latin *The Popes Farwel; or, Queen Ann's Dream*, which was later published in English in 1680. In this poem, Anne's dead uncle—otherwise not identified—comes to her in a dream to warn her that she shall die in thirty days. Her uncle explains why he has come:

> But why should I thus speak? Good Queen attend,
> I only come to tell you as a Friend,
> That Hellish envy lurks in Princes' Court,
> 'Midst all their Games, Divertissements and Sports.

Her uncle warns Anne that there are many who "lurk in Court" and cannot feel secure "whilst you are Queen." While a true Reformation will come to England, "you, oh, Queen, shall never live to see this happy change." He explains to Anne that after Henry will come Edward, but then will come Mary—and Rome:

> Now he who dares the sacred Writ to read
> In his own Tongue, for that offence must Bleed;
> Or he that dares to thwart the See of Rome,
> Has forthwith Fire and Faggot for his Doom.

He then provides hope because after Mary

> by your Child Eliza's bearing sway,
> These wrongs shall cease, and Papists post away.

It will not be easy for Elizabeth, however, because the devilish pope will seek vengeance.

> The Virgin Queen, your Daughter, he will try
> By secret Arts and Methods to Destroy;
> But all in vain, for GOD will Her Defend
> In Peace and Plenty to her utmost end.

The last words her uncle shares with Anne, despite foretelling her impending death, are meant to be comforting.

> For, gentle Queen, your Glass is almost Run,
> Yet Thirty Days, and you'll be Dead and gone:
> But let this cheer you, Your Eliza shall
> Credit her Father, You, her Self and All.[37]

Holinshed's *Chronicles* also has a deceased relative who comes to Anne Boleyn in a dream. This time it is her grandfather, and it is the night before her death, not a month before her execution, that "this good queen was fore-warned of her death in a dream." Her grandfather came to her while she slept. He first gave Anne "a long narration of the vanities of this world (how envy reigns in the courts of princes), maligning the fortunate estate of the vir-tuous," and then assured Anne that "King Henry the eight and his issue should the utter overthrow and expulsion of popery out of England." But his best assurance of the future was "that the government of queen Elizabeth should be established in tranquility & peace."[38]

Even though Elizabeth's father had her mother killed, it was important for Anne Boleyn to be presented, during Elizabeth's reign, as the one who brought forth the reformation in the person of her child. In the above dream, we do not know which of her grandfathers was supposed to bring this message—though it seems more likely that Holinshed would have been think-ing of her maternal grandfather Thomas Howard, second Duke of Norfolk, rather than Sir William Boleyn. We have no evidence of what the historical Anne Boleyn dreamed before her death, or if she dreamed at all. But if she had such a dream, it surely would have brought her comfort and, as a reported dream, would encourage readers to perceive the executed queen as reverent and holy. The section in the *Chronicles* ends with six lines in Latin from Ocland's poem, promising Anne that her daughter Elizabeth would carry the names of her parents to the stars as bringing about the great reformation.[39]

We can never know if such dreams had actually occurred, but those who read these accounts in the reign of Elizabeth would have seen Anne as a virtuous woman who helped to usher in the Reformation rather than believe Henry's depiction of her as an adulterous whore.

Renaissance Drama Enacts Dreams of Katherine and Anne

Henry's passion for Anne Boleyn, his decision to end his marriage with Katherine, the subsequent split with Rome, and Anne's own death were well-known in England and throughout Europe. These events were depicted not only in Shakespeare's play, *Henry VIII,* but also in Pedro Calderón de la Barca's seventeenth-century Spanish play, *La cisma de Inglaterra,* translated into English as *The Schism in England.* George Mariscal argues that Calderón and Shakespeare "are two theatrical practitioners who most forcefully represent the on-going aftershocks" of the crisis of the Reformation.[40]

Calderón, an intensely committed Catholic from Spain, does not present Henry as the monster one might have expected. Rather, it is Wolsey, angry that he did not become pope, who is the architect of the break with Rome. Calderón depicts Anne Boleyn as both evil and seductive—so seductive, in fact, that Henry is drawn into losing his honor because of his lust. Calderón's Henry, released from the constraints of an accurate historical narrative, attempts to make his amends at the end of the play. The play opens with a dream that carefully delineates entire themes of the play. The king's prophetic dream demonstrates the critical role Anne Boleyn plays in causing the Reformation. Gregory Peter Andrachuk contends that "in the first seven lines of the play the whole story is foretold, and the tragedy of Henry's fatal flaw revealed, for his religious fervor is no match for the strength of his physical passion."[41]

The play begins with pipes sounding and a curtain being drawn back, revealing King Henry having fallen asleep as he was writing *Assertio septem sacramentorum,* his defense of the seven sacraments against the assaults of Martin Luther. The phantasm of Anne Boleyn glides by. The king has not yet met Anne in his waking life; he calls to her:

> Stay, divine spirit, beauteous image, sun
>
> In eclipse, lusterless star, beware,
>
> For you offend the sun indeed, in seeking
>
> To blot out such great splendour. Why do you treat me thus,
>
> Your wrath against my heart?[42]

Andrachuk argues that while Henry's speech appears to be a "description of her beauty," what Henry is really referring to are "her heretical tendencies," and that while the king is mesmerized by Anne's beauty, "it is a beauty that, like the Protestantism she represents, is at first attractive and luminous . . . but that ultimately . . . is darkness."[43]

The vision of Anne tells Henry, "I'm going to erase all you write down,"[44] and then vanishes. Calling out in his sleep, Henry begs her to stay. He is still calling to her when Wolsey enters and wakes the king. Henry demands, "Who is the woman who just now left this chamber? Tell me who she is." Wolsey tells him that no one had come that way and that "She must have been an absolute illusion, forged by your dream." When Wolsey asks Henry to tell him about the dream, Henry narrates it with great care, reminding the cardinal that he is writing a book against Luther's "poison and fierce pestilence." He had come to the part on the sacrament of marriage "when, alas, My head grew heavy and my wit was dulled by sleepiness." As he slept, he saw the beautiful woman enter; it made the hair of his beard and on his head stand on end, his blood freeze, and his heart hammer.

> She came towards me, and I was perturbed
> At seeing her, and contemplating her
> I could not go on writing—to be precise,
> However much I wrote and noted down
> With my right hand, my left hand would erase.[45]

Soon after his dream, the king meets the actual Anne Boleyn, a lady-in-waiting to his queen, and he recognizes her as the woman from his dream. Anne seductively dances for Henry, before suddenly falling at his feet. Noting the irony of what Henry had been writing when he dreamed of Anne, Wolsey uses Henry's desire for Anne to convince him to divorce his virtuous wife and leave the Church. Anne persuades Henry to disinherit Princess Mary and exile her, as she then plans to poison Katherine and turn Henry against Wolsey. Toward the end of the play, Henry finally realizes that Anne, who has manipulated him, is also unfaithful. He orders her arrest:

> That woman,
> That fierce animal, that blind enchantment,
> False sphinx, that basilisk, that poisonous serpent,
> That enraged tigress, Anne Boleyn, arrest her,
> And keep her captive for one dismal night
> In the Tower of London.

When Henry sees her as she is being escorted to the Tower, he orders her execution. He then believes that God wishes him to return to Katharine, but he learns that it is too late; his wife is already dead. The Princess Mary comes on stage in mourning to inform Henry of her mother's death. Penitent, Henry begs his daughter, "Give help, since I desire to repent . . . What evil have I done, what evil done!" Henry decides to make amends by promising Mary:

> You shall be Queen of England, and to ensure
> That this is ratified, today the kingdom
> Must swear allegiance to you, that memories
> Of your sainted mother (which will validate it)
> Will be revived in you.

The play ends with the stage filled with citizens coming to take their oath of allegiance to Mary as the future monarch. The king and princess enter and sit upon their thrones. The stage directions detail that "At their feet, instead of a footstool, is to be the body of Anne Boleyn, covered with a silken sheet: and when they are seated, the body is uncovered." Early in the play the seductive Anne had elegantly fallen at the feet of the king; now her body lies there as the Captain proclaims "Henry, the most Christian King . . . in order to satisfy the people who, in their monstrous error, suppose that Katherine was not legitimate Queen, wishes solemnly to proclaim his daughter, Mary, our Princess and Mistress and his sole heir, the Crown Princess."[46]

George Mariscal suggests that the first scene of *The Schism in England* is visually "remarkably like [a] Shakespearean scene."[47] Shakespeare's *Henry VIII*, probably written in collaboration with John Fletcher, also examines the dissolution of Henry's marriage to Katherine and his love affair and subsequent marriage to Anne Boleyn. It also presents a dream on stage. Written in Protestant England instead of Catholic Spain, Shakespeare and Fletcher's play does not demonize Anne Boleyn as Calderón's does. She is the mother of the child who will bring greatness to the realm, but Catholic Katherine is also portrayed as a strong and courageous woman, a steadfast woman of faith.

In the pivotal trial scene where the two cardinals, Thomas Wolsey, close advisor to Henry, and the Italian Campeius, are present to judge the validity of Henry's marriage to Katherine, she presents herself eloquently. She kneels before Henry, telling him:

> Sir, I desire you do me right and justice,
> And to bestow your pity on me . . .
> . . . .
> Heaven witness
> I have been to you a true and humble wife. (2.4.11-12, 20-21)

Later, Henry will acknowledge what a fine wife Katherine had been to him, even as he wants the marriage annulled. When Katherine turns to those who would judge her, her strong sense of agency and integrity make her defiant. She lets Wolsey know that

> I am about to weep; but, thinking that
> We are a queen, or long have dreamed so, certain

The daughter of a king, my drops of tears
I'll turn to sparks of fire. (2.4.68-71)

Her sparks of fire make her decide to refuse to allow those she cannot respect judge her.

I do refuse you for my judge, and here
Before you all appeal unto the Pope,
To bring my whole cause 'fore His Holiness,
And to be judged by him. (2.4.116-19)

Despite Henry VIII's order that Katherine be called to stay, she makes the decision to leave:

I will not tarry: no, nor ever more
Upon this business my appearance make
In any of their courts. (2.4.129-31)

The historical Katherine refused to be the obedient wife when Henry was denying that she was his wife at all. She neither obeyed him nor ever agreed that she was not Queen Katherine, his legally begotten wife and mother of his legal heir, Mary, even if it would have made her life easier. Katherine remained steadfast in her beliefs at whatever cost.

The second scene of Act Four is the final time the audience sees Katherine, who has become seriously ill after Henry broke with the Roman Church and had her declared Dowager Princess. Katherine enters with the aid of Griffith, her gentleman usher, and Patience, her woman servant. Patience tells Griffith that Katherine is "sick to death" (4.2.1). After a discussion about the death of Wolsey, Katherine eventually asks for music and falls asleep as "Sad and solemn music" plays. Katherine's dream is then presented on stage. The stage directions are that "six Personages, clad in white robes, wearing on their heads garlands of bays, and golden vizards on their faces, branches of bays or palm in their hands" (4.2.82.1-82.5) enter one after the other and then dance around the sleeping Katherine. English Renaissance audiences would most likely assume these "personages" were angels who had come to honor Katherine. Two of them hold a garland over her head while the other four curtsey. Pairs of them take turns passing the garland and curtseying to the sleeping former queen. Katherine then in her sleep makes "signs of rejoicing and holdeth up her hands to heaven," (4.2.82.14-82.15) as the dancers vanish. Katherine wakes and calls out to the creatures that had been with her.

Spirits of peace, where are ye? Are ye all gone,
And leave me here in wretchedness behind ye?

She describes her dream as the coming of a "blessed" group who

> Invite me to a banquet, whose bright faces
>
> Cast thousand beams upon me, like the sun?
>
> They promised me eternal happiness,
>
> And brought me garlands, Griffith, which I feel
>
> I am not worthy yet to wear. I shall, assuredly. (4.2.83-84, 88-91)

Her gentleman usher Griffith is "most joyful, madam, such good dreams Possess your fancy" (4.2.92-93). As we have seen in the previous chapter, angels often appeared in early modern English dreams. In *Physiognomie and chiromancie*, Richard Saunders notes that "to speak with an Angel that reveals some secrets to you which you do not yet understand, denotes that you shall come to some great King or Prince."[48] Katherine does not speak to the angels who come to celebrate and welcome her. She has been abandoned by a great king of earth and soon will come, she faithfully believes, to the greatest of all kings.

Patience notices how pale Katherine looks and how drawn her face is. Griffith recognizes "She is going" (4.2.99). One might expect that this would be Katherine's final exit, but before Katherine will go to a place where she can wear her garlands eternally, Caputius, the Holy Roman Emperor's ambassador, comes to visit her at Henry's request. Katherine again strongly expresses her beliefs about herself as the king's wife who had only a chaste, married love for Henry. Her last thoughts are also on what she can do to help her daughter. Katherine asks Caputius to tell Henry

> I have commended to his goodness
>
> The model of our chaste loves, his young daughter
>
> . . . .
>
> She is young, and of a noble modest nature;
>
> I hope she will deserve well. (4.2.131-32, 135-36)

This is the last scene Katherine appears in; she is clearly dying. In her final speech, she instructs her attendant Patience:

> When I am dead, good wench,
>
> Let me be used with honor. Strew me over
>
> With maiden flowers, that all the world may know
>
> I was a chaste wife to my grave. (4.2.167-70)

Even at the very end, Katherine is asserting herself, and this in certain ways creates an insoluble problem in the play. As Gordon McMullan points out, on the one hand, Katherine is an exemplary wife who stands up to her husband in an attempt to sustain her marriage (and loving marriage was key to Reformation theology), while on the other hand, Katherine, a devout Catholic, is intensely committed to the old order. This disjunction in response to Katherine is also present in how her dream is presented on stage and how the audience responds to it. Post–Renaissance productions sometimes portray the dream sparsely in "Protestant" fashion or magnificently and ornately in "Catholic." McMullan demonstrates that the lengthy Folio stage directions were meant to ensure that "original audiences would have seen a spectacular version and therefore have no doubt about Katherine's state of grace." For some of the early seventeenth-century Protestant audience, however, this dream depiction would have been disturbing "since visions of angels are associated with Catholic tradition in a way they are not with Protestantism."[49] Judith Anderson argues that "Katherine's vision is not as reassuring as we might initially assume"[50] since to the very end Katherine rejects the divorce, maintaining her marriage and thus her Catholicism.

Scholars have suggested several possible sources for Shakespeare and Fletcher's description of Katherine's dream. E. E. Duncan-Jones contends that Shakespeare got the idea for Katherine's dream in the play from a dream described by Charles de Sainte Marthe in the funeral oration for Marguerite of Navarre, published in French and Latin in 1550. Soon before Marguerite's death, Duncan-Jones claims, a beautiful woman came to the dying Marguerite in a dream and showed her a coronet of flowers, promising her that she would be crowned with it when she entered heaven. From a reference in Pepys's diary in 1668, this story was apparently known in England in the latter part of the seventeenth century. Duncan-Jones conjectures that, while Shakespeare would not have read the oration himself, "he may easily have talked with those who had," especially when he lodged "with a Huguenot family of Mountjoy in 1604."[51] We have no direct evidence that Shakespeare was familiar with the oration, however, and John Margeson argues that, "although there is marked resemblance in the imagery of the two dreams, the main difficulty lies in determining how Shakespeare might have come across this relatively obscure work." Margeson argues that, in some ways ironically, the source for Katherine's dream is Holinshed's *Chronicles'* depiction of Anne Boleyn's, since both have a "comforting aspect" and each occurs soon before the woman's death.[52] McMullen agrees: "there is no doubt that it is a possible source—a dream-vision of impending death which offers a bright future. . . . it creates a remarkable, and wholly unlikely conflation of personalities and reputations."[53] Of course, Shakespeare—or Fletcher—might have used a number of different readings and remembered previous conversations while they were composing *Henry VIII*.

Just as Calderón ended his Henry VIII play with a projection of the king's daughter Mary as queen, Shakespeare's play closes with Cranmer foretelling England's bright future with Elizabeth.

This royal infant . . .
Though in her cradle, yet now promises

Upon this land a thousand thousand blessings . . .

. . . .

She shall be, to the happiness of England. (5.5.18-20, 57)

John Fletcher's father, Richard, dean of Peterborough and subsequently bishop of Bristol, Worcester, and eventually London, was also Lord Almoner to Elizabeth at court. He preached before her on special feast days, and in these sermons, he would often counsel and praise the queen for her Protestant faith—comments that both precursor and echo in Cranmer's speech.

Dreams of the Young Elizabeth

Both *The Schism of England* and *Henry VIII,* in their portrayal of England's glorious future, fail to mention the child whom the actual Henry VIII was so eager to have—his son Edward, the future Edward VI. His brief reign ended in 1553 when he was fifteen. His early death (and in turn Mary's as well) meant that the daughters Henry declared illegitimate—Mary and Elizabeth— would rule England for the rest of the century. The rule of Mary and the beginning of Elizabeth's were also dramatized in Thomas Heywood's 1605 *If You Know Not Me, You Know Nobody.*[54] In this play as well, dreams caused anxieties, foreshadowed events to come, and demonstrated how in dreams angels could serve as protectors. The subtitle of Heywood's play, produced only two years after the reign of Elizabeth ended, was "The Troubles of Queen Elizabeth." While for most of the play Elizabeth is not yet queen, there are many troubles and the Protestant princess is in much danger.

The play begins with the triumph of Mary and her Catholic lords. Her councilors rejoice that Wyatt and the Kentish rebels' "overthrow is past: The rebel dukes that fought by all means to proclaim queen Jane" (22-23).[55] Later in the scene, word comes that Philip has safely landed in England. When Mary enters, she is triumphant and jubilant as well:

By gods assistance and the power of heaven,

We are instated in our brothers throne,

. . . .

Our heart is joyful Lords, our peace is pure. (48-49, 53)

We also see from the beginning how cruel and dishonorable Mary is as queen. One subject, Dodd, comes and begs Mary to remember

when we first flocked to you

. . . .

Twas thus concluded that we your liegemen

Should still enjoy our consciences, and use that faith

Which in king Edwards days was held Canonical. (81, 83–85)

Mary's response, encouraged by Sir Henry Beningfield and Stephen Gardiner, bishop of Winchester and her chancellor, is to have the man who supported her loyally when her rights to the throne were threatened put in the pillory for three days.

Beningfield suggests that Princess Elizabeth had "a hand in these petitions. . . . She is a favorite of these heretics" (95–97). Winchester agrees and adds, "Is't not probable, that she in Wyatt's expedition . . . was a confederate" (98–101). He urges Mary:

> You must foresee fore-danger, and cut off all such
>
> As would your safety prejudice. (102-3)

Winchester clearly wants Elizabeth "cut off"—in other words, executed—alerting the audience to the danger threatening the princess. The danger becomes keener when Mary agrees to a commission to fetch Elizabeth from Ashridge to London so that she can be examined. One of the lords, Sentlo, exclaims:

> Gracious Queen, she only craves but to behold your face,
>
> That she might clear her self of all supposed treasons
>
> Still protesting, she is as true a subject to your grace,
>
> As lives this day. (116–19)

Winchester is appalled that anyone would come to the defense of the heretic princess. He denounces Sentlo to the queen, who again demonstrates her arrogance and cruelty.

> Away with him, I'll teach him know his place
>
> To frown when we frown, smile on whom we grace. (122-23)

Winchester approves of Mary's action: "Twill be a means to keep the rest in awe." The queen decides to go even further and sends Sentlo to the Tower: "All those that seek our sisters cause to favor, Let them be lodged" (126-27).

If the first scene is presented from the point of view of the powerful Catholic Queen Mary, soon the audience can react firsthand to how Elizabeth and those who serve her are feeling. The scene moves to Ashridge, and we see Gage, her gentleman usher, speaking to one of Elizabeth's servant women, asking her: "How fares her Grace" (149). The response is worrisome:

> O wondrous crazy gentle master Gage,
>
> Her sleeps are all unquiet. (150-51)

Before the princess even appears on stage, we know that she feels terrified by her situation, is having trouble sleeping, and is perhaps suffering from troublesome dreams. Then Mary's entourage arrives with a message, insisting that Elizabeth be brought before the queen. When Elizabeth enters, the audience sees her courage and grace when the princess explains that she is ill but agrees to come since the queen has summoned her.

When Elizabeth arrives at court, she is deeply frightened: "The Queen's displeasure . . . hath made me heart sick, brain sick, and sick even to death" (314-15). But then she tells her servants: "My Innocence yet makes my heart as light, as my front's heavy" (332-33). Later she tells her servants who are also deeply upset:

> weep not I pray,
> Rather you should rejoice:
> If I miscarry in this enterprise, and ask you why,
> A Virgin and a Martyr both I die. (339–42)

Elizabeth insists on demanding: "What's my offence? Who be my accusers" (346). She soon finds out. Mary's commissioners come and accuse her of being involved in Wyatt's rebellion. Elizabeth asserts her innocence, and while it is acknowledged that on the scaffold Wyatt cleared her of any complicity, the constable still tells her, "Madam, the Queen must hear you sing another song" (414). Elizabeth responds: "I can no note but truth. . . . One day in choirs of Angels I shall sing" (416, 418). The councilors leave to consult with the queen, but Elizabeth has little respite. They soon return and Winchester informs Elizabeth:

> It is the pleasure of her majesty
> That you be straight committed to the Tower. (440-41)

Elizabeth is also told that all her servants have been discharged except for Gage, her gentleman usher, and one gentlewoman, Clarentia. The scenes of Elizabeth arriving in the rain at Tower's gate and her ill treatment in the Tower closely echo John Foxe's depiction of the trials of Princess Elizabeth in his *Actes and Monuments*. Finally she is released into the custody of Beningfield. But Elizabeth does not know what this will actually mean and is still deeply frightened. She asks if Lady Jane Grey's scaffold is still standing, and when Beningfield comes to take her away to Woodstock Castle, she exclaims:

> fare-well, fare-well,
> I am freed from limbo to be sent to hell. (832-33)

We see Elizabeth traveling under guard, and her great consternation that those who praise as she passes are punished. Once she arrives at Woodstock, she asks for paper and pen so that she might write to Mary, but Beningfield refuses, telling her it is not in his commission. Finally she is given paper and pen. After writing her letter, she then writes in her book the famous lines the historical Elizabeth actually carved with a diamond into a window at Woodstock when she was imprisoned there: "Much suspected by me, nothing prov'd can be" (1036). Beningfield discovers that what she has written in is an English Bible.

The scenes at Woodstock are where dreams play their most significant role in the drama. After completing her writing, Elizabeth tells Clarentia:

My heart is heavy and my heart doth close,

I am wearing of writing, sleepy on the sudden,

Clarentia . . . command some music

In the with-drawing chamber. (1042-45)

As Elizabeth sleeps, there is a dumb show presented on stage, according to these directions: "Enter Winchester, Constable, Barwick, and Friars: at the other door two Angels: the Friars step to her, offering to kill her: the Angels drive them back. Exeunt. The Angels open the Bible, and put it in her hand as she sleeps, Exeunt Angels, she wakes." As she awakes, Elizabeth remarks on "how pleasant was this sleep to me" (1054), but she is not altogether sure whether what had occurred was a dream or not, and asks Clarentia, "saw'st thou nothing?"(1055) Clarentia assures the princess that she neither saw nor heard anything. Elizabeth realizes that she is holding her English Bible. "Didst not thou put this book into my hand?" (1060) But Clarentia had not done that either. Elizabeth becomes convinced that this dream was miraculous: " 'twas by inspiration" (1062). Her belief is strengthened even more when she looks to read where it is opened and sees

Whoso putteth his trust in the Lord

Shall not be confounded. (1064-65)

Though this dream should be very comforting to Elizabeth, it ends neither her peril nor her fear. She is brought to see Mary, who still hounds her to confess that she is guilty of conspiracy. When Elizabeth weeps, Mary describes them as "tears of spleen" (1259) and later demands: "Will you submit?"(1267) But though Elizabeth responds with deference, she will not admit to any wrongdoing.

My life madam I will, but not as guilty,

Should I confess

Fault done by her, that never did transgress.

. . . .

Exact all torture and imprisonment,

What ere my greatest enemies can devise,

And they all have done their worst, yet I
Will your true subject and true sister die. (1268–70, 1278–81)

Hidden behind the arras, Philip is listening to this conversation and comments to himself:

Mirror of virtue and bright natures pride,
Pity it had been, such beauty should have died. (1282–83)

Heywood's Philip—and perhaps the historical Philip as well—is more impressed with his sister-in-law than with his wife. Though Mary still states that she believes in Elizabeth's guilt, she follows her husband's lead as he appears and agrees that the next day Elizabeth will return to the country, but as a free woman.

Yet Elizabeth still cannot trust Mary, and even while living in the country, she still does not know what her fate will be. Just as at the beginning of the play, one morning Gage inquires of Clarentia if the Princess Elizabeth is up and out of bed.

Yes master Gage, but heavy at the heart,
For she was frighted with a dream this night,
She said, she dreamed her sister was new married,
And sat upon a high Imperial throne,
That she her self was cast into a dungeon,
Where enemies environed her about,
Offering their weapons to her naked breast;
Nay they would scarcely give her leave to pray,
They made such haste to hurry her away. (1342–52)

This is, on the face of it, a worrisome and frightening dream, but a Renaissance audience would also recognize the implications of having a wedding portrayed in a dream. Elizabeth's dream that her sister was newly married had negative connotations in the Renaissance. Gage's concern over the situation deepens when Clarentia narrates her dream from the previous night.

Then did I dream of weddings, and of flowers,
Me thought I was within the finest garden,
That ever mortal eye did yet behold,
Then straight me thought some of the chief were picked
To dress the bride, O, 'twas the rarest show,
To see the bride go smiling along the streets.
As if she went to happiness eternal. (1355–61)

Gage recognizes what wedding dreams represent:

> Oh most unhappy dream, my fear is now
> As great as yours, before it was but small,
> Come let's go comfort her, that joys us all. (1362–64)

Going all the way back to Artemidorus, whose work was available and known in English in the early modern period, "death and marriage represent one another." It was widely believed in Herefordshire that dreaming of a wedding was an omen of death. In *Paroemiologia*, John Clark explained that "after a dream of a wedding comes a corpse." Saunders warned that if someone dreamed that they had been "at a wedding, it is damage by the death of some friend or other."[56]

Heywood emphasizes this final dream of Elizabeth's even more strongly; we have not only Clarentia's description of it, but, later in the scene, Elizabeth appears on stage and informs Gage and Clarentia:

> O God, my last nights dream I greatly fear
> It doth presage my death, good master Gage
> Look to the path-way that doth come from the court,
> I look each minute for death's messenger. (1415–18)

Gage does see a messenger coming—"Madame I see from far a horseman coming" (1421)—but it turns out that it is far from death's messenger. It is Henry Karew, and he has come to tell Elizabeth that death has not come for her, but instead deliverance. "God save the Queen, God save Elizabeth." Mary is dead, and Elizabeth has miraculously survived all danger to become queen. Heywood has given Elizabeth a powerful, upsetting dream—but it turns out not to be a prophetic dream after all. Rather than foretelling imprisonment and death, Elizabeth's future is the opposite of her dream. The play ends with Elizabeth's triumphant entry into London. But in a sense it does end with one of the dreams of the play coming true, as Elizabeth shows the Lord Major of London and the Londoners the book she is carrying—an English Bible. Elizabeth proclaims:

> This was our solace when we were distressed,
> This book that hath so long concealed it self,
> So long shut up, so long hid; now Lords see,
> We here unclasp, for ever it is free:
> Who looks for joy, let him this book adore,
> This is true food for rich men and for poor. (1583–88)

The dream portrayed on stage had angels place the English Bible in her hands. Now Elizabeth is awake, is queen, and is holding out the English

Bible, praising it for all to see. *If You Know Not Me* is dotted with dreams, and McMullen suggests that it, with its depiction of the Princess Elizabeth's dream of angels, is "a further possible source for Katherine's dream" as it was depicted on stage in *Henry VIII:* "the most unlikely conjunction of all."[57]

Late sixteenth and early seventeenth-century dramatists used dreams to emphasize the issues of sexuality and power in the founding of the Tudor dynasty and in the political and religious challenges to that dynasty, as Henry VII established the rule, as Henry VIII broke with the Catholic Church, and as his daughters attempted to establish female rule. Dreams played their part in drama, but they were also a significant part in the actual women's rule in the history of sixteenth-century England. We will turn to this issue in the next chapter.

CHAPTER 5

SACRED BLOOD AND MONARCHY

Early modern English dream books often discussed dreams about monarchs, both kings and queens. Andrew Seyton, the "celebrated seer of Cumberland," suggested that if in a dream one saw the queen, one would soon find honor, joy, and prosperity. But Thomas Hill informed his readers that dreaming of a queen "signifies deceit to follow."[1] The various ways that dreams about queens were interpreted in a century when women were actually ruling monarchs suggest loyalty to a specific ruling queen—Elizabeth—as well as a sense of insecurity brought about by woman's rule, especially in a time of intense religious change. Historical records chronicle dreams both about and by queens of the time. We also have stories of queens' dreams that may or may not have actually occurred but were repeated and used for a variety of political and religious agendas. If some dreams or reported dreams did suggest honor and joy, more were symptomatic of deep cultural, political, and religious divisions and anxiety. Dreaming about the ruler has not been limited to past times. From surveying approximately a thousand individuals about the current British monarchy, Brian Masters found that "quite often, the Queen and her family are the unwitting *dramatis personae* of the plays, masques, farces and dramas which we elaborate in the night." Several hundred people were willing to share their dreams of the royal family with Masters, and he published them in a collection in 1972. Twenty years after the publication of Masters's book, in February 1992, CBS news reported that forty percent of the surveyed British public responded that they dreamed about Queen Elizabeth II. Two years later, in 1994, Julia Anderson-Miller and Bruce Joshua Miller published *Dreams of Bill,* a collection of the dreams of hundreds of people—mostly women—who dreamed about President Bill Clinton. Years before the Monica Lewinsky scandal, many women were having romantic or sexual dreams about the president. The Millers had started to work on the book after Julia had dreamed vividly about Clinton and assumed that others did as well. After they received hundreds of answers to the classified ads they placed throughout the United States, they found their hypothesis was correct.[2]

MEANINGS OF DREAMS ABOUT MONARCHS

Dreaming about kings or queens could have a wide range of meanings according to dream books published in the eighteenth and nineteenth centuries. For example, one could have a dream about speaking to a king, which would mean disappointments in the future for the dreamer, but if one dreamed of a queen who *did not speak,* it would mean good luck. For a young woman to dream she was in the presence of the king meant that she would marry a man whom she would fear.[3] This range of meanings regarding dreaming of royalty was present in sixteenth-century dream books as well. One might, for example, dream that one saw "a Prince long a go dead, with a merry countenance." It might seem odd to see a long-dead ruler looking merry. Hill tells his readers that such a dream "signifies a vain hope to follow." If, on the other hand, someone dreamed that he or she was "kissed of an Emperor or king," or even simply had "talk with him," it was a fortunate dream indeed, as it meant "gain with joy," a very different meaning from one found in the more modern dream book. Symbols in some dreams imply dangers to monarchs even if the rulers are not in the dream. "To see the Sun darkened, signifies the peril or danger of a king." Richard Saunders told his readers that dreaming of a moon represented a queen, but if the moon in the dream darkened "it speaks the treachery of some great and noble woman, as also threatenings, and hatred." If the moon is falling out of heaven, it portends "the death of some Princess, Duchess, Queen, or eminent Lady." Hill assures his readers that dreaming "To be in a fair place furnished with devout images, and be meditating, and that many angels are with you, is a very good dream." But such a dream could turn quite disturbing "if in that place you see deformed figures," since that would mean "treason against the Prince."[4]

AN UNCLE'S WARNING DREAM

One particular dream that happened in 1553 warned of treason against the Prince—in this case against Mary I—and as a result, it saved a family's honor. Nicholas Wotton, who was dean of Canterbury, was at that time the ambassador in France. He dreamed that his nephew Thomas "was inclined to be a party to such a project, as, if he went not suddenly prevented, would turn both to the loss of his life and ruin of family." Thomas Wotton was the father of Sir Henry Wotton, who would write his family history in the next century. Sir Henry was convinced that his great-uncle would have been properly skeptical about whether most dreams had significant meaning: "Doubtless the good dean did well know that common dreams are but a senseless paraphrase on waking thoughts, or of the business of the day past, or are the result of our over-engaged affections when we betake ourselves to rest." Nicholas also could have believed "that prophecies are ceased." When Wotton dreamed the same dream the next night, he considered that "even in these latter times" God might allow "illumination of the soul in sleep" to enable someone to learn something that could thus be prevented.

The dream that so disturbed Wotton was that his nephew Thomas was in grave danger because he was planning to participate in a dangerous enterprise, the soon-to-be rebellion against Mary's marriage to Philip of Spain—a rebellion led by Thomas Wyatt. "There had been an ancient and entire friendship" between the Wyatt and Wotton families. The dean knew that he had to do something or Thomas might be killed and the family disgraced. Wotton decided that he had to secure his nephew's temporary imprisonment in order to save him from worse perils. He wrote to Queen Mary and begged her to send to Kent and have Thomas brought before her council so that "the lords of her council might interrogate him in such feigned questions as might give a color for his commitment into a favorable prison." Wotton promised "that he would acquaint her Majesty with the true reason of his request" the next time he was able "to see and speak to her Majesty." We will never know what excuse Wotton would have given to the queen about why he needed to make such a request. In his description, Henry Wotton further explained that when Nicholas returned to England and visited his nephew in prison, Thomas confessed that he knew "more than an intimation of Wyatt's intentions," and had his uncle not miraculously "so happily dreamed him into a prison" he would have participated and lost his life. Both uncle and nephew "joined in praising God" for the dream, which had saved both the young man and the reputation of his family. This dream was a critical aspect of the family history that Sir Henry knew. He himself would never have been born if his father, as a young man in his early twenties, had participated in the Wyatt rebellion. The authenticity of it cannot be proven, however, but we do know that Thomas Wotton was summoned before Mary's Council on 21 January 1554 "for obstinate standing against matters of religion" and was "committed to the Fleet, to remain there as a close prisoner."[5] We do not know precisely when Thomas was released, but only six days after Mary's death and Elizabeth's accession, Thomas became the sheriff of Kent.[6]

Nicholas Wotton's dream was not the only one known in the Wotton family history. "God, who in days of old did use to speak to his people in visions, did seem to speak to many of this family in dreams." Sir Henry also relates how his father Thomas's "dreams did usually prove true, both in foretelling things to come, and discovering things past." He gave as a specific example that soon before Thomas died, while his son was in Oxford studying, he "dreamed that the university treasury was robbed by townsmen and poor scholars; and that the number was five." The next day Thomas was writing to Henry and added a postscript making "a slight inquiry of it." The letter took three days to arrive from Kent. Henry received the letter "the very morning after the night in which the robbery was committed." Neither the city nor the university could find the thieves, so Sir Henry showed the authorities his father's letter, and it was that assistance which led to "the five guilty persons [being] discovered and apprehended."[7]

THE POWER OF BLOOD

Dreams, and discussions of dreams, can give us information about the most significant issues of this period, especially the sites where religion and politics, death and power, intersect. As we have seen, popular literature and historical records of early modern England include a remarkable number of recorded dreams and considerable discourse on their meanings. Particularly significant is the number of dreams by and about monarchs, dreams that are awash with blood. These dreams reflect deep cultural anxieties, especially given how central the image of blood was in the sixteenth century and the various meanings the word could hold. Writing in 1991, Caroline Bynum argued that in the later Middle Ages "blood became an increasingly powerful symbol." In her recent study, *Wonderful Blood,* she adds that "there is something about blood as physical and physiological stuff—and hence as bodily symbol—that made it particularly appropriate to express the dilemmas and desires of fifteenth-century Christians."[8] Part of the power of blood came from its contradictions and combinations of opposites. As Bettina Bildhauer points out, "Blood can be cleansing and contaminating, nourishing and inedible. Blood both reinforces and violates bodily boundaries."[9] The wine of communion represented the blood of Christ, and in Biblical and theological language to speak of "blood" often represented the blood shed as sacrifice. Blood was also the supposed place of emotion, of passion, in the body. "Blood" could also be used to connote kindred and nationality; "blood royal" or simply "the blood" could mean the royal race or family. Surgeons "let blood" to try to heal the sick.[10] Letting blood could be a terrifying and nightmarish procedure. In the 1641 text, *The Divine Dreamer,* the author Gonzalo told of a wrestler who dreamed he was "in a vessel full of blood, and so deep therein that scarcely the top of his head could be seen." While the dream was interpreted in the text as meaning that the wrestler would recover from an illness if he was bled,[11] the description of someone so deeply in a pool of blood that he might drown in it has its own sense of horror. Thomas Walkington in *The Optick Glasse,* when discussing the different dreams people have depending on their humours, describes the dreams of the sanguine as containing "flowing streams of blood."[12]

The image of blood was central in the sixteenth century, and the dreams discussed in this chapter reflect prevalent cultural anxieties. There were many reported dreams of and about monarchs in early modern England, especially dreams Elizabeth I supposedly experienced over her conflict with her cousin Mary Stuart, which eventually led to her execution in 1587. At the end of the reign was also a series of dreams about Robert Devereux, Earl of Essex, Elizabeth's last favorite, and the one who caused her the most anguish. As a very young man, Essex showed valor fighting in the Netherlands under the command of his stepfather, Robert Dudley, the Earl of Leicester. When he returned to court as a war hero in 1586 he caught the queen's eye. As Paul E. J. Hammer suggests, "To Elizabeth, Essex seemed a handsome, intellectual, and intriguing distraction from the agonizing business of consenting to the death of Mary, queen of Scots."[13] By the 1590s, Essex was the leader of one faction at court, in opposition to William Cecil, Lord Burghley and his son, also named Robert. In 1598 Essex argued passionately for further war against Spain. Finally Burghley responded that Essex "breathed forth nothing but War, Slaughter, and Blood." He took out a book of psalms and read to Essex the verse, "Men of Blood shall not live out half their days."[14]

It all came to a head the summer of 1598 when Elizabeth was trying to decide who should be the new lord deputy for Ireland. In the dispute over whom to appoint, Essex became so angry that he turned his back on the queen, which so outraged her that she boxed his ears. Essex began to reach for his sword and had to be restrained. To make matters worse, as Essex stormed out, he told the queen and his shocked colleagues "that he neither could nor would put up so great an affront and indignity, neither would he have taken it at King Henry the Eighth his hands."[15] Though Essex did make his peace with the queen, he never admitted that he had done anything wrong, and Elizabeth must have become more wary of him. After insisting that no one else was suitable to lead the command in Ireland, he put himself in the situation of either having to accept the position himself or back down entirely. The time in Ireland was so disastrous that Essex returned to London against orders in 1599; two years later, he led a rebellion against Elizabeth's government. The dreams in the last decades of Elizabeth's reign testify to the deep psychological impact felt by the English people due to several events: Mary Stuart's attempts to topple Elizabeth; the resultant execution of the Scottish queen; the intense anxiety as Elizabeth's long reign was coming to an end; and Essex's challenge of the aged queen.

SWIMMING IN BLOOD

Thomas Nashe presented a number of dreams by monarchs that he then claimed were misinterpreted or had no prophetic power. Even if this is the case, the imagery in at least one of them is still compelling. "Louis XI dreamt that he swam in blood on the top of the Alps, which one Father Robert (a holy Hermit of his time) interpreted to present death in his next wars against Italy: though he lived and prospered in all his enterprises a long while after."[16] While Nashe is correct that the dream was certainly no prognostication, or at least Father Robert's analysis was completely inaccurate, it would not be all that surprising for Louis XI to have such a dream in the midst of the bloody wars between the French and the Habsburgs. Dreaming of swimming in blood would be a horrifying but understandable nightmare for a king, on whose conscience lay so many deaths. We might see Louis's dream as a visual parallel to Shakespeare's Henry V's passionate cry from the heart the night before he sends his soldiers off to fight the battle of Agincourt:

Upon the King! Let us our lives, our souls,
Our debts, our careful wives,

Our children, and our sins, lay on the King!
We must bear all. (4.1.228-31)

Henry had to "bear all" though he ended with a great victory, while Louis swam through the blood possibly of those who had died in his wars as he struggled to the top of the mountains, clearly another sign of victory. We have no evidence that Louis actually had this dream, but it powerfully represented values of kingly responsibility and subjects' fears. As we shall see, blood and monarchs came together all too frequently in the reported dreams of the time.

DREAMS OF THE FRENCH ROYAL FAMILY

As we have seen throughout the course of this book, people in the early modern period took dreams seriously; this included people of the highest social status. Some indeed believed that God gave vivid, warning dreams, particularly to those of elevated rank. Marguerite de Valois, for example, wrote of premonitions in dreams:

> Some are of the opinion that God hath an extraordinary and particular protection of illustrious personages, and into those spirits where the rays of his excellence do more brightly shine, he gives them by their good angels some secret advertisements of the accidents which are prepared for them, be they good or evil.[17]

Marguerite, daughter of Henry II of France and his wife Catherine de Medici, sister of Francis II, Charles IX, and Henry III, and first wife to Henry IV, was a woman of intelligence and courage who believed deeply in the importance of dreams in her own life. Marguerite spoke of her gratitude to God for "his goodness and power," adding that "I can declare no extraordinary accident ever befell me, whether fortunate or otherwise, but I received some warning of it, either by dream or in some other way."[18]

Dreams played a significant role in Marguerite's family's history. At the 1547 coronation of her parents Henry II and Catherine de Medici, Henry decided to have four Huguenots burned as part of the celebration. One of the four was a poor tailor. As this man was burned, Henry at first watched and then had to turn away his eyes. When he looked back, although the man's body was almost destroyed, one of his eyes was still staring at the king. According to the French Huguenot theologian Theodore Beza, for the next few nights Henry had terrible nightmares, over and over again seeing the man being burned and the eye staring at him. As a result of the dreams, Henry took an oath that he would never witness another heretic burning. The nineteenth-century historian James Wylie sardonically commented that it would have been far better if he had taken an oath never to order any more burnings.[19]

Contemporaries spoke about Louis de Bourbon, Prince of Condé, the military leader of the Huguenots in the 1560s, who dreamed of his death the night before the battle of Jarnac in 1569. Henry, Duke of Anjou and future king of France, was one of the leaders of the royal French forces against the Huguenots. Condé died that day fighting to save the life of Gaspard de Coligny. Though the Huguenots were badly defeated, Coligny managed to lead a significant portion of the Huguenot army to safety. As for Coligny, he died along with thousands of other Huguenots in August 1572 in the St. Bartholomew's Day massacre. Many people at the time of the massacre were convinced that it had been ordered by Catherine de Medici in an effort to secure the position of her son Charles IX. Afterward, Catherine was pleased to have powerful Catholics believe that was what had happened. This was part of the black legend that developed around Catherine, but what role she actually played in the planning and how much was the responsibility of Charles IX or Italian advisors is much debated.[20] Any role that Charles played in ordering the massacre weighed terribly on him. Although he was only twenty-two, people said that he looked like an old man and had become melancholy and taciturn. Charles was haunted by nightmares in which he heard the agonizing cries of victims and saw their dead bodies floating upon the Seine. Rumors spread that he would wake up in the middle of the night crying out, "Blood, blood!"[21] He died only two years later. (figure 5.1)

Marguerite recorded a number of warning dreams that she claimed her mother Catherine had about her family; the most powerful one was a dream Catherine had foretelling the death of her husband Henry II. These dreams were not only well known in early modern France but were often repeated across the channel in England at the time as well. The death of a monarch was shocking, especially a violent or unexpected death. At the age of forty, Henry II

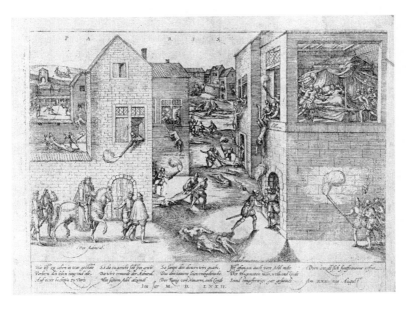

Figure 5.1 Hogenberg, St. Bartholomew's Day Massacre.

Private collection.

Figure 5.2 Hogenberg, Death of Henry II of France.

Private collection.

of France was accidentally killed in a tournament in 1559 when he may have forgotten to put his visor down. According to his daughter Marguerite, "The very night before that inauspicious tournament, [Catherine] dreamed that she saw the King my Father wounded in the eye, as the next day he was, and being awake, she often times besought him that he would not tilt that day."[22] Of course, like Cassandra's, Catherine's warnings, if she did indeed give them, went ignored. We know from chapter 1 in this book that Queen Anna had had a troubling dream that made her beg her husband James I not to travel back to Scotland. James determinedly ignored his wife's warnings and was safe; this was not the case for Henry II. Seemingly, there had long been predictions that Henry II might die at the age of forty in a duel. In 1547, Catherine de Medici had consulted with Nostradamus about her husband's future. He warned Catherine that Henry was in danger of dying in single combat in his forty-first year. If he avoided that danger he would live to be sixty-nine. When Henry was told of the prediction, he laughed it off.[23] In the same way, Henry did not take Catherine's warnings before the tournament seriously either. Whether or not she actually had a dream, Catherine apparently did beg Henry not to joust, but he paid no attention. Catherine was not the only one concerned. As the tournament was nearing completion, it is said that the Marshal de Vielleville, the Master of Ceremonies, begged the king that he be allowed to ride in his place: "Sire, for three nights I have dreamt of calamity."[24]

Catherine's warning dream was well known in Elizabethan England as well, though the queen is called Margaret rather than Catherine, perhaps confusing the mother with the daughter. In his sixteenth-century dream book, Hill reports that "The day before that Henry the French king was wounded in the eye, Queen Margaret his wife as men report, saw in her sleep as she thought the king's eye dug out. But he as by a destiny urging him forward, did neglect the . . . warning."[25] (figure 5.2)

By the seventeenth century, the dream had changed form. *The Divine Dreamer* described Catherine dreaming "that she saw him very sickly, holding down his head as he walked down the streets of Paris, being followed by an infinite company of his people that lamented for him." Ghostly Henry walks the street of his capital city while the people both saw the king's presence and mourned his absence in his death. Supposedly Catherine, awaking from the dream, got on her knees and began wringing her hands; she pleaded with Henry not to tilt that day. What is most interesting about this account is that Catherine, usually demonized in early modern English texts as the architect of the St. Bartholomew's Day massacre, is here depicted as "this great Princess" whom God had sent a premonition by "his good angel." In this version, Catherine is thinking of the good not only of her husband but also of the people of France, while Henry "is more desirous to follow the vanities of the world than the good advertisements of his wife."[26] We might wonder if the years since the death of Catherine were enough to smooth away her horrific image or if in Gonzalo's view the dream warning is that much more powerful if sent to a "great Princess" rather than the fiend who masterminded

Figure 5.3   Death of William II.

Holinshed's *Chronicles*
by permission of the Folger Shakespeare Library.

a massacre of Protestants. The sixteenth-century reports are far more literal representations of what would be Henry's death, while this one almost a century later takes the form of a visual narrative of a dream. Perhaps the passage of time allowed for a more sophisticated rendering.

Even though one of the earliest versions of Catherine's warning dream was presented by her own daughter, we cannot ever truly know if it occurred. But it does suggest how important it was in the early modern period to make some kind of sense of such a horrifying experience. If only Henry had listened to Catherine, he would not have been killed. Perhaps the need to try to go back in time and change the event or somehow place the responsibility on the victim has a universal resonance.

WILLIAM RUFUS DREAMS OF BLOOD

Certainly Henry II of France was not the only historical king to die in a violent accident. Another was the English king William II, called Rufus, who on 2 August 1100 was killed by a stray, or not so stray, arrow while hunting. His death, too, was linked to dreams in the following centuries. In the Middle Ages, chronicles such as Matthew of Westminster's *Flowers of History,* actually a text by Matthew Paris with some additions, described William's many acts of impiety and injustice; the king had even forced Anselm, the archbishop of Canterbury, into exile. According to the chronicle, one night Anselm had a dream that all the saints of England were complaining to God about William's tyranny and his destruction of churches. God said, "Let Alban, the proto-martyr of the English, come hither," and then he handed Alban a flaming arrow. God told Alban: "Behold the death of the man whom you complain before me." Alban received the arrow, saying "And I will give it to a wicked spirit, an avenger of sins." He threw the arrow to earth, sending it flying through the air like a comet. From this vision Archbishop Anselm immediately knew that the king had been shot by an arrow and had died that night. The next morning Anselm celebrated mass, gathered his books, and set forth to his church in Canterbury. (figure 5.3) As he approached the cathedral, he learned that indeed the king, shot with an arrow while hunting in the New Forest, was dead.[27]

As dramatic as Anselm's dream might be, an Elizabethan report of William's death is more startling, and the dreams involved offer a far more complex reading of religion and violence, power and death. Holinshed's *Chronicles* depicted William's rule as one of "willful covetousness, pulling from the rich and wealthy, to waste and spend it out in all excess, vain riot, and gifts bestowed on such as had least deserved the same." The chronicle then described a series of dreams. The main source for these dreams was William of Malmesbury's *Gesta Regum*.[28] One night William dreamed "that the veins of his arms were broken, and that the blood issued out in great abundance."[29] The king had been so disturbed by the dream that he called forth help from the Virgin Mary; he ordered his chamberlains to bring in a light and stay with him, as he could not get back to sleep for a very long time. In the original source for the dream, William was being bled, but this is lost in the sixteenth-century version. His blood spurted out so copiously that it blotted out the sun in the sky and changed day to night. Hill's contemporary dream book states that for a man to dream that "he sees blood issue out of his side, declares peril and danger to follow." We can hardly be surprised by such an interpretation; dreaming that blood is flowing out of one would be terrifying. The image in the dream might also conjure up other fearsome parallels. In 1597, King James, while still only king of Scotland, wrote in his *Daemonologie* about the widely held belief, that "if the dead carcass be any time thereafter handled by the murderer, it will gush out of blood."[30] There was a similar story that is an even closer parallel, as the dead bleeding man is also an English king. Henry II died in 1189 after fighting a civil war with his sons Richard and John. When Henry's body was carried forth to be buried, he "was first appareled in his Princely Robes, having his Crown on his Head . . . a Scepter in his Hand, a Sword by his Side, and so was laid uncovered." The new king Richard came to view the body of his father; as soon as he reached the open casket "the blood gushed out . . . of the dead corpse in great plenty, even as if the spirit of the dead King had disdained and abhorred the presence of him, who was thought to be the chief cause of his death."[31] William, soon to be but dead carcass, was gushing blood in this fearsome dream. The image would be potent for anyone, but for a king the meaning would be even more powerful and frightening, both for him and his subjects. The king was said to be God's representative on earth, even a king such as William with his problematic relationship to churchmen. A king's blood would be sacred, quite different from the blood of an ordinary person. In September 1539, a gunner in the navy was reported to the authorities for stating that if King Henry VIII's blood and his own were side by side in saucers, no one could tell the difference.[32] Such a statement would be a denial of the king's sanctity and special nature. Likewise, William's reported dream would suggest that a king's sacrilegious acts had caused him not only to be threatened with death but also to lose his uniquely divine nature. The intensely symbolic and sacred nature of blood was something that resonated powerfully with sixteenth-century people in a way that is quite separate from the painful connotations blood has today. The belief about William's dream was common enough that it appeared in a commonplace book kept by a John Evans, who wrote "William Rufus the morning before he was unfortunately shot in hunting dreamed that an extreme cold wind passed through his sides."[33]

The significance of the king's blood and its religious connotations are even more extreme in the next dream reported in Holinshed's *Chronicles*. Robert FitzHammon told William that a monk dreamed

how he saw the king gnaw the image of Christ crucified, with his teeth, and that as he was about to bite away the legs of the same image, Christ with his feet should spurn him down to the ground, insomuch that he lay on the earth, there came out of his mouth a flame of fire, and such abundance of smoke, that the air was darkened therewith.

The king attempted to joke about the dream and suggested that the monk who reported the dream should be paid off. He told FitzHammon to "give him therefore an hundred shillings, and bid him dream of better fortune to our person."[34] Despite this outward reaction, according to Holinshed, William worried about the dream and whether or not he should go hunting in the New Forest that day, Lammas Day, as he had planned. William would have been eager to go out hunting that day, as the season for hunting red deer stags had begun only the day before on August 1. Still, for an antireligious king, Lammas Day could have been a particularly disturbing day: It was not only a harvest festival but also a commemoration of St. Peter's miraculous deliverance from prison. At dinner William drank much more than he usually did, and this gave him the courage to go out to hunt—and thus to be killed, shot by an arrow and no doubt having his blood issue out in great abundance. We do know that William did wait until after his midday meal to go hunting that day; his usual custom was to rise before dawn so that the hunting party could be on its way with the first light. As Frank Barlow reminds us, we cannot know why the delay happened. Possibly William was suffering from a hangover from too much partying the night before; perhaps he had important business to take care of first; or indeed "he was held up by warnings of danger to his person."[35] But it is highly doubtful that these dreams have any historical accuracy. As Warren Hollister points out, "In the case of Rufus, if there is any reality at all behind these stories it [is] probably . . . that sinister portents were being discovered constantly throughout the reign. William Rufus was no friend of the Church, and clerics must have often dreamed of his death and damnation. Perhaps he actually did receive a warning before setting out on his last hunt; he had doubtless been receiving them for years."[36]

I think we should not simply dismiss the dream due to its dubious authenticity, but instead we should view it in a different light. Its historical meaning comes not from having actually been reported to the king as a warning on the day of his death but on its development as an explanation or means of understanding this event in the centuries after his death. As I have suggested, the meaning of blood was very significant in this time. One of the most powerful ways to curse was to say "God's blood," which was the means by which "bloody" came into the language as a popular saying. Blood was the most intimate way a believer could encounter God. One of the most critical theological struggles between Catholics and Protestants was over who had access to the wine of the communion supper, which Catholics emphatically believed to be the body and blood of God. William gnawing on the crucifix was a parody of taking communion, one of the most sacred acts for a Christian. William is knocked to the ground by the foot of the son of God.

ELIZABETH DREAMS AND MARY DIES

If the violent, accidental death of a monarch was appalling, how much more cataclysmic, how much bloodier, was the deliberate execution of a queen.

Even though Mary Stuart had been forced to abdicate her throne in Scotland over eighteen years before she was beheaded in England in February 1587, the staged violent death of an anointed monarch shook the foundations of the early modern world. While rulers had been forced to abdicate and then had been secretly done away with in the past, the claim of legality made by the English for the execution of Mary Stuart was quite something else. It is hardly surprising that such an event would disturb the sleep of people across Europe and nightmares over Mary's fate would be used as a metaphor for those who blamed the Protestant Elizabeth. As we saw with Marguerite de Valois, belief in the significance of dreams emerged even from the highest rung of society.

Many people, including queens, believed in prophecy, astrology, omens, and dreams. Elizabeth I certainly did. With the support of Robert Dudley, who had been tutored by the magician/astrologer John Dee, the queen had Dee choose an auspicious day for her coronation. Later in her reign, when an Elizabeth figure was discovered at court stuck with pins, the "doll" was taken to Dee so that any bad spells could be offset. In 1581 Parliament made it a felony to create such figures or to calculate by any sort of prophecy or astrology when the queen might die.[37] From the beginning of the reign, Elizabeth and her advisors, such as Lord Burghley, and Sir Francis Walsingham, were concerned about how ancient prophecies could be used to support contemporary actions against the crown. In 1584, John Birtles was involved in an alleged conspiracy against Elizabeth and in favor of Mary Stuart. Found in his possession was "a certain old book of prophecy, wherein great pictures, some with beards."[38]

Since the beginning of Elizabeth's reign, Catholics in the north of England had circulated prophesies that were used by Mary Stuart's supporters to show that she should be queen of England. Prophecies heard by the Duke of Norfolk were part of what convinced him that he should marry Mary Stuart soon after she fled to England: He had read the prognostications to mean that he and Mary would be king and queen of both Scotland and England. In 1569, Norfolk assured Elizabeth that he would have nothing to do with Mary since he wanted to put his head on a safe pillow; who knows, however, what dreams Norfolk thought he might have on this pillow as a result. Anthony Babington, the leader of what would be the final plot to assassinate Elizabeth so that Mary could rule, owned a copy of prophecies attributed to the magician of King Arthur's court, Merlin. These prophecies were sometimes linked with dreams and used as evidence for Mary's right to rule—and of Elizabeth's wickedness.

Elizabeth was so careful and guarded in her speech, but we might wonder what ideas invaded her dreams, what images floated uncensored through her unconscious. Did all the stress and problems of the reign—concern over religion, fear of foreign invasion, the pressures on her to marry—reappear in her dreams? It is possible that Elizabeth believed that dreams could be warnings in several different modes. While a dream itself could be a warning, she might mention that she had had a particular dream so that she could provide an indirect caution. In several contexts, Elizabeth mentioned dreams she claimed that she had as warnings for her courtiers and servants. On 18 June 1578, Sir Christopher Hatton wrote to Leicester about a dream Elizabeth had told him that she had had. Hatton warned the earl that "since your Lordship's departure the Queen is found in continual great melancholy." Hatton said that the cause of her melancholy "I can but guess at." But, Hatton added, her mood made his life difficult: "notwithstanding that I bear and suffer the whole brunt for her mislike in generality." Hatton got to the heart of Elizabeth's melancholy and mislike. "She dreams of marriage that might seem injurious to her, making myself to be either the man or a pattern of him." Hatton was not the man, but perhaps he was the pattern—that of the favorite.[39]

Hatton may have wondered what marriage was invading Elizabeth's dreams. This conversation took place in the midst of the marriage negotiations with the Duke of Anjou, formerly Alençon. Given how problematic those negotiations turned out to be, Elizabeth might well have had anxious dreams, whether she wanted to share them or not. But it is also possible that it was someone else's marriage that was troubling her. The marriage that would have most troubled Elizabeth, though theoretically she did not know of it, was Leicester's secret marriage to Lettice Knollys, the widowed Lady Essex, in 1578. Unfortunately, we do not know if the queen instructed Hatton to write to Leicester, or if she said anything about her dream that made Hatton think it was somehow aimed at the earl. Elizabeth may well have had some intuition that the secret marriage had occurred but hoped that she was wrong, or she might have been giving a warning to express her annoyance regarding the matter. When Elizabeth did officially learn of the marriage (from the Duke of Anjou's envoy Jehan de Simier), she was furious, and this was the impetus to allow the French prince to visit her court. It is perhaps ironic that Hatton wrote to Leicester about Elizabeth's "dream." Years earlier in 1560, after Dudley's wife Amy Robsart was found with her neck broken and lying dead at the bottom of some stairs, Elizabeth sent him away from court until the Coroner's Inquest could determine the cause of Amy's death. Dudley wrote to William Cecil asking for advice: "I pray you let me hear from you, what you think best for me to do." Dudley confided, "I am sorry so sudden a chance shall breed me so great a change, for I think I am here all this while, as it were in a dream."[40]

If Elizabeth was concerned about Leicester's secret marriage, she would have been far more distressed about whether or not to have Mary Stuart executed after the Babington plot. There had been intense anxiety over Mary's plots since Mary fled to England in 1568. This apprehension worsened in 1571 with the Ridolfi Plot and the execution of Norfolk the next year. By 1586, Protestants were panicked at the thought of Mary's supporters assassinating Elizabeth, while Catholics deeply feared that Elizabeth, who had refused to listen to members of Parliament's calls for Mary's head between 1571 and 1572, would finally agree to Mary's execution. Though by 1587 Elizabeth may well have wanted Mary dead, she was most reluctant to take public responsibility for her execution. The queen hoped that perhaps Sir Amyas Paulet, who had Mary in custody, would solve the problem for her, but he expressed himself horrified at the thought of a private murder instead of a public execution. Burghley and Walsingham were convinced that Mary's execution was essential, but they were aware of the pressure from Scotland and France against it.[41] Elizabeth herself was deeply ambivalent about the execution of one who had once been anointed monarch. Walsingham was ill and away from council; though Burghley suffered from gout and had been in a riding accident, he attended and argued forcefully for the public execution rather than a private assassination. But it was William Davison, recently appointed secretary, who had to get Elizabeth's signature on Mary's death warrant. Once he had it, Davison sent it on; Robert Beale arrived at Fotheringay with the death warrant the evening of February 6, and the next day Mary was informed. The Scottish queen, with bravery and bravado, met her death on 8 February 1587. It took four days for those at court to have the courage to tell Elizabeth the news. The queen responded with tears and fury, and Davison instantly became the scapegoat; he was sent to the Tower. While imprisoned, Davison wrote to Walsingham a report of what had passed between him and Elizabeth over the question of Mary. He included the following description of a conversation that had occurred when she signed the death warrant.

> The next morning her majesty, being in some speech with Mr. Rauley in the Privie Chamber, seeing me come in, called me unto her, and . . . smiling told me how she had been troubled that night upon a dream she [had] that the Scottish Queen was executed. Pretending to have been so greatly moved with the news against my self as in that passion she could have done I know not what.

But Davison did not take Elizabeth's indirect warning as seriously as he might have because, he said, Elizabeth had told him all this "in a pleasant and smiling manner." Davison explained, "I answered her majesty that it was good for me I was not near her so long as that humor lasted." Becoming more serious, "but with all taking hold of her speech," he asked the queen, "in great earnest what it meant, and whether having proceeded thus far she had not a full and resolute meaning to go through with the said execution according to her warrant." Davison assured Walsingham that Elizabeth's "answer was 'Yes,'" and that she "confirmed with a solemn oath in some vehemence, this only she thought, that it might have received a better form, because this threw the whole burden upon her self."[42]

One wonders what the queen was talking about with Walter Raleigh when she broke off that conversation to summon Davison to her side. Did it have anything to do with Mary's execution? Or a dream she had just had? Given how much Elizabeth must have been thinking about Mary those difficult days, she might well have dreamed of the rival whose life was so intertwined with hers, though the two women never met. For Elizabeth, mentioning a dream was a useful way for her to warn Davison that she would be upset to hear about Mary's execution; however, the incongruity between what she said about the dream and the pleasant and smiling manner she used to describe it would certainly have left Davison quite confused. Elizabeth did not send mixed messages to Davison after he sent on the warrant: He was sent to the Tower for twenty months and was severely fined. Though the fine was remitted, Davison was never allowed back into the queen's service.

CATHOLIC DESCRIPTION OF ELIZABETH'S NIGHTMARES

Elizabeth may well have had a dream about Mary Stuart, but it was not the dream reported in Adam Blackwood's 1587 *Martyre de la rayne d'Escosse,* a Catholic propaganda tract that demonized Elizabeth as a "Bastard," referring to "her cruel and barbarous designs" in seeking "the head of the queen," Mary Stuart. Blackwood, the nephew of Robert Reid, the Catholic bishop of Orkney, studied and lived in Paris for most of his adult life due to the generosity of Mary Stuart; he had been her ardent supporter for many years.[43] According to Blackwood, after Elizabeth sent word to the Earl of Shrewsbury to have Mary executed, "the Harpy could not sleep the entire night having another demoness within in her soul who tormented her strangely and vengefully about the execution of her cousin, to such an extent that she repented of having ordered it." In his account, Blackwood also stated that, during this same time frame, the Earl of Leicester was in bed when Sir Walter Mildmay, "one of his familiars," came to him and told him "the evident danger and the ruin of her majesty" if with "inexcusable cruelty" Mary was executed "without right, without reason, without any appearance of justice." Calling Mildmay Leicester's "familiar" also has an implication of witchcraft since in the sixteenth century "familiar" could mean "pertaining to one's family or household" or "a demon." Blackwood then narrates that Leicester "got out of bed, grabbed his robe, and went to find the queen to tell her of these circumstances which could instigate a bloody tragedy, if her commandment were to be executed." At first Elizabeth changed her mind because she found Leicester's argument convincing, but then in the end Elizabeth, the "Harpy," reaffirmed Mary's death sentence. (figure 5.4)

This version, however, was not the only one that Blackwood related. For good measure he added that "there are those who tell it differently," a clear acknowledgement that the recording and interpretation of dreams could be politically driven. His second version has one of Elizabeth's ladies-in-waiting sleeping in the same room with her. The lady-in-waiting, who was Madame de Stratford, cried out in such a terrible voice that she awakened the queen, and then the lady began weeping. Elizabeth asked Madame why she wept and "she declared that she had seen the Queen of Scotland being beheaded and immediately after this Elizabeth's head was cut off as well." Elizabeth responded "that the same vision had appeared to her in her sleep leaving her greatly terrified."[44] In this depiction, Catholic Queen and Protestant Queen are equivalent figures who follow the same trajectory: If one loses her head so, too, will her counterpart. Such a dream could presumably cause terror in Elizabeth, though given the source of this description, it is highly doubtful the queen ever had it. More importantly, though, to the readers of Blackwood's text it reduced Elizabeth's strength and autonomy, and because this version was related second, it showed the "Harpy" and

Figure 5.4   1607 painting of head of Mary Stuart.

by permission of Peterborough Museum.

"demoness" as both terrified and weak, and as deserving of execution herself because of her trafficking with evil. Zacharie Jones in his translation of Pierre de Loyer's *A Treatise of Specters* reported that tyrants and usurpers "have been troubled and tormented with most horrible phantasms and imaginations, which do come into their heads both sleeping and waking."[45] Supporters of Mary Stuart would well believe that Elizabeth was a tyrant and usurper who, deservedly, had horrible dreams.

FRENCH KINGS DREAM AND DIE

Mary Stuart's execution provoked blood-filled dreams. So, too, did the murder of Henry III less than two years later. Henry was the younger brother of Mary's first husband, Francis II, and the brother of Marguerite, whose intense interest in dreams has already been discussed. Henry had ordered the murder of his archrival Henry, the Duke of Guise, in December 1588. In retaliation, a fanatical young Dominican friar, Jacques Clément, decided to kill the king. On 1 August 1589, Clément gained access to Henry by claiming to have important documents to deliver, but when he was handing them to the king he told Henry he also had a secret message to tell him. Henry waved his attendants away to gain privacy, and Clément stabbed him in the stomach when he leaned over to whisper this secret message into the king's ear. Early modern texts described Henry's fearful dream that foretold his death. According to *The Divine Dreamer,* three days before his murder,

Henry dreamed that "all his royal ornaments, to wit, his linen, vesture, sandals, dalmation robe, mantle of azure satin, crown and scepter" were all "bloody and made foul with the feet of religious men." This story also appeared later in the seventeenth century when Louis Guyon wrote about it in his text *Remarques sur plusieurs songes de personnes de qualité*.[46] There were also contemporary stories circulating about dreams that had occurred the night before the Catholic fanatic François Ravaillac assassinated Henry IV on 14 May 1610. In one account, Henry himself dreamed that he saw a rainbow above his head. In another, which was again in John Evans's commonplace book, the king described how his wife, Marie de Medici, dreamed that she was at her coronation, but the diamonds in her crown "mourphised"—changed—into pearls, the emblem of tears.[47]

DREAMS OF STUART MONARCHS

Henry IV's queen was not the only one to dream of pearls as a symbol of tragedy for her husband. According to the seventeenth-century text, *Wonderful Prodigies of Judgment and Mercy,* as James IV was preparing to go to war against England in 1513, he went to church where he had a strange experience. As he was praying, a very old man came to speak to him and told the king that if he went to war it would be his ruin. Then the old man slipped away. After the service, James looked for the old man but could not find him anywhere, "neither could any of the standers by feel or perceive how, or when, or where he passed from them, having as it were vanished." When James told his wife (who was Henry VIII's older sister Margaret, though her name is not mentioned in the narration), she begged him to consider seriously what the old man had told him. She then "acquainted him with the visions and affrightments of her sleep": She had dreamed the gems in her "chains and armlets appeared to be turned into pearl." In her dreams she had also "seen him fall from a great precipice," and he had "lost one of his eyes." James responded, like so many other doubting individuals, by refusing to listen to this prophetic dream that could have saved his life. The king replied, "These were but dreams arising from the many thoughts and cares of the day." The result was what not only those who knew sixteenth-century Anglo-Scottish history would have known but also anyone at all familiar with stories of refusing to listen to dreams would have expected. James "therefore marched on and fought with the English, and was slain in Flodden Field, with a great number of his nobility, and common soldiers, upon Sept. 9, 1513."[48]

If people for generations thought about the death of James IV, they thought even more about the death of his granddaughter Mary Stuart. Perhaps no one thought of her death more than her son, King James. According to Sir John Harington's account in a letter he wrote to Sir Amyas Paulet, James had a lengthy, private conversation with Harington in January 1607 in which James inquired what Harington thought of "the power of Satan in matter of witchcraft." James wondered "why the devil did work more with ancient women than others?" The king also wanted Harington's opinion of tobacco, telling Sir John "it would, by its use, infuse ill qualities on the brain, and that no learned man ought to taste it, and wished it forbidden." Then the conversation turned to "more serious discourse," including a discussion of the king's mother and the role of Sir William Davison in her death. Paulet would have been especially interested in what James had to say about the death of Mary Stuart because his grandfather had been not only Mary's last keeper but also the one in charge of the Scottish queen during her trial and execution. James confided to Harington that Mary's "death was visible in Scotland before it did really happen," that those who had the "power of sight" saw "a bloody head dancing in the air." While James was convinced about second sight and "did remark much on this gift," the seeing of Mary's floating head sounds very much like a nightmare.[49]

ANGELS PROTECT ELIZABETH IN A DREAM

Religious conflict, violence, and monarchy fill the early modern accounts of dreams, whether they are actual dreams or invented ones, private nightmares or publicly created for religious and political purposes. A far more positive—and Protestant—depiction of one of Elizabeth's dreams was also connected to Mary Stuart. Until his injudicious second marriage to a rich widow in 1595, Richard Fletcher was one of Elizabeth's favorite preachers. At the time of Mary's execution, he was dean of Peterborough and served as the chaplain at her execution on 8 February 1587. When Mary refused to listen to Fletcher speak of a Protestant God, George Talbot, Earl of Shrewsbury, had him lead the rest of the company in prayer instead. Four days later when Elizabeth learned of Mary's death, Fletcher preached before the queen at Greenwich; it was a brave move because Elizabeth was consumed with guilt fueled by a towering rage.[50]

In his sermon, Fletcher described to Elizabeth how an angel had protected her during the frightening times of Mary's reign, particularly describing the angel watching over Elizabeth as she slept. Fletcher narrated the dangers Elizabeth had been in before she became queen and how, when as a prisoner she had fallen asleep, God's angel smote Elizabeth's enemies "in the hinder part[s]." After that, the angel struck the sleeping prisoner princess herself "on the side with his right hand" to loosen her chains, and, he reminded Elizabeth, led her through the "iron gate that your enemies would have rampered against your most just and natural succession."[51] This image was presented on stage early in the following century in Heywood's play. As Peter McCullough points out, "Fletcher's angelic deliverance of Elizabeth. . . . anticipates Thomas Heywood."[52] God had sent an angel to protect Princess Elizabeth from those who would have snatched—ramped—the succession so that she might survive to become queen; now queen, she had to accept not just for herself but for the safety of her realm that someone like Mary Stuart, who had threatened her so severely, had to die.

DREAMS OF THREATENING FOREIGNERS

The people in England felt greatly threatened by foreigners, including the Scots. We have evidence of dreams that suggested threats to the queen and threats to the commonwealth, especially by foreigners. Soon after Elizabeth became queen, in February 1559 a man named Nicholas Colman was disturbed enough about what he thought was about to happen that he testified before John Aldrich, the mayor of Norwich, and the aldermen of the city. He told them that there were "seditious persons in diverse places within this realm." These people were strangers, "Scots, Frenchman, Spaniards, and of other foreign nations," and once spring and summer came—Colman specified May, June and July—these dangerous foreigners would travel to various villages and market towns and set them on fire. They would come in disguise, "having beggars' cloaks for their outermost garment, and under that having silk doublets." Colman was particularly upset about these high-status strangers disguised as beggars who would do such damage since he knew they had targeted "the City of Norwich as one specially shall be burned one of these three months either by such strangers or other evil disposed persons." When May had passed and all was still safe in Norwich, the mayor and the aldermen summoned Colman to be examined again "as to what did move him to utter such words." Colman explained that he received "this knowledge by certain visions and dreams that he had in his sleep."[53] We are not able to know if Colman suffered from mental instability or whether he was relieved or disappointed that the marauding strangers never materialized. We do not know if he had other dreams that convinced him of disasters to come, but this specific description demonstrates some of the cultural anxiety felt over England's vulnerability to foreign danger as Mary's reign ended and Elizabeth's began.

WARNING DREAMS FOR ELIZABETH

As we have seen, if people felt threatened and expressed their fears in their dream life from the beginning of Elizabeth's reign, the anxiety only increased as the reign—and the serious threats—continued. The following is described as a visitation by a ghost, but many today would argue that it had been merely a dream. One night in 1587, the year of Mary Stuart's execution and the year before the Spanish Armada was sent to invade England, Mary Cocker, the wife of a Hertfortshire laborer, was lying in bed when she saw what she was sure was a ghost, "a bright thing of long proportion without shape, clothed as it were in white silk." The creature kept passing by her bedside until she finally found the courage to challenge it. "In the name of God, what art thou and why troublest thou me?" The vision or ghost had a clear reply:

> Go to thy Queen and tell her that she receive nothing. . . . of any stranger, for there is a jewel in making for her which the party, if he could, would deliver to her own hands, or else not deliver it at all; which, if she receive, will be her destruction. And if thou dost not tell her this much . . . thou shalt die the cruellest death that ever died any.[54]

The ghost, having had its say, immediately vanished. While Cocker perceived this as the coming of a ghost or vision, it may well seem to a modern reader that Cocker, lying in bed, was actually asleep and had a dream expressing concern for the queen's safety and the need for her to take action to protect the queen, or she herself would "die the cruellest death." The dream could also represent the fears of what tragedies might happen. That the messenger of the warning was a ghost of no clear gender added a frisson of fear to Cocker's experience. Mary's unconscious was, in Keith Thomas's words, "making explicit a great deal which could not be said directly."[55]

In 1588, the Spanish threat materialized, and Elizabeth had one of the most dramatic moments of her reign when she spoke to the troops at Tilbury, addressing them as "My loving people."

> We have been persuaded by some that are careful of our safety, to take heed how we commit our selves to armed multitudes, for fear of treachery; but I assure you I do not desire to live to distrust my faithful and loving people. Let tyrants fear, I have always so behaved myself that, under God, I have placed my chief strength and safeguard in the loyal hearts and good-will of my subjects; and therefore I am come amongst you, as you see, at this time, not for my recreation and disport, but being resolved, in the midst and heat of the battle, to live and die amongst you all; to lay down for my God, and for my kingdom, and my people, my honor and my blood, even in the dust. I know I have the body but of a weak and feeble woman; but I have the heart and stomach of a king, and of a king of England too, and think foul scorn that Parma or Spain, or any prince of Europe, should dare to invade the borders of my realm; to which rather than any dishonor shall grow by me, I myself will take up arms, I myself will be your general.[56]

Through a combination of English naval skill and favorable weather conditions, the Armada was scattered, and the English were delighted with their victory. The concept of a major political event awakening the nation from a dream would have been familiar to Elizabethans. Robert Greene used this metaphor very positively when writing about why God allowed Philip to send the Armada. God "brought in these Spaniards to waken us out of our dreams, to teach the brave men of this realm that after peace comes wars."[57]

Henry VIII Returns in a Dream

Though there was a great sense of victory in 1588, the English were all too aware of the foreign dangers that continued in the 1590s. Part of that danger was expressed by the extensive anti–English Catholic literature demonizing Elizabeth and her government. One text that was aimed particularly at William Cecil was written by the Catholic propagandist Richard Verstegan, who used a monarch appearing in a dream to add strength to his attempt to discredit Elizabeth's closest advisor. Ironically, however, the monarch is Elizabeth's father, Henry VIII, hardly one that Catholics would present as having a correct point of view. Verstegan was the grandson of Theodore

Rowland Verstegan, who had come to England as a refugee from the Netherlands, and his father, a cooper, took the name Rowlands to sound more English. Richard matriculated at Oxford under the name Richard Rowland, but because of his Catholic sympathies, he left in 1569 without taking a degree. His first book, *The Post of the World* (1576), was the earliest English guidebook about travel on the Continent, but in 1581 he secretly printed an account of Edmund Campion's execution and had to flee the country. Once abroad, he adopted his ancestral surname and began publishing accounts of Catholic persecutions in England. From 1590 until the death of Elizabeth, he worked as a publisher, a propagandist, and an intelligence agent for William Allen and Robert Parsons. Elizabeth's government was very concerned about how much Verstegan's writings influenced the way Elizabeth's policies were perceived on the Continent. In 1592, he published *A declaration of the true causes of the great troubles, presupposed to be intended against the realme of England Wherein the indifferent reader shall manifestly perceave, by whome, and by what means, the realme is broughte into these pretented perils,* which immediately went into a second edition. Much of the text was an attack on Elizabeth's closest advisor, William Cecil. Verstegan sought to discredit Cecil because of his "meane" background—a criticism that Verstegan uses to suggest Cecil's low birth. Yet despite that background, Cecil now has "great prosperity," which makes him "forget himself, and doth bereave him of his judgment." Verstegen also taunted that not only Cecil's "own parentage . . . is but mean" but also how little "he has bettered himself by his matches." Verstegan dismissed Cecil's first wife, Mary Cheke, as "but the sister of a Pedant"—a teacher. Verstegan was far more disdainful of Cecil's second wife, Mildred Cooke, who was known as one of the best-educated women of Elizabethan England. According to Verstegan, she had "so lately come out of the kitchen, that her posterities for some descents, must need smell of the fat of the frying pan." But the way Verstegan demeaned Cecil the most severely was to relate "what Sir Walter Raleigh dreamed of." In Raleigh's supposed dream, "King Henry VIII told him, that he did very much wonder" that someone named Cecil "was now come to bear so great sway in the court" when, said Henry, in his time the Cecil name "was so obscure in the country."[58] In Verstegan's dream, Henry seems very concerned with the status of the men at his daughter's court; given Raleigh's own status and ambitions, even if he had such an unlikely dream, it is highly doubtful he would have repeated it.

DREAMS OF LOVE AND POWER

While Verstegan would have created the Raleigh dream that included Henry as a character, in June 1597 Anthonius Green actually dreamed not just of royalty but of becoming royalty himself, in what might be construed as a potential threat to the queen. In his dream, Anthonius "was told that the Emperor Rudolph II was dead, and that a certain Thomas Green of Aldbury, in Hertfordshire, who when at Moscow, had married a noble lady of the ancient imperial stock, had left this Anthonius Green as his heir, and also undoubted heir to the empire." As is typical with the form of dreams, we do not know who gave Anthonius this information, but in some ways it sounds like the Elizabethan equivalent to the email announcing that some stranger has left you millions of dollars. The dream went on to give other great news. Nicholas Green, son of Anthonius's older brother Thomas, would marry Lady Arabella "and should be King of Bohemia." As for Anthonius, he "should be Duke of Hertford, . . . [and] should also have the bishopric of Salisbury."[59] While this sounds like a lovely dream of wish fulfillment, Arabella Stuart, daughter of Henry Stuart, Lord Darnley's younger brother Charles, as an English-born cousin of Elizabeth was thought by some to be a stronger contender as heir to the throne than Scottish-born James, and any who married her could be powerful indeed. In fact, neither Elizabeth nor James ever allowed Arabella to marry. When James learned of Arabella's secret marriage to William Seymour in 1610, he was furious, and he ordered that they be separated. Arabella tried unsuccessfully to flee to France to join William, who had managed to escape there, but she died in the Tower in 1615.

The same year as Green's dream, the astrologer Simon Forman, whose dreams were discussed in previous chapters, had two dreams about Elizabeth. He recorded in his diary on 23 January 1597 that he dreamed "that I was with the Queen." According to his description, Elizabeth certainly did not appear very regal. "She was a little elderly woman in a coarse white petticoat all unready," meaning in sixteenth-century terms that she was in the state of being partly undressed. Though the woman was elderly and wearing coarse clothing, there is also, as Louis Montrose has brilliantly observed,[60] a strong element of sexual attraction that in part came from the queen's power. Forman's description of the queen in his dream also implies an element of misogynistic contempt for the woman who rules the kingdom. Forman and Elizabeth "walked up and down through lanes and closes, talking and reasoning." Unfortunately, Forman does not record—or perhaps remember—the nature of their conversation. They finally "came over a great close where were many people, and there were two men at hard words. One of them was a weaver, a tall man with a reddish beard, distract of his wits." Elizabeth spoke to him, "and he spoke very merrily unto her, and at last did take her and kiss her." Forman did not appreciate Elizabeth's familiarity with another person, so he "took her by the arm and did put her away; and told her the fellow was frantic." Forman and Elizabeth moved away from the weaver who had "her by the arm still." Then, Forman and the queen "went through a dirty lane." While earlier the queen had been wearing a petticoat and was partially undressed, in the way of dreams she now had on "a long white smock very clean and fair," but because of where they were walking "it trailed in the dirt and her coat behind." As someone ought to do when with any lady of quality, but especially the queen, Forman took her coat and did carry it up a good way, but then it hung too low as before. "I told her she should do a favor to let me wait on her, and she said I should." Then Forman's meaning becomes much more overtly sexual: "I mean to wait upon you and not under you, that I might make this belly a little bigger to carry up this smock and coat out of the dirt." This comment led to Forman and the queen talking "merrily; then she began to lean upon me, when we were past the dirt and to be very familiar with me, and I thought she began to love me. When we were alone, out of sight, I thought she would have kissed me."[61] But before Forman could experience what the weaver had earlier in the dream, he awoke.

Forman's dream, with its sexual overtones, suggests the contradictory domination of queen over subject, yet male over the female. The woman in the dream is both queen and lover, both subordinate and in power. Though there is an obvious sexual component to the dream, the queen is not presented as a traditionally appealing object of sexual desire. Forman did not dream Elizabeth in the idealized and flattering form in which she preferred to be described. Instead, Forman's dreamer's eye created a realistic portrait of an aging woman. Her attraction comes from her powerful position, the desire for sexual intimacy, and a desire for the power intimacy with the sovereign confers. Montrose argues that "The aged Queen's body exerts a power upon the mind of Doctor Forman; and, in his dream, he exerts a reciprocal power upon the body of the Queen. . . . In the context of the crosscutting relationships between subject and prince, man and woman, the dreamer insinuates into a gesture of homage, a will to power." Montrose delights in the connection between the weaver in Forman's dream and William Shakespeare's *A Midsummer Night's Dream*. "It is strange and admirable that the dreamer's rival for the Queen should be a weaver—as if Nick Bottom had wandered out of Shakespeare's *Dream* and into Forman's."[62] I, however, find A. L. Rowse's identification of the weaver, "a tall man with reddish beard," as Essex to be far more compelling. In the late 1590s, those in the capital might easily dream of an Essex who fought with others with "hard words," would speak "very merrily" to the queen, and as one who would "at last . . . take her and kiss her." But what may be the most interesting about the description of the weaver is that he was "distract of his wits. . . . frantic," which was certainly how some would have described Essex in the last years of his life. By 1597 Forman, and others in London, may have already perceived the earl's dangerous and erratic mood swings. Three years later, in 1600, after Essex's disgrace because of his abrupt and unauthorized return from Ireland, Elizabeth's godson Sir John Harington visited him. He found the earl "shifts from sorrow and repentance to rage and rebellion so suddenly as will prove him devoid of good reason or right mind . . . he uttered strange words bordering on such strange designs, that made me hasten for and leave his presence."[63]

A month after his first dream, Forman had another about Elizabeth, this time "coming to him all in black, with a French hood."[64] In the first dream Elizabeth wore white; in the second she was completely in black. White and black together were the Renaissance colors representing virginity and purity, and Elizabeth often wore them. Much earlier in her reign she referred to them as "my colors."[65] But if her white dress might well suggest Elizabeth's virginity, as well as the concerted attack on it by both the tall red-headed weaver and Forman himself, the later dream has a more somber tone. The queen, all in black, may suggest Forman's recognition that the reign is ending and that a dark time is coming for all of England, especially with Elizabeth's refusal to name an heir. When Elizabeth did die in 1603, at her funeral John Clapham described how "first went two hundred and sixty poor women, four in a rank, appareled in black, with linen kerchiefs over their heads."[66] Elizabeth's head covering is particularly interesting. A French hood was a headdress English women wore in the sixteenth and seventeenth centuries, but it could have a more specific meaning. There are cases in the late sixteenth century where women were forced to wear it as punishment for charges of lasciviousness, again expressing at its deepest roots the discomfort with an unmarried female monarch and the intersections of sexuality and power in considering Elizabeth the queen.

DREAMS OF THE EARL OF ESSEX

If the Earl of Essex may have been the weaver in Forman's 1597 dream, he more overtly haunted other dreams. His own dreams deeply disturbed him as well. Essex confided in Lord Henry Howard, later Earl of Northampton, who wrote about Essex's nightmare and other related dreams. Northampton described how in November 1598, before Essex left for Ireland, the earl told him "that he could not sleep all night by reason of a fearful dream that preparing himself toward Ireland a great beam fell upon his head." If this was not frightening enough, the dream was so vivid that "at his waking he did feel a great p[ai]n in the place and such a soreness as amazed him." Clearly, Essex was deeply worried about the difficult situation into which his pride had led him.

It may be ironic that Essex dreamed of great trauma to his head, as he was found guilty of treason for his attempted coup and beheaded 25 February 1601. At about the time of Essex's aborted rebellion, a preacher in Ipswich, who obviously felt very invested in Essex, dreamed "that he saw my Lord and diverse after him walking through the streets of London." The earl and those with him had drawn their swords. The preacher followed Essex to see "what should become [of] him." At about the time Essex came to St. Paul's, "he thought that my Lord was apprehended by officers and carried to the Tower which caused him to awake in agony." The preacher was about to "send to London for advertisements how matters stood but before he sent word came of the tragedy." Before Essex's execution, "the same person dreamed that he saw my Lord's head stricken off and related both the first and second dream to two or three ministers that by occasion did come to visit him." An old woman to whom Essex had been generous also "dreamed that she saw him with a number more perplexed and disquieted walk through London streets and at the last brought to the scaffold where he lost his head."[67]

While some who dreamed of Essex were distressed at what could happen to him, others feared what Essex might do to the queen. Just as Mary Cocker had a nocturnal warning for Elizabeth, so did Joan Notte, though unlike Cocker, she knew they were dreams and was convinced they were dreams that had to be taken seriously. On two successive Saturdays in early 1601, Notte had warning dreams "against assassination to be addressed to the Queen."[68] Notte's dreams are filled with fear over the role Essex was determined to play in the politics of England and what danger this posed for Elizabeth. These dreams were so powerful that John Notte "importunately moved by my wife," informed John Garnons, a former justice of the peace whom they knew well, of the warning dreams. Garnons took these warning dreams seriously, and he in turn sent the account of them on to Robert Cecil. Cecil, of course, was getting these dreams fourth hand—from Notte's wife to Notte to Garnons and now to Cecil—and still hundreds of years later to us. The dreams and the conversations that Joan Notte reported at the same time greatly concerned Garnons. "Though some part of the said writings seems to be fantastical dreams, yet other part are to be tried out and the offenders punished. Had I been still in the commission of the peace, I would have searched out some of it myself. Had age and health permitted, I would have brought you the papers with my own hand."[69]

Joan Notte had two dreams she thought important enough to share with the government. In each of the dreams there were a variety of beasts that threaten both Elizabeth and Robert Cecil. In one of the dreams Anne Boleyn is also a character. Although Anne had been dead for nearly seventy years, Joan Notte described how "Queen Anne Boleyn . . . appeared warning Queen Elizabeth not to go further from London than St. James." Anne Boleyn died long before Joan Notte was born; therefore, Joan would never have seen her. We do not know if she had ever seen Elizabeth either, though she might well have. Joan Notte had been to London during the last few years and Elizabeth also went on progress throughout the countryside. Of course, we can never know even with our own dreams why certain people and symbols appear much less than we can know about the dream of a woman who lived hundreds of years earlier. But we might speculate as to why, in Joan Notte's dream, it is Elizabeth's mother rather than her father Henry VIII who comes back to deliver the warning. Perhaps Joan Notte as a woman imagined that the mother would be the one to most care, even more than the father, about what happened to a child, especially a daughter as opposed to the son Henry had so intently craved. Or was Anne Boleyn's own spectacular and horrific death so much a matter of public memory that any worry over the fate of Elizabeth would coalesce with the image of that ritualized slaughter, the beheading, of the earlier queen? Did Joan Notte see a connection between Anne Boleyn, a queen consort whose vulnerability was expressed by attacks on her sexual reputation and her inability to have a living son, and Elizabeth, queen regnant, who was called whore by some of her subjects and also had no heir of her body? Anne Boleyn was killed by her husband, the man who had so desired her, had written her impassioned love letters, and had waited almost seven years to make her his queen. Though over thirty years younger than the queen, Essex beseeched her favors by acting like a lover. The rumors of sexual misconduct that had been circulating throughout the reign about Leicester and Hatton had their last appearance in whispers about Elizabeth and Essex. Henry the king had had his wife Anne executed. Would Essex kill Elizabeth to become the king? And why does Anne Boleyn warn her daughter not to leave the city? In Joan Notte's unconscious, what does Anne Boleyn see as so dangerous for the queen were she to go into the countryside? Do the court and London represent the center of power, and for Elizabeth to leave, to abandon that power, would put her at terrible risk? We cannot know the answers, but the very questions are provocative. We saw in the previous chapter how Anne Boleyn was presented in chronicles and eventually on stage; her image must have been very powerful that it would still be affecting dreams long after her death.

Joan Notte's second dream even more explicitly deals with the dangers of Essex and fears over the succession. Worries about Essex's role must have been in Notte's mind for a long time as we can see from the conversations she reportedly heard about Essex and his claims over the last few years. She described an actual trip she made to London, and how she was staying at an inn near Charing Cross, while she sent one of her men to see if her lodgings at Paul's Wharf were ready. She was alone in her room near the window and overheard in the courtyard below a serving man ask another: "Is great Robin out?" After some other speeches, which she could not completely understand since some strangers were coming in and out, one of them swore, "By God's wounds, the very city will set him up, for they have offered to pay all his debts for him." As the two men were leaving, one said to the other, "Thou shall see good sport among them before the end of the summer, if they walk abroad." Joan Notte was not sure whom they were discussing, "but by imagination since, and by hearing, which before she knew not, that the great man's name was Robert."[70]

The Nottes were concerned not only about the Earl of Essex himself but also about his supporters, one of whom they apparently knew personally. It is clear from the nature of the information that John Notte presented to Garnons that the three of them were acquainted with Sir Gelly Meyrick, a close confederate of Essex. Meyrick was the eldest son of the bishop of Bangor. He was still a boy when his father died, and from an early age, he had made his fortune as a soldier, eventually serving with the young Earl of Essex in the Netherlands in the mid-1580s. Meyrick was the steward of Essex's household and accompanied Essex on a number of his expeditions, including ones to Portugal, Normandy, Cadiz, and eventually the ill-fated Irish campaign. Meyrick, like so many others, received his knighthood from Essex and was fanatically loyal to the earl. Joan Notte reported how, at Christmas two years before, she had talked with Edward Reavell, "gentleman, a valiant soldier of the Low Country, that served under Sir Thomas Baskerville, and the son of Thomas Reavell, of Kilgarren in Pembrokeshire," and he had told her about a conversation between two soldiers, one a follower of Meyrick and one of Mr. Roger Vaughan; both Meyrick and Vaughan were supporters of Essex. According to Reavell as reported by Notte, when the soldiers saw Essex, Meyrick's follower told the other man, "There goes [one] that will be King of England one day." The other replied, "Yea!" but it would not be until "the old woman were dead," meaning of course Elizabeth. The first one responded, "Tush! Dead or dead not, he will be king one day." This made the other so excited that he claimed, "if it so fall out, thy master [meaning Meyrick] will sure be a Duke and my master [meaning Vaughan] will be an Earl at the least."[71]

Joan Notte also reported how at "another time"—she does not say when or how recent this conversation was—she had mentioned Meyrick to a Mrs. Powell, who also knew him. Mrs. Powell replied that Meyrick "the priest's son hopes for that day that I trust he never shall see," demonstrating that Mrs. Powell knew enough about his background to know who his father was. Joan asked her to what day she was referring. "Mary!" said Mrs Powell, "he hopes to see his master king of England one day." Joan Notte expressed herself amazed. "What does the two legged ass mean? For there is no color nor likelihood thereof. I would I might hear one of the best of them dare to speak it." Mrs. Powell admitted that "they will keep their speeches secret enough, but sure I am this is their hope." This conversation translated itself into a dream in which Meyrick appeared. In one dream a gentleman Notte could not name was walking with Meyrick and asked him "who after her Majesty should carry the crown. 'Who,' quoth he, 'but my Lord of Essex.'" To make the dream even more frightening, wild beasts also threatened Elizabeth.

The dreams and the statements John Notte gave Garnon about his wife's experiences were quite incendiary. Of course we cannot know if she actually had the dreams or overheard the conversations, though clearly Garnon believed she had and accepted Notte's assurance that his purpose was not to cause trouble. "I speak this only of my fervent love to her Majesty." Essex found that the city did not rise for him, but rather supported the queen, and his own followers were arrested. Essex was executed February 25 and Meyrick March 13.

Did Elizabeth Dream of Hell?

Blackwood claimed that Elizabeth experienced horrible dreams at the time of Mary's execution. Elizabeth died only two years after Essex's execution. The final reported dream by Elizabeth is also from a Catholic source and again is perhaps questionable as an actual dream but powerful as an image presented by those on the other side of the religious divide. Elizabeth Southwell eloped to Italy with Leicester's illegitimate son Sir Robert Dudley dressed as his page. She subsequently married him there after they both converted to Catholicism and the pope had annulled his first marriage. In 1607, she wrote "A true relation of what succeeded at the sickness and death of Queen Elizabeth." While Sir John Neale has found the manuscript lacking in credibility, particularly the description of the dead Elizabeth's exploding body, Catherine Loomis has recently argued that scholars should give it another look.[72] Whatever did or did not happen to Elizabeth after her death, in Southwell's manuscript, Southwell claimed that soon before Elizabeth died she told Lady Scrope, in a "very private and confident" manner that "she saw one night in her bed her body exceeding lean and fearful in a light of fire." Lady Philadelphia Scrope was a Lady of the Bedchamber and the great-aunt to Southwell. While Loomis suggests that Scrope repeated "the Queen's words about her fiery visions," proving herself not a good confidante, we actually do not know if Scrope told this to Southwell or if Southwell simply invented the story, as the only account of it is in Southwell's memoir.[73] Southwell's manuscript is well worth examining but not because we can trust that we know more about what actually happened in the last days of Elizabeth's life. Rather, it demonstrates how powerful the idea of a dreaming monarch would be, and the pleasure Elizabeth's enemies would have in believing her last dream was of watching herself burning in hell. (figure 5.5)

Figure 5.5   William Clarke, Death of Elizabeth I.

Private collection.

DREAMS OF ELIZABETH FROM FAR AWAY

Elizabeth's image was so powerful that not only did her own subjects dream about her but foreigners did as well. The final dreams considered in this chapter occurred not in England but in Spain. The story of Mary Stuart's execution, and Elizabeth's role in it, spread throughout Europe and influenced the dreams of those far away from England, reflecting a wide range of religious and political anxieties. In 1590, a twenty-one-year-old woman, Lucrecia de Leon, daughter of a legal clerk in Madrid, was arrested on the order of Philip II himself and brought before the Spanish Inquisition because of the widespread publicity her dreams had received. Lucrecia's dreams were highly critical of King Philip II; critics of the king encouraged Lucrecia to tell her dreams; they then recorded them, using the dreams to prophesize disaster for Spain because of the king's misguided policies. Richard Kagan argues that "the real importance of these dreams lies in their social and political criticism of Philip's Spain . . . as glosses on historical events."[74]

Lucrecia's dreams reflected the political concerns and worries of many people as Spain was preparing for war with England. In some of Lucrecia's dreams, her guides, who are referred to as the Ordinary Man, the Lion Man, and the Old Man, took her to visit foreign countries; England was a frequent destination. Lucrecia had a number of dreams not only about the dangerous seafarer Francis Drake but also about Elizabeth herself. Her most vivid and horrifying dream of the queen occurred on 18 December 1587. Lucrecia dreamed that she and her guide "flew across the seas and came to a seaport, where there were many ships, medium-sized and large, being made ready." She had seen Drake before in a dream, and he was there again, ready to pay the sailors who would fight against Spain. So that he could pay them, Drake went to his house, and "we saw how he took out from a safe place a hoard of treasure that he had hidden—this was something I had seen in another dream." In the way of dreams, Drake's house then became the queen's palace. "From there we came into another room, where I saw a woman who looked a little more than fifty years old. The Ordinary Man said to me, 'Look, there is Elizabeth, queen of England.'"

Elizabeth was sitting on a low stool. In her lap was a dead lamb, cut open. Lucrecia saw her "taking up with both hands the blood that was held inside the lamb and was drinking it with great relish." Sitting beside Elizabeth "was a very beautiful woman, though very pale and dressed in the black of a widow." Elizabeth told the beautiful widow woman to drink of the lamb's blood, but the woman in black refused. The refusal made the queen very angry, "and stood up and, taking a sword from her side, she struck suddenly at the woman, cutting off her head." But the dream did not end there. Elizabeth then washed the blood of the lamb off her hands and gave the lamb to Drake, who ordered that the remaining meat and skin be given to his soldiers. Drake ordered his men "that they should hang the flesh of the lamb from their banners," which Lucrecia interpreted as intended as an insult to

Philip II. "Then the Ordinary Man took me back across the sea to the Old Man. As he did so, I heard the sound of war drums."[75]

A week later on the 23rd of December, Lucrecia had another dream that suggested how strongly the Spanish feared Elizabeth. Lucrecia saw "the English Queen Mary who appeared with a rope in her hands and about her throat. The Old Fisherman asked her, 'Why do you appear like that?'" Mary's answer in the dream might well have been one that the historical Mary would have given at that moment had she had the opportunity. "Does it not seem to you that I deserve it since all of the sins committed by my sister fall upon me? There was a time when I could have remedied the situation and I did not." One wonders, too, if Lucrecia was aware that it was in part Philip's influence when he was Mary's consort that saved Elizabeth's life. The dream reflected a shiver of guilt that Catholics had not taken care of Elizabeth years earlier when they had had the chance.

The imagery in Lucrecia's dreams is powerful and horrific indeed. Lucrecia's dream guide does not explain the symbolism of the grisly scene of the queen and the dead lamb, but the lamb, a particularly potent religious image that often represented Christ himself, might well suggest persecuted Catholics; Kagan and Roger Osborne's identification of the widow as Mary Stuart, executed ten months earlier, is convincing. Lucrecia's contemporaries also found this dream powerful and disturbing, demonstrating Elizabeth's ruthlessness as an enemy of Spain. Lucrecia had met Doctor Alonso de Mendoza, a canon attached to the cathedral of Toledo, three months earlier. Kagan tells us that "It was after studying this particular dream that Mendoza avowed that Lucrecia's dreams 'do not proceed from an evil spirit, nor do they appear to be fictions composed either by human or diabolical invention; rather, they are truths advising us about the rigorous justice from heaven that we deserve for our sins.'"[76]

This is a powerful, masculinized queen, not afraid of blood or slaughter, who actually offers blood to drink and expertly wields her sword against those who refuse her commands. The dream about William Rufus reported in Holinshed's *Chronicles,* with the king actually chewing on the body of Christ, served as a parodic inversion of the mass itself. Lucrecia's dream of Elizabeth, with the queen offering her rival blood to drink, echoes this symbolism. In the dream, the ritual, with sword as well as blood, expresses not redemption but death.

Throughout history, dreams have offered powerful ways to explore deep fears and anxieties. Even when the dreams described were probably apocryphal, they still give us valuable insights into the psyche of a long vanished time. The dreams about Elizabeth and Mary Stuart, invented as propaganda in texts such as Blackwood, perhaps a rhetorical ploy by Elizabeth herself in discussion with Davison, an example of warning to a beloved queen in Cocker's ghost story, and a nightmare of danger in the dream of the Spanish Lucrecia, are all windows into a way of understanding Elizabeth and Mary, religious and political crisis, in late sixteenth-century England.

AFTERWORD

This book begins with the court of James I and ends with the reign of his predecessor Elizabeth and the execution of James's mother. In the ways of dreams, this book has come full circle. Studying dreams, and ideas about dreams, allows us to understand more about the mentality of the English Renaissance. Some dreams were intensely private; others were spoken of publicly. People's dreams could be about the most personal aspect of their lives or about the most major of public events. Dreams could be ominous or joyful, mundane or significant, silly or spiritual. Some aspects of early modern people's beliefs about dreams were lighthearted and not to be taken seriously, such as the Topsell dragon tongue in wine recipe to prevent nightmares or the commonplace book that argued that putting an ape's heart under the pillow would allow one to have exciting dreams. Others, such as dreams of loved ones who might soon die or already had, were solemnly and painfully experienced. Kenelm Digby's letter to his brother about the dreams he had of his dead wife is filled with an anguish that we can recognize centuries after it was written. The vivid dreams about Elizabeth, such as those by the English woman Joan Notte or the Spanish woman Lucrecia de Leon, also show how important dreams were to people's considerations of public as well as private experience.

Dreams of people in sixteenth- and early seventeenth-century England allow us to understand how external events intensely penetrated the deepest recesses of the unconscious. Dreams reflected and interrelated with the most significant political, religious, and cultural values of the time. This is especially evident when examining the dreams about monarchs such as Elizabeth I, dreams that were perceived as warnings or dreams that saw her as the enemy. As we saw, dreams were highly significant both to men and to women, those of the highest social classes as well as those of lower status, and across the entire religious divide. People had widely differing views of dreams. Dreams could be considered as sent from God and angels or as temptations placed in one's mind by devils, and nightmares might be caused by a succubus sitting on the chest of the sleeper. Some people thought dreams were the result of the body's dominant humour: The blood-filled dreams of the sanguine were markedly different from the phlegmatic's dreams of water, the choleric's of fire, or the melancholic's frightening dreams of graves and cells. Other people argued that one should interpret a dream experienced by someone of sanguine humour very differently from that same dream if related by one of melancholic humour. Still others maintained that dreams had no meaning but were merely the fragments of the day retold—a shoemaker might dream of footwear while a fisherman of his catches. But the most common and deeply felt belief was that dreams could foretell the future if one could only understand the symbolism, and thus we saw the large number of texts that explained how to interpret dreams. Yet also in this period, there was a significant shift toward a more modern understanding of dreams. Thomas Nashe, for example, argued that feelings of guilt were the cause of dreams, at least many of the disturbing ones. Perhaps the most clear and economical statement is in the early seventeenth-century translation of Wilhelm Adolf Scribonius's *Naturall Philosophy:* "A dreame is an inward act of the mind."[1] Through the great concern and discussion English Renaissance people had about their vivid and sometimes emotionally wrenching dreams, we can see how much the interior sense of individual self developed in this period.

Some dreams described in this study appear to be actual experiences; others were created for reasons of art and drama, politics and power. Dreams "invented" by playwrights can be as revelatory of cultural beliefs as the dreams people described to their closest friends or wrote down in their journals. A study such as this also opens up what we can see as history; this book is not only a history of dreams but also a history of early modern England. Dreams can tell us more about history, and in turn, a thorough knowledge of a specific historical period can allow us to understand more about its people's dreams. Symbols in dreams are not universal; they hold specific meanings in the historicity of the experience. Dreams tied people to their past or to their memories, even as early modern English people saw their dreams as a way to know and lead them into the future. Dreams are another language to express not only deepest fears and desires but also a period's cultural anxieties.

We can never completely know anyone's dreams; we have only fragmented memories, images that are recreated and conveyed in words. But even given those difficulties of translation, dreams of the English Renaissance are revelatory, giving us a new insight into a vanished age.

NOTES

INTRODUCTION

1. Anthony Stevens, *Private Myths: Dreams and Dreaming* (Cambridge, MA: Harvard University Press, 1995), 301; Charles Carlton, *Archbishop William Laud* (London and New York: Routledge & Kegan Paul, 1987), 144.
2. Alan MacFarlane, *The Family Life of Ralph Josselin, a Seventeenth-Century Clergyman: An Essay in Historical Anthropology* (Cambridge, UK: Cambridge University Press, 1970), 186.
3. William C. Dement, *The Promise of Sleep: A Pioneer in Sleep Medicine Explores the Vital Connection between Health, Happiness, and a Good Night's Sleep* (New York: Delacorte Press, 1999), 293.
4. Philip Goodwin, *The mystery of dreames, historically discoursed* (London, 1658), 292. Thomas Nash, *The terrors of the night. Or, A Discourse of apparitions* (London, 1594), C3v.
5. Jean-Claude Schmitt, "The Liminality and Centrality of Dreams in the Medieval West," Stéphane Moses, "The Cultural Index of Freud's Interpretation of Dreams," *Dream Cultures: Explorations in the Comparative History of Dreaming,* ed. David Shulman and Guy Stroumsa (Oxford, NY: Oxford University Press, 1999), 274.
6. John Foxe, *Acts and Monuments* [. . .] *The Variorum Edition* [online] (hrOnline, Sheffield 2004), 1662. Available from: http://www.hrionline .shef.ac.uk/foxe/[Accessed: 20 Nov 2007].
7. Jacques Le Goff, *The medieval imagination,* trans. Arthur Goldhammer (Chicago: University of Chicago Press, 1988), 194, 229.
8. Zacharie Jones, *A Treatise of Specters or straunge Sights, Visions and Apparitions appearing sensibly unto men. Wherein is delivered, the Nature of Spirites, Angels, and Divels: their power and properties: as also of Witches, Sorcerers, Enchanters, and such like. Newly done out of French into English* (London, 1605), 2.
9. R. B., *Wonderful Prodigies of Judgment and Mercy: Discovered in Above Three Hundred Memorable Histories* (London, 1685), 111.
10. Thomas Hobbes, *Leviathan* (1651), ed. C. B. Macpherson (London: Penguin, 1968), 91.
11. Gervase Holles, *Memorials of the Holles Family, 1493–1656,* ed. A. C. Wood (Camden Third Series, vol. LV; London: Camden Society, 1937), 190.
12. David R. Como, *Blown by the Spirit: Puritanism and the Emergence of an Antinomian Underground in Pre-Civil War England* (Stanford: Stanford University Press, 2004), 150; Nigel Smith, *Perfection Proclaimed: Language and Literature in English Radical Religion, 1640–1660* (Oxford, UK: Clarendon Press, 1989), 73–75; Keith Thomas, *Religion and the Decline of Magic* (London: Weidenfeld and Nicolson, 1971), 153.

13. Goodwin, *mystery of dreames*, 265.

14. Gonzalo, *The Divine Dreamer: or, A Short Treatise Discovering the True Effect and Power of Dreams* (London, 1641), n.p.

15. W. Vaughan, *Directions for Health, Naturall and Artificiall*, the seventh edition reviewed by the Author (London, 1633), 163.

16. Goodwin, *mystery of dreames*, 8–9.

17. William Laud, *The works of the Most Reverend Father in God, William Laud, D. D., sometime Lord Archbishop of Canterbury*, ed. William Scott and James Bliss (Oxford, UK: J. H. Parker, 1847–1860), iii, 170.

18. Moise Amyraut, *A discourse concerning the divine dreams mention'd in Scripture, together with the marks and characters by which they might be distinguish'd from vain delusions*, in a letter to Monsieur Gaches, by Moses Amyraldus, trans. Ja. Lowde (London, 1676), 19.

19. William Basse, *A helpe to discourse. Or, A misselany of merriment Consisting of witty philosophicall, and astronomicall questions and ansvvers. As also, of epigrams, epitaphs, riddles, and jests. Together with The country-mans counsellour, next his yearely oracle or prognostication to consult with. Contayning divers necessary rules and observations, of much use and consequence being knowne* (London, 1623), 209.

20. Nash, *Terrors of the Night*, D3v.

21. Thomas Cooper, *The Mystery of Witch-Craft* (London, 1617), 146.

22. Moses, "The Cultural Index of Freud's Interpretation of Dreams," 306.

23. Thomas Hill, *The Pleasant Art of the Interpretation of Dreams* (London, 1576); Jeffrey Masten, "The Interpretation of Dreams, Circa 1610," *Historicism, Psychoanalysis, and Early Modern Culture*, ed. Carla Mazzio and Douglas Trevor (New York and London: Routledge, 2000), 163-64; Charles Mackay, *Extraordinary Popular Delusions and the Madness of Crowds* (Boston: L. C. Page, 1932), 293–97; Josiah Dare, *Counsellor Manners: His last legacy to His Son (1672)*, ed. Ira Webster Porter (New York: Coward-McCann, 1929), 131.

24. Paul Edward Dutton, *The Politics of Dreaming in the Carolingian Empire* (Lincoln: University of Nebraska Press, 1994); Steven F. Kruger, *Dreaming in the Middle Ages* (Cambridge, UK: Cambridge University Press, 1992); R. Po-Chia Hsia, "Dreams and Conversions: A Comparative Analysis of Catholic and Buddhist Dreams in Ming and Qing China: Part 1," *Journal of Religious History* 29, no. 3 (2005), 223–40; Carla Gerona, *Night Journeys: The Power of Dreams in Transatlantic Quaker Culture* (Charlottesville: University of Virginia Press, 2004); Mechal Sobel, *Teach Me Dreams: The Search for Self in the Revolutionary Era* (Princeton, NJ: Princeton University Press, 2000); Charlotte Beradt, *The Third Reich of Dreams* (Chicago: Quadrangle Books, 1968); Irina Paperno, "Dreams of Terror: Dreams from Stalinist Russia as a Historical Source," *Kritika: Explorations in Russian and Eurasian History* 7, no. 4 (2006), 793–824. These are only a sampling from a large number of very fine studies on the subject.

25. George Steiner, "The Historicity of Dreams (two questions to Freud)," *Salmagundi* 61 (1983), 9.

26. Henry Howard, Earl of Northampton, *A defensative against the poyson of supposed prophecies Not hitherto confuted by the pen of any man, which being grounded, either vpon the warrant and authority of old painted bookes, exposi-*

tions of dreames, oracles, reuelations, invocations of damned spirits, judicials of astrologie, or any other kinde of pretended knowledge whatsoeuer, de futuris contingentibus; have beene causes of great disorder in the common-wealth, especially among the simple and vnlearned people. Very needfull to be published, considering the great offence, which grew by most palpable and grosse errors in astrologie (1583; reprint London, 1620), 42.

27. There have been a number of excellent recent studies on this topic. Among those to which I will refer throughout the book are the following: Katherine Hodgkin, Michelle O'Callaghan, and S. J. Wiseman, eds., *Reading the Early Modern Dream: The Terrors of the Night* (New York and London: Routledge, 2008); Peter Brown, ed., *Reading Dreams: The Interpretation of Dreams from Chaucer to Shakespeare* (Oxford, UK: Oxford University Press, 1999), especially Peter Holland, " 'The Interpretation of Dreams' in the Renaissance," 125–46; Derek Alwes, "Elizabethan Dreaming: Fictional Dreams from Gascoigne to Lodge," *Framing Elizabethan Fictions: Contemporary Approaches to Early Modern Narrative Prose,* ed. Constance C. Relihan (Kent, OH: The Kent State University Press, 1996), 153–67; Jeffrey Masten, "The Interpretation of Dreams, Circa 1610," *Historicism, Psychoanalysis, and Early Modern Culture,* ed. Carla Mazzio and Douglas Trevor (New York and London: Routledge, 2000), 157–85. Though it does not deal with dreams, one of the books that has shaped modern Renaissance studies is Stephen Greenblatt, *Renaissance Self-Fashioning: From More to Shakespeare* (Chicago: University of Chicago Press, 1980). This book has greatly influenced the idea of the developing sense of self in Tudor and early Stuart England. Most significant for this study is Stephen Greenblatt, *Hamlet in Purgatory* (Princeton, NJ: Princeton University Press, 2001). Also helpful is Stephen Greenblatt's essay "Psychoanalysis and Renaissance Culture," in *Literary Theory/Renaissance Texts,* eds. Patricia Parker and David Quint (Baltimore: Johns Hopkins University Press, 1986). See also, Elizabeth Jane Bellamy, "Desires and Disavowals: Speculations on the Aftermath of Stephen Greenblatt's 'Psychoanalysis and Renaissance Culture,' " *Clio* 34, no. 3 (2005), 297–315.

CHAPTER 1

1. Also spelled Monteagle.
2. Henry Paul, *The royal play of Macbeth; when, why, and how it was written by Shakespeare* (New York: Macmillan, 1950), 114. Historical Manuscripts Commission, *Calendar of the Manuscripts of the Most Honourable the Marquess of Salisbury Preserved at Hatfield House, Part XVII,* ed. M. S. Guiseppi (London: Her Majesty's Stationery Office, 1938), 37, 121.
3. Joel Hurstfield, "Gun-Powder Plot and the Politics of Dissent," in *Early Stuart Studies: Essays in Honor of David Harris Willson,* ed. Howard S. Reinmuth, Jr. (Minneapolis: University of Minnesota Press, 1970), 96–97; G.P.V. Akrigg, *Jacobean Pageant, or the Court of King James I* (Cambridge, MA: Harvard University Press, 1962), 73.
4. See especially Mark Nicholls, *Investigating Gunpowder Plot* (Manchester, UK: Manchester University Press, 1991); James Sharpe, *Remember, Remember: A Cultural History of Guy Fawkes Day* (Cambridge, MA: Harvard University

Press, 2005); Antonia Fraser, *The Gunpowder Plot: Terror & Faith in 1605* (London: Weidenfeld and Nicolson, 1996); Jenny Wormald, "Gunpowder, Treason, and Scots," *Journal of British Studies* 24 (1985), 141–68.

5. Sharpe, *Remember, Remember, 7*; *Calendar of State Papers and Manuscripts Relating to English Affairs, Existing in the Archives and Collections of Venice, and in Other Libraries of Northern Italy,* ed. Horatio F. Brown (1900; repr., Nendeln, Liechtenstein: Kraus Reprint, 1970), x, 297.

6. J. H., *The Divell of the Vault, Or the Unmasking of Murther in a brief declaration of the Cacolicke-complotted Treason, lately discovered* (London, 1606), C2v.

7. *The Returne of the knight of the poste from Hell* (London: John VVindet, 1606), C1; William Barlow, *The Sermon Preached at Paules Crosse, the tenth day of November* (London: Matthew Law, 1606), preface, D. For Andrewes's sermon and an excellent discussion on the sermons about the Gunpowder Plot, see Lori Anne Ferrell, *Government by Polemic: James I, the King's Preachers, and the Rhetorics of Conformity, 1603–1625* (Stanford: Stanford University Press, 1998), chap. 3 and particularly p. 94. William Hubbard, *Greate Britianes Resurrection* (London, 1606), B2. Arthur Kinney tellingly compares this to Lady Macduff. For an excellent discussion of the cultural context of Macbeth and its connection with the Gunpowder Plot, see Kinney, *Lies Like Truth: Shakespeare, Macbeth, and the Cultural Moment* (Detroit, MI: Wayne State University Press, 2001), 119, 123.

8. *Minor Prose Works of King James VI and I,* ed. James Craigie (Edinburgh, UK: Scottish Text Society, 1982), 48; Ludwig Lavater, Robert Harrison, John Dover Wilson, and May Yardley, *Of Ghostes and Spirites Walking by Nyght, 1572,* edited with introduction and appendix by J. Dover Wilson and May Yardley (Oxford, UK: Printed for the Shakespeare Association at the University Press, 1929), 6. For more on Lavater, see Bruce Gordon, "Malevolent Ghosts and Ministering Angels: Apparitions and Pastoral Care in the Swiss Reformation," in *The Place of the Dead: Death and Remembrance in Late Medieval and Early Modern Europe* (Cambridge, UK: Cambridge University Press, 2000), 87–109.

9. *The political works of James I, reprinted from the edition of 1616,* ed. Charles Howard McIlwain (Cambridge, MA: Harvard University Press, 1918), 45.

10. In one case of 1614, John Smith, "the Leicester boy," accused a number of people of bewitching him. While some were executed, James began to investigate. He became convinced that Smith was a fraud and, therefore, saved the lives of several of the accused.

11. Arthur Wilson, *The History of Great Britain, being the life and reign of King James the First, relating to what passed from his first accesse to the crown, till his death* (London, 1653), 111.

12. Sir Richard Baker, *A Chronicle of the kings of England from the time of the Romans Government unto the Death of King James* (London: George Sawbridge, 1674), 506.

13. [State papers 14 /13; Film Acc., 560 reel 131], at the Folger Shakespeare Library.

14. Sarah Bakewell, "Haydock, Richard (1569/70–ca. 1642)," *Oxford Dictionary of National Biography* (Oxford University Press, 2004). Available from: http://0-www.oxforddnb.com.library.unl.edu:80/view/article/12746 [Accessed: 8 Feb 2007]. See also, Paul, *Royal play of Macbeth,* 117–18.

15. Frederick Hard, "Richard Haydocke and Alexander Browne: Two Half-Forgotten Writers on the Art of Painting," *PMLA* 55, no. 3 (1940), 729.

16. *Letters of King James VI & I*, ed. G.P.V. Akrigg (Berkeley: University of California Press, 1984), 268.

17. James Sharpe, *The Bewitching of Anne Gunter: A Horrible and True Story of Deception, Witchcraft, Murder, and the King of England* (New York: Routledge, 2000), 194. This text provides a complete discussion of the case and is very useful. See also, Paul, *Royal play of Macbeth*, 118–27.

18. Historical Manuscripts Commission, *Calendar of the Manuscripts of the Most Honourable the Marquess of Salisbury*, 136-37.

19. Edmund Lodge, *Illustrations of British History* (London: John Childley, 1838), iii, 153.

20. Wilson, *History of Great Britain*, 111.

21. This is how it is reported in James Travers. *James I: The Masque of Monarchy* (Surrey, UK: National Archives, 2003), 34.

22. Lodge, *Illustrations of British History*, 157; *The Letters of John Chamberlain*, ed. Norman Egbert McClure (Philadelphia: American Philosophical Society, 1939), i, 206.

23. Historical Manuscripts Commission, *Calendar of the Manuscripts of the Most Honourable the Marquess of Salisbury*, xvii, 162.

24. Baker, *Chronicle of the kings of England*, 506.

25. Richard Haydocke [Dreams—dated in ms. 20 November 1605] *ONEIROLOGIA: or A briefe discourse of the nature of Dreames: Discoveringe how farre the reasonable Soule exerciseth her operations in the time of Sleepe: And prooveinge that in Sleep there can bee noe reasonable and Metholdicall*. This manuscript is at the Folger Shakespeare Library, and I am deeply indebted to Letitia Yendle for pointing it out to me.

26. *Calendar of the Manuscripts of the Most Honourable the Marquess of Salisbury*, xvii, 163.

27. SP 78/52/141. This microfilm is at the Folger Shakespeare Library.

28. *Letters of King James VI & I*, 266.

29. Harold Spencer Scott, ed., "The Journal of Sir Roger Wilbraham, Solicitor-General in Ireland and Master of the Requests, for the Years 1593–1616," in *The Camden Miscellany: Volume the Tenth* (Camden Society, third series, 4, 1902), 69-70.

30. Paul, *Royal play of Macbeth*, 127.

31. Pierre de Loyer, *A Treatise of Specters or straunge Sights, Visions and Apparitions appearing sensibly unto men. Wherein is delivered, the Nature of Spirites, Angels, and Divels: their power and properties: as also of Witches, Sorcerers, Enchanters, and such like*. Newly done out of French into English by Zacharie Jones (London, 1605), 101.

32. Edmond Howes, *The annales, or a generall chronicle of England, begun first by maister Iohn Stow, and after him continued and augmented with matters forreyne, and domestique, auncient and moderne, vnto the ende of this present yeere 1614* (London, 1615), 864-65; Baker, *Chronicle*, 444-45.

33. Gerald Schofield, "Lower Darwen: A History." Available from: http://www.cottontown.org/page.cfm?pageid=2572&language=eng [Accessed: 20 Nov 2007].

34. John Webster, *The Displaying of Supposed Witchcraft* (London, 1677), 295–97; L. Valentine, *Picturesque England: Its Landmarks and Historical*

Haunts, as Described in Lay and Legend (London: Frederick Warne, 1891), 389; R. B., *Wonderful Prodigies of Judgment and Mercy: Discovered in above Three Hundred Memorable Histories* (London, 1685), 174.

35. Geoffrey Chaucer, *The workes of our ancient and learned English poet, Geffrey Chaucer, newly printed* (London, 1602), fol. 82.

36. Thomas Walkington, *The optick glasse of humors or The touchstone of a golden temperature, or the Philosophers stone to make a golden temper Wherein the foure complections sanguine, cholericke, phligmaticke, melancholicke are succinctly painted forth and their externall intimates laid open to the purblind eye of ignorance it selfe, by which euery one may iudge, of what complection he is, and answerably learne what is most sutable to his nature* (Oxford, 1631), A Photoprint with an introduction by John A. Popplestone and Marion White McPherson (Delmar, NY: Scholars' Facsimiles & Reprints, 1981), 144; W. Vaughan, *Directions for Health, Naturall and Artificiall* (London, 1633), 163-64; Josiah Dare, *Counsellor Manners: His Last Legacy to his Son* (1672), ed. Ira Webster Porter (New York: Coward-McCann, 1929), 132, 133.

37. John Stow, *The annales of England faithfully collected out of the most autenticall authors, records, and other monuments of antiquitie, lately corrected, encreased, and continued, from the first inhabitation vntill this present yeere 1600* (London, 1600), 864.

38. John Bellamy, *Strange, Inhuman Deaths: Murder in Tudor England* (Westport, CT: Praeger, 2006), 1-2.

39. Frances Dolan, *Dangerous Familiars: Representations of Domestic Crime in England, 1550–1700* (Ithaca, NY: Cornell University Press, 1994), 25.

40. Bellamy, *Strange, Inhuman Deaths,* 53-54, 81; Dolan, *Dangerous Familiars,* 71–79; Garthine Walker, *Crime, Gender and Social Order in Early Modern England* (Cambridge, UK: Cambridge University Press, 2003), 138–48; Gregory Durston, *Crime & Justice in Early Modern England, 1500–1750* (Little London, Chichester: Barry Rose Law Publishers, 2004), 682–87.

41. John Foxe, *Acts and Monuments [. . .] The Variorum Edition* [online] (Online, Sheffield 2004), 1018. Available from: http://www.hrionline.shef .ac.uk/foxe/ [Accessed: 20 Nov 2007].

42. Henry Kirkham, *A true reporte or description of an horrible, woful, and moste lamentable murther, doen in the citie of Bristowe by one Jhon Kynnestar, a Sherman by his occupation, declarying howe wickedly he murthered his owne wife, in the monethe of August laste paste, and being taken, was hanged the same moneth 1572* (London, 1573).

43. *The Bloudy booke, or The Tragicall and desperate end of Sir John Fites (alias Fitz)* (London, 1605). Apparently in the modern period as well, people have killed people while sleepwalking or have been encouraged by their dreams to commit murder. See William C. Dement, *The Promise of Sleep: A Pioneer in Sleep Medicine Explores the Vital Connection Between Health, Happiness, and a Good Night's Sleep* (New York: Delacorte Press, 1999), 208–16.

44. Philip Goodwin, *The mystery of dreames, historically discoursed* (London, 1658), 223.

45. Vavasour Powell, *Spirituall experiences, of sundry beleevers Held forth by them at severall solemne meetings, and conferences to that end. With the recommendation of the sound, spiritual, and savoury worth of them, to the sober and spir-*

ituall reader, by Vavasor Powel, minister of the gospel (London, 1653), 160, 167, 168.

46. Samuel Clarke, *The lives of sundry eminent persons in this later age in two parts: I. of divines, II. of nobility and gentry of both sexes/by Samuel Clark . . . ; printed and reviewed by himself just before his death; to which is added his own life and the lives of the Countess of Suffolk, Sir Nathaniel Barnardiston, Mr. Richard Blackerby and Mr. Samuel Fairclough, drawn up by other hands* (London, 1683), ii, 190; N. H. Keeble, "Margaret Baxter (*bap.* 1636, *d.* 1681)," *Oxford Dictionary of National Biography* (Oxford University Press, Sep 2004); online edn, May 2007. Available from: http://0-www.oxforddnb.com.library.unl.edu:80/view/article/1734 [Accessed: 31 July 2007].

47. James Sharpe, "Introduction: The Lancashire Witches in Historical Context," in *The Lancashire Witches: Histories and Stories,* ed. Robert Poole (Manchester and New York: Manchester University Press, 2002), 6.

48. Sharpe, "Introduction," 9; Kirsteen Macpherson Bardell, "Beyond Pendle: The 'Lost' Lancashire Witches," in Poole, *Lancashire Witches,* 106; James Sharpe, *Instruments of Darkness: Witchcraft in England, 1550–1750* (London: Hamish Hamilton, 1996), 126.

49. Thomas Cooper, *The Mystery of Witch-Craft* (London, 1617), 15.

50. Moise Amyraut, *A discourse concerning the divine dreams mention'd in Scripture, together with the marks and characters by which they might be distinguish'd from vain delusions,* in a letter to Monsieur Gaches, by Moses Amyraldus, trans. Ja. Lowde (London, 1676), 10. It has only been relatively recently that scientists have discovered "that virtually everyone dreams every night," though "some people *remember* their dreams more frequently than others." Stanley Krippner and William Hughes, "Everybody Dreams Every Night," in *The New World of Dreams,* ed. Ralph L. Woods and Herbert B. Greenhouse (New York: Macmillan, 1974), 287–88.

51. Haydocke, *ONEIROLOGIA.* All of the quoted statements are from this manuscript.

52. Hurstfield, "Gun-Powder Plot and the Politics of Dissent," 97.

53. I am grateful to Paul Hammer for sharing his research on this with me. See also Rebecca Lemon, *Treason by Words: Literature, Law, and Rebellion in Shakespeare's England* (Ithaca, NY: Cornell University Press, 2006).

54. Fraser points out that while government accounts spelled the family name as Winter, it was never spelled so in any of its variations that the Wintours themselves used. *Gunpowder Plot,* 48.

55. Nicholls, *Investigating Gunpowder Plot,* 9-10.

56. Brown, *Calendar of State Papers,* x, 289; Caroline Bingham, *The Making of a King: The Early Years of James VI and I* (London: Collins, 1968), 48–51.

57. Keith Thomas, *Religion and the Decline of Magic* (London: Weidenfeld and Nicolson, 1971), 312; Fraser, *The Gunpowder Plot,* 172, 186.

58. Fraser, *Gunpowder Plot,* 169.

59. Brown, *Calendar of State Papers,* x, 292.

60. Thomas Bayly Howell, *Complete collection of state trials and proceedings for high treason and other crimes and misdemeanors from the earliest period to the present time* (London: R. Bagshaw, 1809–1826), ii, 186-87.

61. Howell, *Complete Collection of State Trials,* ii, 342.

62. Thomas Nash, *The terrors of the night or, A discourse of apparitions* (London, 1594), 15.

63. John Vicars, *November 5 1605: The Quintessence of Cruelty, or Master-piece of Treachery, the Popish Pouder-Plot, Invented by Hellish-Malice, Prevented by Heavenly-mercy. Truly related, and from the Latine of the Learned, Religious, and Reverend D. Herring, translated and very much dilated* (London, 1641), 69.

64. Nicholls, *Investigating Gunpowder Plot*, 25.

65. William, Lord Bishop of Rochester, *The Sermon Preached at Paules Cross, the tenth day of November, being the next Sunday after the Discoverie of this late Horrible Treason* (London, 1606), E.

66. Thomas, *Religion and the Decline of Magic*, 128; *Calendar of State Papers, Domestic Series, of the Reign of James I, 1611–1618*, ed. Mary Anne Everett Green (London: Longman, Brown, Green, Longmans, & Roberts, 1858), 438. There is some confusion over when Anne actually had this dream. Agnes Strickland dates it in May and argues that Anne sent a special messenger to James begging him to cut short his visit and return home, which he refused. Strickland, *Lives of the Queens of England from the Norman Conquest*, new and revised edn. (London: George Bells and Sons, 1888), iv, 124.

67. Thomas Birch, *The Court and Times of James the First: Containing a Series of Historical and Confidential Letters* (London: Henry Colburn, 1849), ii, 301; *Calendar of State Papers*, xvii, 444-45. Again there is some discrepancy about when this dream actually occurred. Reverend Mead asserts that Downham had told him that the dream had taken place three years earlier; on the other hand, Lando reports that it was "some months" before his report.

CHAPTER 2

1. *The Diary of Abraham de la Pryme, the Yorkshire Antiquary,* ed. Charles Jackson (Publications of the Surtees Society, vol. 54; Durham, UK: Andrews, 1870), 219-20. De la Pryme got this version of the tale word for word from William Winstanley, *The new help to discourse: or, Wit, mirth, and jollity intermixt with more serious matters. Consisting of pleasant astrological, astronomical, philosophical, grammatical, physical, chyrurgical, historical, moral, and poetical questions and answers. As also histories, poems, songs, epitaphs, epigrams, anagrams, acrosticks, riddles, jests, poesies, complements, &c. With several other varieties intermixt* (London, 1669), 74–76. Sir William Dugdale sent a version of this story to Sir Roger Twisden in a letter dated 29 January 1653. For this letter, see Jennifer Westwood, *Albion: A Guide to Legendary Britain* (London: Granada, 1985), 163. This story is also the subject of a children's book. Gail E. Haley, *Dream Peddler* (New York: Dutton, 1993). See also, Adam Fox, *Oral and Literature Culture in England, 1500–1700* (Oxford, UK: Clarendon Press, 2000), 32-33; and A.J.J. Ratcliff, *A History of Dreams* (Boston: Small, Maynard, 1923), 53–55; A. Roger Ekirch, *At Day's Close: Night in Times Past* (New York: W. W. Norton, 2005), 319; Robert L. van de Castle, *Our Dreaming Mind* (New York: Ballantine Books, 1994), 21-22; "The Swaffam Tinker," in *The World of Dreams,* ed. R. L. Woods (New York: Random House, 1974), 378–80.

2. Though this story is most often told about Swaffham, there are variants told about other towns in England, Ireland, and Wales. Variants of this story can

also be found in German, Jewish, Japanese, and Middle Eastern folklore, and it is one of the *Thousand and One Nights*. It is listed as "The Man Who Became Rich through a Dream" Aarne-Thompson type 1645 folktale. For more versions, see D. L. Ashliman, ed., "The Man Who Became Rich through a Dream: Folktales of Type 1645." Available from: http://www .pitt.edu/~dash/type1645.html#swaffham [Accessed: 4 Dec 2007]; Story Lovers, "Pedlar of Swaffham." Available from: http://www.story-lovers.com/listspedlarswaffham.html [Accessed: 21 Nov 2007].

3. Just Tour Limited, "Swaffham Norfolk Tourist Information Guide," Tour UK. Available from: http://www.touruk.co.uk/norfolk/nor_swaf.html [Accessed: 9 Nov 2007].

4. Frank Seafield, *The Literature and Curiosities of Dreams* (London: Chapman and Hall, 1865), 154–57; Local Authority Publishing, "Swaffham Town Council Official Guide," Swaffham Town Council Official Guide. Available from: http://www.localauthoritypublishing.co.uk/councils/swaffham/history .html [Accessed: 9 Nov 2007].

5. Isaac Ambrose, *Ministration of, and Communion with Angels* in *The Compleat Works* (London, 1674), 129.

6. Richard L. Greaves, *Dublin's Merchant-Quaker: Anthony Sharp and the Community of Friends, 1643–1707* (Palo Alto, CA: Stanford University Press, 1998), 242.

7. For more on Artemidorus and the impact of his work, see S.R.F. Price, "The Future of Dreams: From Freud to Artemidorus," *Past and Present* 113 (1986), 3–37.

8. For more on Hill, see Francis R. Johnson, "Thomas Hill: An Elizabethan Huxley," *The Huntington Library Quarterly* 4 (1944), 329–51.

9. Jacques Le Goff, *The Medieval Imagination*, trans. Arthur Goldhammer (Chicago: University of Chicago Press, 1988), 199.

10. William Lilly, *A groats worth of wit for a penny, or, The interpretation of dreams* (London, 1670), 5.

11. Alice Wandesford Thornton, *The autobiography of Mrs. Alice Thornton, of East Newton, Co. York*, ed. Charles Jackson (Durham, UK: Published for the Surtees Society by Andrew, 1875), 123.

12. Anne Clifford Herbert, *Countess of Pembroke, Lives of Lady Anne Clifford Countess of Dorset, Pembroke and Montgomery (1590–1676) and of her parents*, with an introduction by J. P. Gibson (London: Printed for Presentation to the members of the Roxburghe Club by Hazell, Watson and Viney, 1916), 23–24.

13. C. H. Herford and Percy Simpson, eds., *Ben Jonson* (Oxford, UK: Clarendon Press, 1925), i, 139–40. See also David Lee Miller, "Writing the Specular Son: Jonson, Freud, Lacan, and the (K)not of Masculinity," *Desire in the Renaissance: Psychoanalysis and Literature*, ed. Valeria Finucci and Regina Schwartz (Princeton, NJ: Princeton University Press, 1994), 233–60 and David Riggs, *Ben Jonson: A Life* (Cambridge, MA: Harvard University Press, 1989), 95–96.

14. Francis Bacon, *Novum Organum: With Other Parts of The Great Instauration*, trans. and ed. Peter Urback and John Gibson (Chicago: Open Court, 1994), 58; *The Works of Francis Bacon*, collected and edited by James Spedding, Robert Leslie Ellis, and Douglas Denon Heath (London: Longman, 1857), ii, 666–67.

15. Thomas Heywood, *The Hierarchie of the blessed Angells. Their names, orders and Offices. The fall of Lucifer with his Angells* (London: Printed by Adam Islip, 1635), 223.

16. Gervase Holles, *Memorials of the Holles Family, 1493–1656*, ed. A. C. Wood (Camden Third Series, vol. LV; London: Camden Society, 1937), 190, 230, 231.

17. Robert Burton, *The Anatomy of Melancholy*, ed. Thomas C. Faulkner and Nicolas K. Kiessling (Oxford, UK: Clarendon Press, 1989–2000), i, 84, 111, 127, 138, 140, 156; Robert Ashley, British Library, Sloane MSS 2131, fols. 16–20; Masten, "The Interpretation of Dreams," 163; William Basse, *A helpe to Discourse. Or, A misselany of merriment Consisting of witty philosophicall, and astronomicall questions and ansvvers. As also, of epigrams, epitaphs, riddles, and iests. Together with The country-mans counsellour, next his yearely oracle or prognostication to consult with. Contayning diuers necessary rules and obseruations, of much vse and consequence being knowne* (London, 1623), 330. There are many other examples, including Moise Amyraut, *A discourse concerning the divine dreams mention'd in Scripture, together with the marks and characters by which they might be distinguish'd from vain delusions*, in a letter to Monsieur Gaches, by Moses Amyraldus, trans. Ja. Lowde (London, 1676), 22.

18. Richard Saunders, *Physiognomie* (1653, 2nd edn. London, 1671), 260.

19. Philip Goodwin, *The mystery of dreames, historically discoursed* (London, 1658), 348.

20. Le Goff, *Medieval Imagination*, 202; Ekirch, *At Day's Close*, 322.

21. Reginald Scot, *The Discovery of Witchcraft* (London, 1584), 104; John Palsgrave, Gulielmus Gnaphaeus, and P.L. Carver, *Acolastus: The Comedy of Acolastus Translated from Discourse of the Sight: Of Melancholike Diseases; of Rheumes, and of Old Age from the Latin of Fullonius*, ed. P. L. Carver (London: H. Milford, Oxford University Press, 1937), 66; W. Vaughan, *Directions for Health, Naturall and Artificiall*, the seventh edition reviewed by the author (London, 1633), 163.

22. Lauren Kassell, *Medicine & Magic: In Elizabethan London; Simon Forman; Astrologer, Alchemist, & Physician* (Oxford, UK: Clarendon Press, 2005), 33, 59, 205; *The Diaries of John Dee,* ed. Edward Fenton (Oxfordshire, UK: Day Books, 1998), 288; Barbara Howard Traister, *The Notorious Astrological Physician of London: Works and Days of Simon Forman* (Chicago: University of Chicago Press, 2001), 110.

23. Derek Parker, *Familiar to All: William Lilly and Astrology in the Seventeenth Century* (London: Jonathan Cape, 1973), 162.

24. Michael Hunter, "Ashmole, Elias (1617–1692)," *Oxford Dictionary of National Biography* (Oxford University Press, Sep 2004); online edn., May 2006. Available from: http://0-www.oxforddnb.com.library.unl.edu:80/view/article/764 [Accessed: 9 Feb 2007].

25. C. H. Josten, ed., *Elias Ashmole (1617–1692): His Autobiographical and Historical Notes, his Correspondence, and Other Contemporary Sources Relating to his Life and Work* (Oxford, UK: Clarendon Press, 1966), ii, 369.

26. Gonzalo, *The Divine Dreamer: or, A Short Treatise Discovering the True Effect and Power of Dreams* (London, 1641), n.p.

27. Ella Mary Leather, *The Folk-Lore of Herefordshire* (Hereford, UK: Jakeman and Carver, 1912), 64.

28. John Symonds Udal, *Dorsetshire Folklore* (Hertford, UK: Stephen Austins and Sons, 1922), 276; T. F. Thiselfton-Dyer, *Folklore of Women* (Chicago: A. C. McClurg, 1906), 223.

29. Saunders, *Physiognomie*, 229.

30. Thomas Hill, *The Pleasant Art of the Interpretation of Dreams* (London, 1576), n.p.

31. M. Andreas Laurentius, *A Discourse of the Sight: of Melancholike Diseases; of Rheumes, and of Old Age*, trans. Richard Surphlet (1599), with an introduction by Sanford V. Larkey (Oxford, UK: Oxford University Press, 1938), 99–100.

32. *Culpeper's English Physician; and Complete Herbal*, ed. E. Sibly (London: Lewis and Hamblin, 1807), ii, 4.

33. Wilhelm Adolf Scribonius, *Naturall Philosophy: or, A description of the world, and of the severall creatures therein contained viz. of angels, of mankinde, of the heavens, the starres, the planets, the foure elements, with their order, nature and government: as also of minerals, mettals, plants, and precious stones; with their colours, formes, and virtues*, trans. Daniel Widdowes (London, 1631), 52.

34. Thomas Wright, *The Passions of the Minde in Generall* (London, 1620), 111.

35. These dream books were very popular. *A Helpe to Discourse* went through eight editions between 1619 and 1682 (London, 1623), 208. *The Optick Glasse* also went through four editions in the seventeenth century. Thomas Walkington, *The optick glasse of humors or The touchstone of a golden temperature, or the Philosophers stone to make a golden temper Wherein the foure complections sanguine, cholericke, phligmaticke, melancholicke are succinctly painted forth and their externall intimates laid open to the purblind eye of ignorance it selfe, by which euery one may iudge, of what complection he is, and answerably learne what is most sutable to his nature, 1631*, a photoprint with an introduction by John A. Popplestone and Marion White McPherson (Delmar, NY: Scholars' Facsimiles & Reprints, 1981), 148; Levinus Lemnius, *The touchstone of complexions. Generallye appliable, expedient and profitable for all such, as be desirous & carefull of their bodylye health. Contayning most easie rules & ready tokens, whereby every one may perfectly try, and throughly know, as well the exacte state, habite, disposition, and constitution, of his owne body outwardly: as also the inclinations, affections motions, & desires of his mynd inwardly. First written in Latine, by Leuine Lemnie, and now englished by Thomas Newton* (London, 1576). This book went through three editions. Nicolas Abraham de la Framboisiere, *An easy method to know the causes and signs of the humour most ruleth in the body* (London, 1640), 7, 8. The quote about women is on page 7.

36. Laurentius, *Discourse of the Sight*, xv.

37. Burton, *Anatomy of Melancholy*, 242.

38. Laurentius, *Discourse of the Sight*, 82, 98. See also Lawrence Babb, *The Elizabethan Malady: A Study of Melancholia in English Literature from 1580 to 1642* (East Lansing: Michigan State College Press, 1951), 31, 191.

39. Thomas Nash, *The terrors of the night. Or, A Discourse of apparitions* (London, 1594), C4v.

40. Babb, *Elizabethan Malady*, 29.

41. Burton, *Anatomy of Melancholy*, i, 84, 111, 127, 138, 140, 156; Pierre de Loyer, *A Treatise of Specters or straunge Sights, Visions and Apparitions*

appearing sensibly unto men. Wherein is delivered, the Nature of Spirites, Angels, and Divels: their power and properties: as also of Witches, Sorcerers, Enchanters, and such like. Newly done out of French into English by Zacharie Jones (London, 1605), 101.

42. Saunders, *Physiognomie*, 227, 229.

43. Steven R. Fischer, *The Complete Medieval Dream Book* (Berne: Peter Lang, 1982), 74.

44. Walkington, *The Opticke Glasse*, 17, viii.

45. Walkington, *The Opticke Glasse*, 146–47.

46. Timothy Bright, *A Treatise on Melancholie,* reproduced from the 1586 edition printed by Thomas Vautrollier, with an introduction by Hardin Craig (New York: Published for the Facsimile Text Society by Columbia University Press, 1940), 117, 124.

47. Saunders, *Physiognomie*, 225.

48. Nash, *Terrors of the Night*, D3v, E4.

49. Charles Nicholl, *A Cup of News: The Life of Thomas Nashe* (London: Routledge & Kegan Paul, 1984), 150.

50. Nash, *Terrors of the Night*, C3v, C4v, E3v, E4.

51. Nash, *Terrors of the Night*, B3, C3v.

52. Owen Felltham, "Of Dreams," in *Resolves Divine, Morall and Politicall* (London: J. M. Dent, 1904), 145–47; John Evans, *Hesperides or The Muses Garden,* compiled ca. 1655–1659, V.b.93. This manuscript is held at the Folger Shakespeare Library.

53. Hieronymus Brunschwig, *A most excellent and perfecte homish apothecarye or homely physik booke, for all the grefes and diseases of the bodye.* Translated out the Almaine speche into English by Ihon Hollybush (Collen, 1561), 10a; Adam Fox, *Oral and Literate Culture in England, 1500–1700* (Oxford, UK: Clarendon Press, 2000), 195.

54. Scribonius, *Naturall philosophy*, 53.

55. James N. Wise, *Sir Thomas Browne's Religio Medici and Two Seventeenth-Century Critics* (Columbia: University of Missouri Press, 1973), 15.

56. *The Works of Sir Thomas Browne,* ed. Charles Sayle (Edinburgh, UK: John Grant, 1927), i, 105; *The Works of Sir Thomas Browne,* iii, 550, 553; Reid Barbour, *Literature and Religious Culture in Seventeenth-Century England* (Cambridge, UK: Cambridge University Press 2002), 115–16.

57. Goodwin, *mystery of dreames,* 108.

58. Eldred Jones, *The Elizabethan Image of Africa* (Charlottesville: Published for the Folger Shakespeare Library by the University Press of Virginia), 5.

59. Burton, *Anatomy of Melancholy,* 393.

60. Thomas Nicols, *Arcula Gemmea, or, A Cabinet of Jewels* (London, 1653), 51.

61. *English Medieval Lapidaries,* ed. Joan Evans and Mary S. Serjeantson. Early English Text Society, no. 190 (London: Humphrey Milford, Oxford University Press, 1933), 119; Jean de Renou, *A medical Dispensatory, containing the whole Body of Physick,* trans. Richard Tomlinson (London, 1657), 415, 419.

62. Vaughan, *Directions for Health,* 26.

63. Edward Topsell, *The historie of serpents,* 2nd edn. (London, 1608), 173.

64. *A Miscellaneous Collections of Recipes—Household, Medical & Veterinary—* compiled ca.1600 and bound together with an index ca. 1750, 12vol., 14vls;

The Secrets of Alexis: Containing many excellent Remedies Against Divers Diseases, Wounds and other Accidents (London, 1615), 132.

65. Nash, *Terrors of the Night*, 237.
66. *Works of Sir Thomas Browne*, iii, 553.
67. Gonzalo, *Divine Dreamer;* Burton, *Anatomy of Melancholy*, i, 138–39.
68. Thomas Cogan, *The haven of health chiefely gathered for the comfort of students, and consequently of all those that have a care of their health, amplified upon five words of Hippocrates* (London, 1584), 49. Subsequent editions were published in 1584, 1588, 1589, 1596, and 1605. There were also two editions, in 1612 and 1636, after Cogan's death in 1607.
69. William Turner, *A Book of Wines*, 1568, ed. Sanford V. Larkey and Philip M. Wagner (New York: Scholars' Facsimiles & Reprints, 1941), 12.
70. Henry Butts, *Dyets Dry Dinner* (London, 1599), 7r.
71. Judith Cook, *Dr Simon Forman: A Most Notorious Physician* (London: Chatto & Windus, 2001), 165.
72. Le Goff, *Medieval Imagination*, 209.
73. Burton, *Anatomy of Melancholy*, i, 611.
74. Burton, *Anatomy of Melancholy*, i, 414.
75. Gonzalo, *Divine Dreamer*, Bv.
76. Richard Brathwaite, *A strange metamorphosis of man, transformed into a wildernesse Deciphered in characters* (London, 1634), chap. 37, 12.
77. [(Ephemeris for 1651, G3v) in ODNB]. Patrick Curry, "Culpeper, Nicholas (1616–1654)," *Oxford Dictionary of National Biography* (Oxford University Press, 2004). Available from: http://www.oxforddnb.com/view/article/6882 [Accessed: 7 Apr 2007].
78. Gent J. B., *Faire in Spittle Fields, whereall the Knick Knacks of Astrology are Exposed to open sale, to all that will see for their Love, and buy for their money* (London, 1652), 6.
79. *Nicholas Culpeper's English Physician and Complete Herbal*, ii, 177.
80. *Nicholas Culpeper's English Physician and Complete Herbal*, i, 291, 297–308, 302.
81. William Turner, *The first and seconde partes of the herbal of William Turner Doctor in Phisick, lately ouersene, corrected and enlarged with the thirde parte*, 2nd edn. (Collen, 1568), ii, 84.
82. *Nicholas Culpeper's English Physician and Complete Herbal*, ii, 178.
83. *Secrets of Alexis*, 132.
84. Leather, *Folk-Lore of Herefordshire*, 120.
85. *English Medieval Lapidaries*, ed. Joan Evans and Mary S. Serjeantson. Early English Text Society, no. 190 (London: Humphrey Milford, Oxford University Press, 1933), 122.
86. "A Letter to a Friend upon occasion of the Death of His Intimate Friend," in *The Works of Sir Thomas Browne*, i, 380–81.
87. Charles Carlton, "The Dream Life of Archbishop Laud," *History Today* 36 (Dec 1986), 11.
88. Simonds D'Ewes, *The Autobiography and Correspondence of Sir Simonds D'Ewes*, ed. James Orchard Halliwell (London: Richard Bentley, 1845), i, 37–38.
89. Vittorio Gabrieli, *Sir Kenelm Digby: un Inglese italianato nell'età della Controriforma* (Roma: Edizioni di storia e letteratura, 1957), 241–42, 243.

90. *The Diary of Bulstrode Whitelocke, 1605–1675,* ed. Ruth Spalding (Oxford, UK: Published for the British Academy by Oxford University Press, 1990), 238–39.

91. Bruce Gordon, "Malevolent Ghosts and Ministering Angels: Apparitions and Pastoral Care in the Swiss Reformation," in *The Place of the Dead: Death and Remembrance in Late Medieval and Early Modern Europe* (Cambridge, UK: Cambridge University Press, 2000), 97.

92. Saunders, *Physiognomie,* 260.

93. Le Goff, *Medieval Imagination,* 211. Penance for seeking dream interpretation was established at the Council of Ankara, in the year 314 AD.

94. Nicholl, *Cup of News,* 197.

95. A. L. Rowse, *Simon Forman: Sex and Society in Shakespeare's Age* (London: Weidenfeld and Nicolson, 1974), 268; Cook, *Dr Simon Forman,* 3; Kassell, *Medicine & Magic,* 15.

96. *The Works of Sir Thomas Browne,* iii, 553–54.

97. Rowse, *Simon Forman,* 66; Cook, *Dr Simon Forman,* 98.

98. Kassell, *Medicine & Magic,* 58; Rowse, *Simon Forman,* 181; Traister, *Notorious Astrological Physician of London,* 109.

99. Traister, *Notorious Astrological Physician of London,* 122; Cook, *Dr Simon Forman,* 99.

100. Patricia Crawford and Laura Gowing, eds., *Women's Worlds in Seventeenth-Century England: A Sourcebook* (London and New York: Routledge, 2000), 277.

101. *The Lives of those eminent Antiquaries Elias Ashmole, Esquires and Mr. William Lilly, written by themselves; containing first William Lilly's History of His life and Times, with Notes, by Mr. Ashmole: Secondly Lilly's Life and Death of Charles the First; and lastly, the Life of Elias Ashmole, Esquire, by Way of Diary. With Several Occasional Letters,* ed. Charles Burman, Esquire (London: T. Davies, 1784), 7.

102. *Elias Ashmole,* ed. Josten, 38.

103. Patrick Curry, "Lilly, William (1602–1681)," *Oxford Dictionary of National Biography* (Oxford University Press, 2004). Available from: http://www .oxforddnb.com/view/article/16661 [Accessed: 6 Apr 2007].

104. *Elias Ashmole,* ed. Josten, vol. II, 363n1.

105. *Elias Ashmole,* ed. Josten, vol. II, 381–83.

106. *Elias Ashmole,* ed. Josten, vol. II, 395, 424, 442, 445.

107. *The Diary of Abraham de la Pryme,* 26–27.

Chapter 3

1. Keith Thomas, *Religion and the Decline of Magic* (London: Weidenfeld and Nicolson, 1971), 128; Thomas Cranmer, *The Works of Thomas Cranmer,* ed. Rev. John Edmund Cox (Cambridge, UK: Cambridge University Press, 1844–1846), ii, 43; David G. Selwyn, *The Library of Thomas Cranmer* (Oxford, UK: Oxford Bibliographical Society, 1996), 148. The book was *Paaedictiones siue prognostica,* trans. L. Laurentianus and G. Copus (Paris, 1516).

2. Andre Gerhard, *The true tryall and examination of a mans owne self,* trans. Thomas Newton (London, 1586), 34–35.

3. Laurence Vaux, *A catechisme or christian doctrine necesssarie for children and ignorante people* (Louvain, 1583), sig. CIIIIV.

4. Walter Stephens, *Demon Lovers: Witchcraft, Sex, and the Crisis of Belief* (Chicago and London: University of Chicago Press, 2000), 158.

5. Richard Day, *A Book of Christian Prayers, collected out of the auncie[n]t writers, and best learned in our tyme, worthy to be read with an earnest mynde of all Christians, in these daungerous and troublesome dayes, that God for Christes sake will yet still be mercyfull unto us* (London, 1578), 9–10.

6. John Foxe, *Acts and Monuments [. . .] The Variorum Edition* [online] (Online, Sheffield 2004), 199, 201. Available from: http://www.hrionline. shef.ac.uk/foxe/ [Accessed: 20 Nov 2007].

7. John Foxe, *Acts and Monuments [. . .] The Variorum Edition* [online] (Online, Sheffield 2004), 333. Available from: http://www.hrionline .shef.ac.uk/foxe/ [Accessed: 20 Nov 2007].

8. John Foxe, *Acts and Monuments [. . .] The Variorum Edition* [online] (Online, Sheffield 2004), 1715–16. Available from: http://www.hrionline .shef.ac.uk/foxe/ [Accessed: 20 Nov 2007].

9. D. Andrew Penny, "Bradford, John (ca. 1510–1555)," *Oxford Dictionary of National Biography* (Oxford University Press, 2004). Available from: http://0-www.oxforddnb.com.library.unl.edu:80/view/article/3175 [Accessed: 23 Aug 2007].

10. John Foxe, Acts and Monuments [. . .] (1576 edition) [online] (hriOnline, Sheffield 2004), 160–65. Available from: http://www.hrionline.shef.ac.uk/ foxe/ [Accessed: 20 Nov 2007].

11. John Foxe, *Acts and Monuments [. . .] The Variorum Edition* [online] (hrOnline, Sheffield 2004), 2072. Available from: http://www.hrionline.shef .ac.uk/foxe/ [Accessed: 20 Nov 2007].

12. John Foxe. Acts and Monuments [. . .] (1576 edition) [online] (hriOnline, Sheffield), 1663. Available from: http://www.hrionline.shef.ac.uk/foxe/ [Accessed: 20 Nov 2007].

13. Arthur F. Marotti, "The Catholic Martyrdom Account," in *Print, Manuscript, and Performance: The Changing Relations of the Media in Early Modern England,* ed. Arthur F. Marotti and Michael D. Bristol (Columbus: Ohio State University Press, 2000), 176; John Hungerford Pollen, *Acts of English martyrs hitherto unpublished* (London: Burns and Oates, 1891), 56.

14. Philip Goodwin, *The mystery of dreames, historically discoursed* (London, 1658), 263, 264–65, 276, 296.

15. David Hill, "Dreams," Richard J. Clifford, "Joseph (son of Jacob)" in *The Oxford Companion to the Bible,* ed. Bruce M. Metzger and Michael D. Coogan (Oxford, NY and Oxford, UK: Oxford University Press, 1993), 171, 382–83.

16. Goodwin, *mystery of dreames,* A4, 67–68.

17. W. Patten, Londoner, *The Expedicion into Scotlande of the most woorthely fortunate prince Edward, Duke of Soomerset, uncle unto our most noble sovereign lord the kinges majestie Edward the VI* (London, 1548), 83.

18. Patten, *Expedicion,* 81, 82, 83.

19. Patten, *Expedicion,* 86, 87.

20. John Foxe, *Acts and Monuments [. . .] The Variorum Edition* [online] (hrOnline, Sheffield 2004), 1814. Available from: http://www.hrionline .shef.ac.uk/foxe/ [Accessed: 20 Nov 2007].

21. Arise Evans, *An Eccho to the Book, called A Voyce from Heaven* (London, 1653), 8, 10.

22. Elizabeth Allen, "Everard, John (ca. 1584–1640/41)," *Oxford Dictionary of National Biography* [online] (Oxford University Press, 2004). Available from: http://www.oxforddnb.com/view/article/8998 [Accessed: 1 May 2007].

23. Goodwin, *mystery of dreames*, 222.

24. Anthony Cade, *A sermon of the nature of conscience which may well be tearmed, a tragedy of conscience in her,* 2nd edn. (London, 1621), 33. Cade was very concerned with the issue of conscience, and he continued to work on his notions of it by it publishing another sermon on the same topic in 1636—a sermon that was republished in 1639 and then again in 1661 (twenty years after his death).

25. Goodwin, *mystery of dreames*, 22.

26. Howard, *defensative against the poyson of supposed prophecies*, 42v.

27. John Webster, *Displaying of Supposed Witchcraft*, 288–89.

28. King James Bible, Matthew 1:19–1:20; Matthew 2:13, 2:19. Webster, *Displaying of Supposed Witchcraft*, 288–89. Goodwin also mentions the dream, *mystery of dreames*, 269.

29. Goodwin, *mystery of dreames*, A4, 209, 210.

30. Goodwin, *mystery of dreames*, 86, 196–97, 198, 327–29, 350.

31. Goodwin, *mystery of dreames*, 97.

32. Goodwin, *mystery of dreames*, 37.

33. Thomas Cooper, *Mystery of Witch-Craft*, 146.

34. Goodwin, *mystery of dreames*, 95–96, 100, 106, 109, 124, 125, 128.

35. John Foxe, *Acts and Monuments [. . .] The Variorum Edition* [online] (hrOnline, Sheffield 2004), 1583, 1816. Available from: http://www.hrion line.shef.ac.uk/foxe/ [Accessed: 20 Nov 2007].

36. Goodwin, *mystery of dreames*, 227–28.

37. Adam Fox, *Oral and Literate Culture in England, 1500–1700* (Oxford, UK: Clarendon Press, 2000), 195–96; John Bunyan, *Grace Abounding to the Chief of Sinners,* ed. Roger Sharrock (Oxford, UK: Oxford University Press, 1962), 6, 49–50. For more on Spira, see Michael Macdonald, "The Fearefull Estate of Francis Spira: Narrative, Identity, and Emotion in Early Modern England," *Journal of British Studies* 31, no. 1 (1992), 32–61.

38. Wilhelm Adolf Scribonius, *Naturall Philosophy: or, A description of the world, and of the severall creatures therein contained,* trans. Daniel Widdowes (London, 1631), 1–2.

39. Thomas Hill, *The moste pleasuante arte of the Interpretation of dreames* (London, 1576), n.p.; Goodwin, *mystery of dreames*, 272.

40. Joseph Hall, *The invisible world, bound with The great mystery of godliness* (London, 1652), 143.

41. Moise Amyraut, *A discourse concerning the divine dreams mention'd in Scripture, together with the marks and characters by which they might be distinguish'd from vain delusions,* trans. Ja. Lowde (London, 1676), 19.

42. BL, Sloane MSS 2131, fols. 16–20.

43. Lauren Kassell, *Medicine & Magic in Elizabethan London: Simon Forman: Astrologer, Alchemist, & Physician* (Oxford, UK: Clarendon Press, 2005), 55.

44. Alan MacFarlane, *The Family Life of Ralph Josselin, A Seventeenth-Century Clergyman: An Essay in Historical Anthropology* (Cambridge, UK: Cambridge University Press, 1970), 165–66.

45. *The Diary of Ralph Josselin, 1616–1683,* ed. Alan MacFarlane (London: Published for the British Academy by the Oxford University Press, 1976), 237, 335.

46. Vavasour Powell, *Spirituall experiences, of sundry beleevers Held forth by them at severall solemne meetings, and conferences to that end. With the recommendation of the sound, spiritual, and savoury worth of them, to the sober and spirituall reader, by Vavasor Powel, minister of the gospel* (London, 1653), 357–68.

47. Henry Jessey, *The Exceeding Riches of Grace Advanced By the Spirit of Grace, in an Empty Nothing Creature, viz. Mris. Sarah Wight, Lately hopeles and restles, her soule dwelling as far from Peace or hopes of Mercy, as ever was any. Now hopeful, and joyfull in the Lord, that hath caused LIGHT to shine out of DARKNES* (London, 1647), 148–50.

48. Paul S. Seaver, *Wallington's World* (Stanford: Stanford University Press, 1985), 186.

49. Josten, ed., *Elias Ashmole*, ii, 386.

50. John Foxe, *Acts and Monuments [. . .] The Variorum Edition* [online] (hrOnline, Sheffield 2004), 2012. Available from: http://www.hrionline.shef.ac.uk/foxe/ [Accessed: 20 Nov 2007].

51. Margery Kempe, *The Book of Margery Kempe: A New Translation, Contexts, Criticism,* trans. and ed. Lynn Staley (New York: Norton, 2001), 6–8.

52. Sylvia Bowerbank, *Speaking for Nature: Women and Ecologies of Early Modern England* (Baltimore: Johns Hopkins University Press, 2004), 199–220.

53. Patricia Crawford, *Women and Religion in England 1500–1720* (London: Routledge, 1993), 112, 115.

54. David Booy, *Autobiographical Writings by Early Quaker Women* (Aldershot, UK: Ashgate, 2004), 52, 60–61. For more on Evans, see Stefano Villani, "Evans, Katharine (ca. 1618–1692)," *Oxford Dictionary of National Biography* [online] (Oxford, UK: Oxford University Press, 2004). Available from: http://0-www.oxforddnb.com.library.unl.edu:80/view/article/45814 [Accessed: 11 Aug 2007].

55. John Rogers, *Ohel Ohel or Beth-shemesh. A tabernacle for the sun: or Irenicum evangelicum. An idea of church-discipline, in the theorick and practick parts; which come forth first into the world as bridegroom and bride, hand in hand; by whom you will have the totum essentiale of a true Gospel-Church state, according to Christ's rules and order, left us when he ascended. In which you may finde the hidden mystery of whole Christ, in head, neck, and body. Hidden in former ages from the sons of men* (London, 1653), 412–13.

56. *Experiences in the Life of Mary Penington* (written by Herself), edited with introduction and notes by Norman Penney (Philadelphia: Biddle Press, 1911; new edition 1992 with preface by Gil Skidmore), x, 22–23.

57. Marie H. Loughlin, "Penington, Mary [*other married name* Mary Springett, Lady Springett] (*bap.* 1623, *d.* 1682)," *Oxford Dictionary of National Biography* [online] (Oxford, UK: Oxford University Press, Sep 2004). Available from: http://0-www.oxforddnb.com.library.unl.edu:80/view/article/45819 [Accessed: 7 Aug 2007].

58. *Experiences in the Life of Mary Penington,* 48–52.

59. Douglas Gwyn, *Seekers Found: Atonement in Early Quaker Experience* (Walingford, PA: Pendle Hill, 2000), 266.

60. For more on Penington's dreams, see Linda S. Coleman, "Gender, Sect, and Circumstances: Quaker Mary Penington's Many Voices," in *Women's Life-Writing: Finding Voice/Building Community,* ed. Linda S. Coleman

(Bowling Green, OH: Bowling Green State University Popular Press, 1997), 93–107.

61. *Experiences in the Life of Mary Penington,* 48–52.

62. Henry Jenkyns, ed., *The Remains of Thomas Cranmer, D.D. Archbishop of Canterbury* (Oxford, UK: Oxford University Press, 1833), ii, 194.

63. Richard Baxter, *The Certainty of the World of Spirits, full evinced by unquestionable histories of Apparitions and Witchcrafts* (London, 1691), 175.

64. Francis Hutchinson, *An historical essay concerning witchcraft* (London, 1718), 102.

65. *The most strange and admirable discouerie of the three witches of Warboys arraigned, conuicted and executed at the last Assises at Huntington, for the bewitching of the fiue daughters of Robert Throckmorton Esquier, and diuers other persons, with sundrie diuelish and grieuous torments. And also for the bewitching to death of the Lady Crumwell, the like hath not bene heard of in this age* (London, 1593), n.p.

66. Richard Bernard, *A guide to grandjury men divided into two bookes: in the first, is the authors best advice to them what to doe, before they bring in a billa vera in cases of witchcraft, with a Christian direction to such as are too much given upon every crosse to thinke themselves bewitched. In the second, is a treatise touching witches good and bad, how they may be knowne, evicted, condemned, with many particulars tending thereunto* (London, 1627), 190–91.

67. *The Most strange and admirable discouerie of the three Witches of Warboys, arraigned, convicted, and executed at the last Assises at Huntington, for the bewitching of the five daughters of Robert Throckmorton, Esquire and divers others person, with sundrie Divelish and grievous torments: And also for the bewitching to death of the Lady Crumwell, the like hath not been heard of in this age* (London, 1593), n.p.

68. Bernard, *Guide to grandjury men,* 190.

69. Burton, *Anatomy of Melancholy,* 465.

70. John Brinley, *A discovery of the impostures of witches and astrologers* (London, 1680), 25–26; Hutchinson, *Historical essay concerning witchcraft,* 103.

71. Henry More, *An Antidote Against Atheisme* (London, 1653), 116.

72. Thomas Potts, *The vvonderfull discouerie of witches in the countie of Lancaster VVith the arraignement and triall of nineteene notorious witches, at the assizes and general gaole deliuerie, holden at the castle of Lancaster, upon Munday, the seuenteenth of August last, 1612* (London, 1613), B3.

73. David Kathman, "Stanley, Ferdinando, fifth earl of Derby (ca. 1559–1594)," *Oxford Dictionary of National Biography* (Oxford University Press, Sep 2004); online edn., May 2006. Available from: http://0-www.oxforddnb .com.library.unl.edu:80/view/article/26269 [Accessed: 9 Sep 2007].

74. The descendants of Katherine Grey and Edward Seymour were tainted with illegitimacy, since their marriage could not be proven.

75. Christopher Devlin, "The Earl and the Alchemist," *The Month* 1, no. 9 (1953), 103, 165 [whole article 25–38, 92–104, 153–66].

76. John Stow, *The annales of England faithfully collected out of the most autenticall authors, records, and other monuments of antiquitie, lately corrected, encreased, and continued, from the first inhabitation vntill this present yeere 1600* (London, 1600), 307.

77. Devlin, "The Earl and the Alchemist," 163.

78. Hutchinson, *historical essay concerning witchcraft,* 97–98.

79. Brian P. Levack, *The Witch-hunt in Early Modern Europe* (London: Longman, 1987), 77. Diane Purkiss, *The Witch in History: Early Modern and Twentieth-Century Representations* (London: Routledge, 1996), 234.

80. Christina Hole, *Witchcraft in England* (Totowa, NJ: Rowman and Littlefield, 1977), 20.

81. Hutchinson, *historical essay concerning witchcraft*, 53.

82. Purkiss, *Witch in History*, 235; Gail Kern Paster, *The Body Embarrassed: Drama and the Disciplines of Shame in Early Modern England* (Ithaca, NY: Cornell University Press, 1993), 254.

83. H. R. Ellis Davidson, "Hostile Magic in the Icelandic Sagas," in *The Witch Figure: Folklore essays by a group of scholars in England honouring the 75th birthday of Katharine M. Briggs,* ed. Venetia Newall (London and Boston: Routledge and Kegan Paul, 1973), 31.

84. Richard Boulton, *The possibility and reality of magick, sorcery, and witchcraft, demonstrated, or, A vindication of a compleat history of magick, sorcery and witch craft: in answer to Dr. Hutchinson's Historical essay* (London, 1722), 64; Reginald Scot, *The discovery of witchcraft proving that the compacts and contracts of witches with devils and all infernal spirits or familiars are but erroneous novelties and imaginary conceptions: also discovering, how far their power extendeth in killing, tormenting, consuming, or curing the bodies of men, women, children, or animals by charms, philtres, periapts, pentacles, curses, and conjurations: wherein likewise the unchristian practices and inhumane dealings of searchers and witch-tryers upon aged, melancholly, and superstitious people, in extorting confessions by terrors and tortures, and in devising false marks and symptoms, are notably detected* (London, 1665), chap. 8; G. R. Quaife, *Godly Zeal and Furious Rage: The Witch in Early Modern Europe* (London: Croom Helm, 1987), 200, 106; Joseph Granvil, *A blow at modern sadducism in some philosophical considerations about witchcraft* (London, 1668), 4; Richard Bovet, *Pandaemonium, or, The devil's cloyster being a further blow to modern sadduceism, proving the existence of witches and spirits, in a discourse deduced from the fall of the angels, the propagation of Satans kingdom before the flood, the idolatry of the ages after greatly advancing diabolical confederacies, with an account of the lives and transactions of several notorious witches: also, a collection of several authentick relations of strange apparitions of daemons and spectres, and fascinations of witches, never before printed* (London, 1684), 32.

CHAPTER 4

1. John Stow, *The Chronicle of England* (London, 1580), 602.

2. Stow, *Chronicle of England,* 627.

3. Christopher Devlin, "The Earl and the Alchemist," *The Month* 1, no. 9 (1953), 27.

4. All Shakespeare quotations are from *The Complete Works of Shakespeare,* ed. David Bevington, 4th edn. (New York: Harper Collins, 1992).

5. Nicholas Grene, *Shakespeare's Serial History Plays* (Cambridge, UK: Cambridge University Press, 2002), 140.

6. Robert K. Presson, "Two Types of Dreams in Elizabethan Drama, and Their Heritage: Somnium Animale and the Prick-of-Conscience," *Studies in English Literature, 1500–1900* 7 (1967), 249.

7. For more on the parallels between the Duchess of Gloucester and Lady Macbeth, see Nina Levine, "The Case of Eleanor Cobham: Authorizing History in *2 Henry VI*," *Shakespeare Studies* 22, no. 10 (1994), 104–21; Naomi C. Liebler and Lisa Scancella Shea, "Shakespeare's Queen Margaret: Unruly or Unruled," in *Henry VI: Critical Essays,* ed. Thomas Pendleton (New York: Routlege, 2001), 84–85.

8. Grene, *Shakespeare's Serial History Plays,* 141.

9. *The Mirror for Magistrates,* ed. Lily B. Campbell (Cambridge, UK: Cambridge University Press, 1938; republished New York: Barnes & Noble, 1960), 441.

10. *Mirror for Magistrates,* 262. For more on *The Mirror for Magistrates,* see Paul Budra, *A mirror for magistrates and the de casibus tradition* (Toronto: University of Toronto Press, 2000).

11. Emrys Jones, *The Origins of Shakespeare* (Oxford, UK: Clarendon Press, 1977), 205, 207.

12. Thomas More, *The History of King Richard III and Selections from the English and Latin Poems,* ed. Richard S. Sylvester (New Haven, CT: Yale University Press, 1976); Sir Richard Baker, *A Chronicle of the kings of England from the time of the Romans Government unto the Death of King James* (London: George Sawbridge, 1674), 223.

13. Baker, *Chronicle of the kings of England,* 223; Raphael Holinshed, *The Chronicles of England, Scotland and Ireland* (London, 1587), iii, 723.

14. More, *History of King Richard III,* 89, 90.

15. Baker, *Chronicle of the Kings of England,* 227.

16. Holinshed, *Chronicles,* iii, 755.

17. Baker, *Chronicle of the Kings of England,* 233.

18. Marjorie B. Garber, *Dream in Shakespeare: From Metaphor to Metamorphosis* (New Haven, CT: Yale University Press, 1974), 18–19.

19. John Fisher, *There after foloweth a mornynge remembraunce had at the moneth mynde of the noble prynces margarete countesse of Rychemonde & Darbye moder unto kynge Henry the Vii. & granddame to oure soverayne lorde that nowe is upon whose soule almighty god have mercy* (London, 1509), 4.

20. Michael K. Jones and Malcolm G. Underwood, "Beaufort, Margaret, countess of Richmond and Derby (1443–1509)," *Oxford Dictionary of National Biography* (Oxford University Press, 2004). Available from: http://0-www .oxforddnb.com.library.unl.edu:80/view/article/1863 [Accessed: 21 Oct 2007]; Michael K. Jones and Malcolm G. Underwood, *The King's Mother: Lady Margaret Beaufort, Countess of Richmond and Derby* (Cambridge, UK: Cambridge University Press, 1992), 37–38. See also, *English works of John Fisher, Bishop of Rochester (1469–1535): sermons and other writings, 1520–1535,* ed. Cecilia A. Hatt (Oxford, NY: Oxford University Press, 2002), 8, 15; Linda Simon, *Of Virtue Rare: Margaret Beaufort, Matriarch of the House of Tudor* (Boston: Houghton Mifflin, 1982), 20.

21. Michael J. Bennett, "Simnel, Lambert (*b.* 1476/7, *d.* after 1534)," *Oxford Dictionary of National Biography* (Oxford University Press, Sep 2004); online edn., May 2006. Available from: http://0-www.oxforddnb.com.library .unl.edu:80/view/article/25569 [Accessed: 21 Oct 2007].

22. Pedro de Ayala to Ferdinand and Isabella, 26 March 1499, *Calendar of Letters, Despatches, and State Papers, Relating to the negotiations between*

England and Spain (London: Longman, Green, Longman, & Roberts, 1862), i, 206.

23. Edward Hall, *Chronicle* (London: J. Johnson, 1809), 490.

24. *Great Chronicle of London,* ed. A. H. Thomas and I. D. Thornley (London: G. W. Jones, 1938), 289; J. Gunn, "Wilford, Ralph (ca. 1479–1499)," *Oxford Dictionary of National Biography* (Oxford University Press, 2004). Available from: http://0-www.oxforddnb.com.library.unl.edu:80/view/article/30094 [Accessed: 22 Oct 2007]

25. Hall, *Chronicle,* 490; *The Anglica Historia of Polydore Vergil, A.D. 1485–1537,* edited with a translation by Denys Hay (London: Royal Historical Society, 1950), 117.

26. Francis Bacon, *History of the Reign King Henry VII,* ed. J. Lawson Lumby (Cambridge, UK: Cambridge University Press, 1880), 177; Baker, *Chronicles of the Kings of England,* 152; Stow, *Chronicle of England,* 873; *The Reign of Henry VII from Contemporary Sources,* 204; Eric N. Simons, *Henry VII: The First Tudor King* (New York: Barnes & Noble, 1968), 213–14; Ann Wroe, *The Perfect Prince* (New York: Random House, 2003), 474.

27. Philip Goodwin, *the mystery of dreames, historically discoursed* (London, 1658), 93, 97, 100.

28. Thomas Hobbes, *Elements of Law, Natural and Politic (1640),* ed. J.C.A. Gaskin (Oxford, UK: Oxford University Press, 1999), 27.

29. Tho Buoni, *Problemes of Beautie and all humane affections,* Written in Italian by Tho Buoni, citizen of Lucca, *With* a *discourse of Beauty,* by the same Author. Translated into English, by S. L. Gent (London, 1606), 63.

30. Lording Barry, *Ram Alley: Or Merry Tricks,* ed. Peter Corbin and Douglas Sedge (Nottingham, UK: Nottingham University Press, 1981), 56.

31. Thomas Campion, "Sleepe, Angry Beauty," in *Poems of Sleep and Dreams,* ed. Peter Washington (New York: Random House, 2004), 38.

32. Ella Mary Leather, *The Folk-Lore of Herefordshire* (Hereford, UK: Jakeman and Carver, 1912), 64.

33. *Oxford English Dictionary,* 2nd edn. (Oxford, UK: Oxford University Press, 1989), s.v. yew (n).

34. *Letters and papers, foreign and domestic of the reign of Henry VIII preserved in the Public Record Office, the British Museum, and elsewhere* (London: Her Majesty's Stationery Office, 1862–1920), vii, 1609.

35. Gotthelf Wiedermann, "Alesius [Allane or Alan], Alexander (1500–1565)," *Oxford Dictionary of National Biography* (Oxford University Press, 2004). Available from: http://0-www.oxforddnb.com.library.unl.edu:80/view/article/ 320 [Accessed: 12 Nov 2007].

36. *Calendar of State Papers, Foreign Series, of the Reign of Elizabeth, 1558–1559,* ed. Rev. Joseph Stevenson (London: Longman, Green, Longman, Roberts, and Green, 1863), 528.

37. Christopher Ocland, *The Popes Farwel; or, Queen Ann's Dream. Containing a true Prognostick of her own Death, Written Originally in Latine Verse by Mr. Christopher Ocland, and Printed in the Year 1582* (London, 1680), 4–7.

38. Raphael Holinshed, *The Chronicles of England, Scotland and Ireland* (London, 1587), iii, 940.

39. I am deeply grateful to Linda Shenk for her help with the translation.

40. George Mariscal, "Calderón and Shakespeare: the Subject of Henry VIII," *Bulletin of the Comediantes* 39, no. 2 (1987), 191.

41. Gregory Peter Andrachuk, "Calderón's View of the English Schism," in *Parallel Lives: Spanish and English National Drama, 1580–1680,* ed. Louise and Peter Fothergill-Payne (Lewisburg, PA: Bucknell University Press, 1991), 226.

42. Pedro Calderón de la Barca, *The Schism in England (La cisma de Inglaterra),* trans. Kenneth Muir and Ann L. Mackenzie (Westminster: Aris & Phillips, 1990), 49.

43. Andrachuk, "Calderón's View of the English Schism," 226.

44. De la Barca, *Schism in England,* 49.

45. De la Barca, *Schism in England,* 53.

46. De la Barca, *Schism in England,* 175, 183, 185, 187.

47. Mariscal, "Calderón and Shakespeare," 198.

48. Richard Saunders, *Physiognomie and chiromancie,* 205.

49. Gordon McMullen, "Introduction," William Shakespeare and John Fletcher, *King Henry VIII,* ed. Gordon McMullen (London: Thomson Learning, 2000), 122, 123.

50. Judith H. Anderson, *Biographical Truth: The Representation of Historical Persons in Tudor-Stuart Writing* (New Haven, CT: Yale University Press, 1984), 134.

51. E. E. Duncan-Jones, "Queen Katherine's Visions and Queen Margaret's Dreams," *Notes and Queries* 206 (1961), 142–43.

52. John Margeson, "Introduction," William Shakespeare, *King Henry VIII,* ed. John Margeson (Cambridge, UK: Cambridge University Press, 1990), 19.

53. McMullen, *King Henry VIII,* 134.

54. For more insights into this play, see Marsha S. Robinson, *Writing the Reformation: Actes and Monuments and the Jacobean History Play* (Burlington, VT: Ashgate, 2002), 16–17; John Watkins, *Representing Elizabeth in Stuart England: Literature, History, Sovereignty* (Cambridge, UK: Cambridge University Press, 2002), 36–55.

55. Thomas Heywood, *If You Know Not Me, You Know Nobody, Part I* (Oxford, UK: The Malone Society Reprints at the Oxford University Press, 1934). All quotations are from this edition.

56. Artemidorus, *The interpretation of dreams, digested into five books by that ancient and excellent philosopher, Artimedorus. Compiled by him in Greek; and translated afterwards into the Latine, the Italian, the French, and Spanish, tongues. And now more exactly rendred into English. It being a work of great esteem in all ages, and pleasant and profitable to peruse, for all conditions of people whatsoever* (London, 1644), 101; Leather, *Folk-lore of Herefordshire,* 118; John Clark, *Paroemiologia Anglo-Latina* (London, 1639), 236; Saunders, *Physiognomie,* 229.

57. McMullen, *King Henry VIII,* 134.

CHAPTER 5

1. Andrew Seyton, *The Seytonian Dreamer's Sure Guide Collected from the Writings of Andrew Seyton, Celebrated Seer of Cumberland* (London: R. Walwyn, 1820), 24; Thomas Hill, *The moste pleasuante arte of the Interpretation of dreames* (London, 1576), n.p.

2. Brian Masters, *Dreams about H.M. the Queen and Other Members of the Royal Family* (London: Blond & Briggs, 1972), 11; Julia Anderson-Miller and Bruce Joshua Miller, *Dreams of Bill: A Collection of Funny, Strange and Downright Peculiar Dreams about Our President* (Secaucus, NJ: Carol Pub. Group, 1994).

3. Masters, *Dreams about H.M. the Queen and Other Members of the Royal Family,* 127–29.

4. Hill, *moste pleasuante arte of the Interpretation of dreames,* n.p.; Richard Saunders, *Physiognomie* (2nd edn. London, 1671), 244.

5. *Acts of the Privy Council, New Series,* ed. John Dasent (London: Printed for H.M.S.O. by Eyre & Spottiswood, 1890–1949), iv, 385, 389.

6. A.F.P., "Thomas Wotton," *Dictionary of National Biography Archive,* first published 1900.

7. Sir Henry Wotton, *Reliquiae wottonianae* (London, 1651), B4.

8. Caroline Walker Bynum, *Fragmentation and Redemption: Essays on Gender and the Human Body in Medieval Religion* (New York: Zone, 1991), 101; Caroline Walker Bynum, *Wonderful Blood: Theology and Practice in Late Medieval Northern Germany and Beyond* (Philadelphia: University of Pennsylvania Press, 2007), 21.

9. Bettina Bildhauer, "Blood," in *Medieval Folklore: A Guide to Myths, Legends, Tales, Beliefs, and Customs,* ed. Carl Lindahl, John McNamara, and John Lindow (Oxford, NY and Oxford, UK: Oxford University Press, 2002), 45.

10. *Oxford English Dictionary,* 2nd edn. (Oxford, UK: Oxford University Press, 1989), s.v. blood (n).

11. Gonzalo, *The Divine Dreamer: or, A Short Treatise Discovering the True Effect and Power of Dreams* (London, 1641), n.p.

12. Thomas Walkington, *The optick glasse of humors or The touchstone of a golden temperature, or the Philosophers stone to make a golden temper Wherein the foure complections sanguine, cholericke, phligmaticke, melancholicke are succinctly painted forth and their externall intimates laid open to the purblind eye of ignorance it selfe, by which euery one may iudge, of what complection he is, and answerably learne what is most sutable to his nature, 1631,* a photoprint with an introduction by John A. Popplestone and Marion White McPherson (Delmar, NY: Scholars' Facsimiles & Reprints, 1981), 48.

13. Paul E. J. Hammer, "Devereux, Robert, second earl of Essex (1565–1601)," *Oxford Dictionary of National Biography* (Oxford University Press, Sep 2004); online edn., Oct 2007. Available from: http://0-www.oxforddnb .com.library.unl.edu:80/view/article/7565 [Accessed: 5 Dec 2007].

14. William Camden, *The History of the Most Renowned and Victorious Princess Elizabeth, Late Queen of England,* 4th edn. (London: M. Flesher, 1688), 555.

15. Camden, *History of the Most Renowned and Victorious Princess Elizabeth,* 556.

16. Thomas Nash, *Terrors of the Night. Or, A Discourse of apparitions* (London, 1594), C3v, 259.

17. Marguerite, Queen Consort of Henry IV, *The History of M. de Valois,* trans. Robert Codrington (London: R. H., 1650), 49.

18. The Project Gutenberg EBook of Memoirs of Marguerite de Valois, Complete by *Marguerite de Valois, Queen of Navarre.* www.gutenberg

.net: Title: *Memoirs of Marguerite de Valois, Complete;* Author: Marguerite de Valois, Queen of Navarre; Release Date: Sep 27, 2006 [EBook #3841], n.p.

19. James A. Beza, tom.il, livr.ii, p. 51 in James A. Wylie, *The History of Protestantism* (London: Cassell Petter Galpin, 1870s), ii, 519.

20. See Denis Crouzet, *La nuit de la Saint-Barthélemy: un rêve perdu de la Renaissance* (Paris: Fayard, 1994); Elaine Kruse, "The Blood-Stained Hands of Catherine de Médicis," in *Political Rhetoric, Power, and Renaissance Women,* ed. Carole Levin and Patricia A. Sullivan (Albany: SUNY Press, 1995), 139–55; Elaine Kruse, "The Woman in Black: The Image of Catherine de Medici from Marlowe to Queen Margot," in *"High and Mighty Queens" of Early Modern England: Realities and Representations* (New York: Palgrave Macmillan, 2003), 223–37.

21. Wylie, *History of Protestantism,* 611.

22. Marguerite deValois, *History of M. De Valois,* 49.

23. Frederic J. Baumgartner, *Henry II, King of France 1547–1559* (Durham, NC and London: Duke University Press, 1988), 250.

24. Quoted in Hugh Ross Williamson, *Catherine de' Medici* (London: Michael Joseph, 1973), 81.

25. Thomas Hill, *The Pleasant Art of the Interpretation of Dreams* (London, 1576), n.p.

26. Gonzalo, *Divine Dreamer,* n.p.

27. Matthew of Westminster, *Flowers of History,* cited in Frank Seafield, *The Literature and Curiosities of Dreams: A commonplace book of speculations concerning the mystery of dreams and visions* (London: Lockwood, 1869), 108–9.

28. Frank Barlow, *William Rufus* (Berkeley and Los Angeles: University of California Press, 1983), 427; C. Warren Hollister, "The Strange Death of William Rufus," *Speculum: A Journal of Medieval Studies* 48, no. 4 (Oct 1973), 640–41.

29. Raphael Holinshed et al., *Holinshed's Chronicles of England, Scotland, and Ireland,* ed. Henry Ellis (originally published in 1577; this edn. 1809; reprint London: J. Johnson, New York: AMS Press, 1965), iii, 44.

30. *Minor Prose Works of King James VI and I,* ed. James Craigie (Edinburgh, UK: Scottish Text Society, 1982), 56.

31. Webster, *Displaying of Supposed Witchcraft,* 305.

32. *Letters and Papers of Henry VIII,* xiii, Part I, 595.

33. John Evans, *Hesperides or The Muses Garden,* n.p.

34. *Holinshed's Chronicles,* iii, 44. This dream appears almost word for word also in Sir Richard Baker, *A Chronicle of the kings of England from the time of the Romans Government unto the Death of King James* (London: George Sawbridge, 1674), 36.

35. Barlow, *William Rufus,* 425.

36. Hollister, "The Strange Death of William Rufus," 642.

37. Keith Thomas, *Religion and the Decline of Magic* (London: Weidenfeld and Nicolson, 1971), 344.

38. Thomas, *Religion and the Decline of Magic,* 404; L. O. Pike, *A History of Crime in England* (1873–1876), ii, 23.

39. Derek Wilson, *Sweet Robin: A Biography of Robert Dudley, Earl of Leicester* (London: Hamilton, 1981), 229–30; E. M. Tenison, *Elizabethan England,*

vol. III: 1575–1580 (Royal Leamington Spa, Warwick, issued by the author, 1933), 148.

40. William Cecil, *A Collection of State papers Relating to Affairs in the Reign of Queen Elizabeth from 1542 to 1596 by William Cecil, Lord Burghley*, ed. William Murdin and Samuel Haynes (London: William Bowyer, 1740–1759), i, 361–62.

41. See for example, Susan Doran, "Revenge Her Foul and Most Unnatural Murder? The Impact of Mary Stewart's Execution on Anglo-Scottish Relations," *History* 85 (2000), 589–612.

42. William K. Boyd, ed., *Calendar of State Papers Relating to Scotland and Mary Queen of Scots, Volume IX: 1586–1588* (Glasgow: HMSO, 1915), 287–95, Item 284: "A discourse sent by Secretory Davisone, beinge then prisonere in the Towere of London, unto Secretarye Walsyngham, contaynynge a somary reporte of that which passed between hir majestie and him in the case of the Skotyshe Queene, from the signynge of the warrante to the tyme of his restrainte."

43. Georgianna Ziegler, "Mary Stuart," in *Elizabeth I: Then and Now* (Washington, DC: The Folger Shakespeare Library, 2003), 107; James Emerson Phillips, *Images of a Queen: Mary Stuart in Sixteenth-Century Literature* (Berkeley and Los Angeles: University of California Press, 1964), 106–9.

44. Adam Blackwood, *Martyre de la rayne d'Escosse* (Paris, 1587), 345–49. My great thanks to Carolyn Biltoft and Jordan Stump for providing the translation.

45. Pierre de Loyer, *A Treatise of Specters or straunge Sights, Visions and Apparitions appearing sensibly unto men. Wherein is delivered, the Nature of Spirites, Angels, and Divels: their power and properties: as also of Witches, Sorcerers, Enchanters, and such like*, newly done out of French into English by Zacharie Jones (London, 1605), 112.

46. Gonzalo, *The Divine Dreamer: or, A Short Treatise Discovering the True Effect and Power of Dreams* (London, 1641), n.p.; Guyon's book was published in 1690 and is cited in Grillot de Givry, *Witchcraft, Magic & Alchemy*, trans. J. Courtenay Locke (New York: Dover, 1971; orig. published by Houghton Mifflin, 1931), 323.

47. Raymond de Becker, *The Understanding of Dreams and Their Influence on the History of Man*, trans. Michael Heron (New York: Bell, 1948), 63–64; Givry, *Witchcraft, Magic & Alchemy*, 323; John Evans, *Hesperides or The Muses Garden*, n.p.

48. R. B., *Wonderful Prodigies of Judgment and Mercy: Discovered in Above Three Hundred Memorable Histories* (London, 1685), 62.

49. Sir John Harington, *Nugae Antiquae: Being a Miscelleaneous Collection of Original Papers, in Prose and Verse*, ed. Thomas Park (London: Vernon and Hood, 1804; New York: AMS Press, 1966), i, 367–70.

50. Brett Usher, "Fletcher, Richard (1544/5–1596)," *Oxford Dictionary of National Biography* (Oxford University Press, 2004). Available from: http://0-www.oxforddnb.com.library.unl.edu:80/view/article/9739 [Accessed: 25 Nov 2007]; Peter E. McCullough, "Out of Egypt: Richard Fletcher's Sermon before Elizabeth I after the Execution of Mary Queen of Scots," *Dissing Elizabeth: Negative Representations of Gloriana*, ed. Julia M. Walker (Durham, NC: Duke University Press, 1998), 118–49.

51. McCullough, "Out of Egypt," 129.

52. McCullough, "Out of Egypt," 129.

53. Thomas, *Religion and the Decline of Magic*, 130; *Depositions taken before the mayor & aldermen of Norwich, 1449–1567 and Extracts from the Court Books of the City of Norwich, 1666–1688*, ed. Walter Rye (Norwich, UK: Printed for the Norfolk and Norwich Archaeological Society by A. H. Goose, 1905), 61–66.

54. P.R.O., SP 12/200, f. 65 in Thomas, *Religion and the Decline of Magic*, 600.

55. Thomas, *Religion and the Decline of Magic*, 600.

56. *Cabala, Mysteries of State and Government: in Letters of Illustrious Persons and Great Ministers of State* (London, 1663), 173.

57. Robert Greene, *The Spanish Masquerado Wherein under a pleasant devise, is discovered effectuallie, in certaine breefe sentences and mottos, the pride and insolencie of the Spanish estate: with the disgrace conceived by their losse, and the dismaied confusion of their tronbled [sic] thoughts* (London, 1589), B4.

58. Richard Verstegan, *A declaration of the true causes of the great troubles, presupposed to be intended against the realme of England VVherein the indifferent reader shall manifestly perceaue, by whome, and by what means, the realme is broughte into these pretented perils* (Antwerp, 1592), 63–64.

59. *Calendar of State Papers, Domestic Series, of the Reigns of Edward VI, Mary, Elizabeth, and James, 1547–1625*, ed. Robert Lemon and Mary Anne Everett Green, 12 vols. (London: Longman, Brown, Green, Longmans, and Roberts, 1856–1872), iv, 446.

60. Louis Montrose, "Shaping Fantasies: Figurations of Gender and Power in Elizabethan Culture," *Representations* 1, no. 2 (1983), 61–94.

61. Rowse, *Simon Forman*, 20.

62. Montrose, "Shaping Fantasies," 65.

63. Harington, *Nugae Antiquae*, i, 178–79.

64. Rowse, *Simon Forman*, 20.

65. *Calendar of the Letters and State papers Relating to English Affairs Preserved in, originally belonging to, the Archives of Simancas*, ed. Martin Hume (London: Her Majesty's Stationery Office, 1892–1900), i, 633.

66. John Clapham, *Elizabeth of England*, ed. Evelyn Plummer Read and Conyers Read (Philadelphia: University of Pennsylvania Press, 1951), 111.

67. Cotton Vitellius, CXVII 42–42b, 42 with great thanks to Paul E. J. Hammer.

68. Historical Manuscript Commission, *Calendar of the Manuscripts of the Most Honourable, the Marquis of Salisbury . . . Preserved at Hatfield House*, ed. R. A. Roberts (London, 1883–1976), xi, 135.

69. Historical Manuscript Commission, ix, 132.

70. Historical Manuscript Commission, ix, 134–35.

71. Historical Manuscript Commission, ix, 134.

72. J. E. Neale, "The Sayings of Queen Elizabeth," *History* 10 (Oct 1925), 212–33; Catherine Loomis, "Elizabeth Southwell's Manuscript Account of the Death of Queen Elizabeth," *ELR* 26 (1996), 482–509.

73. Loomis, "Elizabeth Southwell's Manuscript," 485, 489.

74. Richard Kagan, *Lucrecia's Dream: Politics and Prophecy in Sixteenth-Century Spain* (Berkeley: University of California Press, 1990), 2. For more on Lucrecia, see Roger Osborne, *The Dreamer of Calle de San Salvador: Visions of Sedition and Sacrilege in Sixteenth-Century Spain* (London: Jonathan

Cape, 2001). I am very grateful to Anne Cruz, who called my attention to Osborne's book and lent me a copy.

75. Osborne, *Dreamer of Calle de San Salvador,* 61.
76. Kagan, *Lucrecia's Dream,* 71.

Afterword

1. Scribonius, *Naturall Philosophy,* 52.

BIBLIOGRAPHY

PRIMARY SOURCES

Acts of the Privy Council, New Series, ed. John Dasent. London: Printed for H.M.S.O. by Eyre & Spottiswood, 1890–1949.

Alessio, Piemontese. *The Secrets of Alexis: Containing many excellent Remedies Against Divers Diseases, wounds and other Accidents,* newly corrected and amended. London, 1615.

Ambrose, Isaac. *Ministration of, and Communion with Angels,* in *The Compleat Works.* London, 1674.

Amyraut, Moise. *A discourse concerning the divine dreams mention'd in Scripture, together with the marks and characters by which they might be distinguish'd from vain delusions,* trans. Ja. Lowde. London, 1676.

The Anglica Historia of Polydore Vergil, A.D. 1485–1537, ed., trans. Denys Hay. London: Royal Historical Society, 1950.

Artemidorus, *The interpretation of dreames, digested into five books by that ancient and excellent philosopher, Artimedorus. Compiled by him in Greek; and translated afterwards into the Latine, the Italian, the French, and Spanish, tongues. And now more exactly rendred into English. It being a work of great esteem in all ages, and pleasant and profitable to peruse, for all conditions of people whatsoever.* London, 1644.

Ashmole, Elias, and William Lilly. *The Lives of those eminent Antiquaries Elias Ashmole, Esquires and Mr. William Lilly, written by themselves; containing first William Lilly's History of His life and Times, with Notes, by Mr. Ashmole: Secondly Lilly's Life and Death of Charles the First; and lastly, the Life of Elias Ashmole, Esquire, by Way of Diary. With Several Occasional Letters,* ed. Charles Burman, Esquire. London: T. Davies, 1784.

R. B. *Wonderful Prodigies of Judgment and Mercy: Discovered in Above Three Hundred Memorable Histories.* London, 1685.

Bacon, Francis. *History of the Reign King Henry VII,* ed. J. Lawson Lumby. Cambridge, UK: Cambridge University Press, 1880.

———. *Novum Organum: With Other Parts of the Great Instauration,* ed., trans. Peter Urback and John Gibson. Chicago: Open Court, 1994.

———. *The Works of Francis Bacon,* ed. James Spedding, Robert Leslie Ellis, and Douglas Denon Heath. London: Longman, 1857.

Baker, Sir Richard. *A Chronicle of the kings of England from the time of the Romans Government unto the Death of King James.* London, 1674.

Barca, Pedro Calderón de la. *The Schism in England (La cisma de Inglaterra),* trans. Kenneth Muir and Ann L. Mackenzie. Warminster, UK: Aris & Phillips, 1990.

Barlow, William. *The Sermon Preached at Paules Crosse, the tenth day of November.* London, 1606.

Barry, Lording. *Ram Alley: Or Merry Tricks,* ed. Peter Corbin and Douglas Sedge. Nottingham, UK: Nottingham University Press, 1981.

Basse, William. *A helpe to discourse. Or, A misselany of merriment Consisting of witty philosophicall, and astronomicall questions and ansvvers. As also, of epigrams, epitaphs, riddles, and iests. Together with The country-mans counsellour, next his yearely oracle or prognostication to consult with. Contayning diuers necessary rules and obseruations, of much vse and consequence being knowne.* London, 1623.

Baxter, Richard. *The Certainty of the World of Spirits, full evinced by unquestionable histories of Apparitions and Witchcrafts.* London, 1691.

Bernard, Richard. *A guide to grandjury men divided into two bookes: in the first, is the authors best advice to them what to doe, before they bring in a billa vera in cases of witchcraft, with a Christian direction to such as are too much given upon every crosse to thinke themselves bewitched. In the second, is a treatise touching witches good and bad, how they may be knowne, evicted, condemned, with many particulars tending thereunto.* London, 1627.

The Bloudy booke, or The Tragicall and desperate end of Sir John Fites (alias Fitz). London, 1605.

Booy, David. *Autobiographical Writings by Early Quaker Women.* Aldershot, UK: Ashgate, 2004.

Boulton, Richard. *The possibility and reality of magick, sorcery, and witchcraft, demonstrated, or, A vindication of a compleat history of magick, sorcery and witch craft: in answer to Dr. Hutchinson's Historical essay.* London, 1722.

Bovet, Richard. *Pandaemonium, or, The devil's cloyster being a further blow to modern sadduceism, proving the existence of witches and spirits, in a discourse deduced from the fall of the angels, the propagation of Satans kingdom before the flood, the idolatry of the ages after greatly advancing diabolical confederacies, with an account of the lives and transactions of several notorious witches: also, a collection of several authentick relations of strange apparitions of daemons and spectres, and fascinations of witches, never before printed.* London, 1684.

Brathwaite, Richard. *A strange metamorphosis of man, transformed into a wildernesse Deciphered in characters.* London, 1634.

Bright, Timothy. *A Treatise on Melancholie,* reproduced from the 1586 edition printed by Thomas Vautrollier, with an introduction by Hardin Craig. New York: Published for the Facsimile Text Society by Columbia University Press, 1940.

Brinley, John. *A discovery of the impostures of witches and astrologers.* London, 1680.

Browne, Sir Thomas. *The Works of Sir Thomas Browne,* ed. Charles Sayle. Edinburgh, UK: John Grant, 1927.

Brunschwig, Hieronymus. *A most excellent and perfecte homish apothecarye or homely physik booke, for all the grefes and diseases of the bodye. Translated out the Almaine speche into English by Ihon Hollybush.* Collen, 1561.

Buoni, Thommaso. *Problemes of Beautie and all humane affections, Written in Italian by Tho: Buoni, citizen of Lucca, With a discourse of Beauty, by the same Author,* trans. S. L. Gent. London, 1606.

Bunyan, John. *Grace Abounding to the Chief of Sinners,* ed. Roger Sharrock. Oxford, UK: Oxford University Press, 1962.

Burton, Robert. *The Anatomy of Melancholy,* ed. Thomas C. Faulkner and Nicolas K. Kiessling. Oxford, UK: Clarendon Press, 1989–2000.

Butts, Henry. *Dyets Dry Dinner.* London, 1599.

Cabala, Mysteries of State and Government: in Letters of Illustrious Persons and Great Ministers of State. London, 1663.

Cade, Anthony. *A sermon of the nature of conscience which may well be tearmed, a tragedy of conscience in her.* 2nd ed. London, 1621.

Calendar of State Papers, Domestic Series, of the Reign of James I, 1611–1618, ed. Mary Anne Everett Green. London: Longman, Brown, Green, Longmans, & Roberts, 1858.

Calendar of State Papers and Manuscripts Relating to English Affairs, Existing in the Archives and Collections of Venice, and in Other Libraries of Northern Italy, ed. Horatio F. Brown. London, 1900; Nendeln, Liechtenstein: Kraus Reprint, 1970.

Calendar of State Papers Relating to Scotland and Mary Queen of Scots, Volume IX: 1586–1588, ed. William K. Boyd. Glasgow, Scotland: Her Majesty's Stationery Office, 1915.

Calendar of the Letters and State Papers Relating to English Affairs Preserved in, originally belonging to, the Archives of Simancas, ed. Martin Hume. London: Her Majesty's Stationery Office, 1892–1900.

Calendar of State Papers, Domestic Series, of the Reigns of Edward VI, Mary, Elizabeth, and James, 1547–1625, ed. Robert Lemon and Mary Anne Everett Green. London: Longman, Brown, Green, Longmans, and Roberts, 1856–1872.

Calendar of State Papers, Foreign Series, of the Reign of Elizabeth, 1558–1559, ed. Rev. Joseph Stevenson. London: Longman, Green, Longman, Roberts, and Green, 1863.

Camden, William. *The History of the Most Renowned and Victorious Princess Elizabeth, Late Queen of England,* 4th edn. London, 1688.

Chaucer, Geoffrey. *The workes of our ancient and learned English poet, Geffrey Chaucer, newly printed.* London, 1602.

Clark, John. *Paroemiologia Anglo-Latina.* London, 1639.

Clarke, Samuel. *The lives of sundry eminent persons in this later age in two parts : I. of divines, II. of nobility and gentry of both sexes / by Samuel Clark . . . ; printed and reviewed by himself just before his death; to which is added his own life and the lives of the Countess of Suffolk, Sir Nathaniel Barnardiston, Mr. Richard Blackerby and Mr. Samuel Fairclough, drawn up by other hands.* London, 1683.

Cogan, Thomas. *The haven of health chiefely gathered for the comfort of students, and consequently of all those that have a care of their health, amplified upon five words of Hippocrates.* London, 1584.

Cooper, Thomas. *The Mystery of Witch-Craft.* London, 1617.

Cranmer, Thomas. *The Works of Thomas Cranmer,* ed. Rev. John Edmund Cox. Cambridge, UK: Cambridge University Press, 1844–1846.

Culpeper, Nicholas. *Nicholas Culpeper's English Physician and Complete Herbal,* ed. E. Sibly. London: Lewis and Hamblin, 1807.

Dare, Josiah. *Counsellor Manners, his last legacy to his son,* ed. Ira Webster Porter. New York: Coward-McCann, 1929.

Day, Richard. *A Book of Christian Prayers, collected out of the auncie[n]t writers, and best learned in our tyme, worthy to be read with an earnest mynde of all Christians, in these daungerous and troublesome dayes, that God for Christes sake will yet still be mercyfull unto us.* London, 1578.

Dee, John. *The Diaries of John Dee,* ed. Edward Fenton. Oxfordshire, UK: Day Books, 1998.

D'Ewes, Simonds. *The Autobiography and Correspondence of Sir Simonds D'Ewes,* ed. James Orchard Halliwell. London: Richard Bentley, 1845.

English Medieval Lapidaries, ed. Joan Evans and Mary S. Serjeantson. Early English Text Society, no. 190. London: Humphrey Milford, Oxford University Press, 1933.

Evans, Arise. *An Eccho to the Book, called A Voyce from Heaven.* London, 1653.

Evans, John. *Hesperides or The Muses Garden.* Compiled ca. 1655–1659.

Felltham, Owen. "Of Dreams," in *Resolves Divine, Morall and Politicall.* London: J. M. Dent, 1904.

Fisher, John. *English works of John Fisher, Bishop of Rochester (1469–1535): sermons and other writings, 1520–1535,* ed. Cecilia A. Hatt. New York: Oxford University Press, 2002.

———. *There after foloweth a mornynge remembraunce had at the moneth mynde of the noble prynces margarete countesse of Rychemonde & Darbye moder unto kynge Henry the Vii. & granddame to oure soverayne lorde that nowe is upon whose soule almighty god have mercy.* London, 1509.

Foxe, John. *Acts and Monuments [. . .] The Variorum Edition* [online] (Online, Sheffield 2004). Available from: http://www.hrionline.shef.ac.uk/foxe/ [Accessed: 20 Nov 2007].

Framboisiere, Nicholas Abraham de la. *An easy method to know the causes and signs of the humour most ruleth in the body.* London, 1640.

Gerhard, Andre. *The true tryall and examination of a mans owne self,* trans. Thomas Newton. London, 1586.

Gonzalo. *The Divine Dreamer: or, A Short Treatise Discovering the True Effect and Power of Dreams.* London, 1641.

Goodwin, Philip. *The mystery of dreames, historically discoursed.* London, 1658.

Granvil, Joseph. *A blow at modern sadducism in some philosophical considerations about witchcraft.* London, 1668.

Great Chronicle of London, ed. A. H. Thomas and I. D. Thornley. London: G. W. Jones, 1938.

Greene, Robert. *The Spanish Masquerado Wherein under a pleasant devise, is discovered effectuallie, in certaine breefe sentences and mottos, the pride and insolencie of the Spanish estate: with the disgrace conceived by their losse, and the dismaied confusion of their tronbled [sic] thoughtes.* London, 1589.

Hall, Edward. *Chronicle.* London: J. Johnson, 1809.

Hall, Joseph. *The great mysterie of godliness, laid forth by way of affectuous and feeling meditation. Also, the invisible world, discovered to spirituall eyes, and reduced to useful meditation.* Holborn, 1651.

Harington, Sir John. *Nugae Antiquae: Being a Miscelleaneous Collection of Original Papers, in Prose and Verse,* ed. Thomas Park. London: Vernon and Hood, 1804; New York: AMS Press, 1966.

Haydocke, Richard. *ONEIROLOGIA: or A briefe discourse of the nature of Dreames: Discoveringe how farre the reasonable Soule exerciseth her operations in the time of Sleepe: And prooveinge that in Sleep there can bee noe reasonable and Metholdicall,* owned by the Folger Shakespeare Library.

A helpe to memory and discourse: with table-talke, as musicke to a banquet of wine. London, 1630.

Heywood, Thomas. *The Hierarchie of the blessed Angells. Their names, orders and Offices. The fall of Lucifer with his Angells.* London, 1635.

———. *If You Know Not Me, You Know Nobody, Part I.* Oxford, UK: The Malone Society Reprints at the Oxford University Press, 1934.

Hill, Thomas. *The moste pleasuante arte of the Interpretation of dreames*. London, 1576.

Historical Manuscripts Commission. *Calendar of the Manuscripts of the Most Honourable the Marquess of Salisbury preserved at Hatfield House, Part XVII*, ed. M. S. Guiseppi. London: Her Majesty's Stationery Office, 1938.

——. *Calendar of the Manuscripts of the Most Honourable, the Marquis of Salisbury . . . Preserved at Hatfield House*, ed. R. A. Roberts. London, 1883–1976.

Hobbes, Thomas. *Elements of Law, Natural and Politic*, ed. J.C.A. Gaskin. New York Oxford University Press, 1999.

——. *Leviathan* (1651), ed. C. B. Macpherson. London: Penguin, 1968.

Holinshed, Raphael. *The Chronicles of England, Scotland and Ireland*. London, 1587.

Holles, Gervase. *Memorials of the Holles Family, 1493–1656*, ed. A. C. Wood. Camden Third Series, vol. LV; London: Camden Society, 1937.

Howard, Henry, Earl of Northampton. *A defensative against the poyson of supposed prophecies Not hitherto confuted by the pen of any man, which being grounded, either vpon the warrant and authority of old painted bookes, expositions of dreames, oracles, reuelations, invocations of damned spirits, judicials of astrologie, or any other kinde of pretended knowledge whatsoeuer, de futuris contingentibus; have beene causes of great disorder in the common-wealth, especially among the simple and vnlearned people. Very needfull to be published, considering the great offence, which grew by most palpable and grosse errors in astrologie.* (1583); reprint London, 1620.

Howell, Thomas Bayly. *Complete collection of state trials and proceedings for high treason and other crimes and misdemeanors from the earliest period to the present time*. London: Printed by T. C. Hansard, published by R. Bagshaw, 1809–1926.

Howes, Edmond. *The annales, or a generall chronicle of England, begun first by maister Iohn Stow, and after him continued and augmented with matters forreyne, and domestique, auncient and moderne, vnto the ende of this present yeere 1614*. London, 1615.

Hubbard, William. *Greate Britianes Resurrection*. London, 1606.

Hutchinson, Francis. *An historical essay concerning witchcraft*. London, 1718.

I.H., *The Divell of the Vault, Or the Vnmasking of Murther in a briefe declaration of the Cacolicke-complotted Treason, lately discovered*. London, 1606.

J. B., Gent. *Faire in Spittle Fields, whereall the Knick Knacks of Astrology are Exposed to open sale, to all that will see for their Love, and buy for their money*. London, 1652.

Jenkyns, Henry, ed. *The Remains of Thomas Cranmer, D.D. Archbishop of Canterbury*. Oxford, UK: Oxford University Press, 1833.

Jessey, Henry. *The Exceeding Riches of Grace Advanced By the Spirit of Grace, in an Empty Nothing Creature, viz. Mris. Sarah Wight, Lately hopeles and restles, her soule dwelling as far from Peace or hopes of Mercy, as ever was any. Now hopeful, and joyfull in the Lord, that hath caused LIGHT to shine out of DARKNES*. London, 1647.

Jones, Zacharie. *A Treatise of Specters or straunge Sights, Visions and Apparitions appearing sensibly unto men. Wherein is delivered, the Nature of Spirites, Angels, and Divels: their power and properties: as also of Witches, Sorcerers, Enchanters, and such like. Newly done out of French into English*. London, 1605.

Josselin, Ralph. *The Diary of Ralph Josselin, 1616–1683*, ed. Alan MacFarlane. London: Published for the British Academy by the Oxford University Press, 1976.

Kempe, Margery. *The Book of Margery Kempe: A New Translation, Contexts, Criticism*, trans. and ed. Lynn Staley. New York: Norton, 2001.

Kirkham, Henry. *A true reporte or description of an horrible, woful, and moste lamentable murther, doen in the citie of Bristowe by one Jhon Kynnestar, a Sherman by his occupation, declarying howe wickedly he murthered his owne wife, in the monethe of August laste paste, and being taken, was hanged the same moneth 1572.* London, 1573.

Laud, William. *The works of the Most Reverend Father in God, William Laud, D. D., sometime Lord Archbishop of Canterbury,* ed. William Scott and James Bliss. Oxford, UK: J. H. Parker, 1847–1860.

Laurentius, M. Andreas. *A Discourse of the Sight: of Melancholike Diseases; of Rheumes, and of Old Age,* trans. Richard Surphlet (1599), with an introduction by Sanford V. Larkey. Oxford, UK: Oxford University Press, 1938.

Lavater, Ludwig, Robert Harrison, John Dover Wilson, and May Yardley. *Of Ghostes and Spirites Walking by Nyght, 1572,* edited with introduction and appendix by J. Dover Wilson and May Yardley. Oxford, UK: Printed for the Shakespeare Association at the University Press, 1929.

Lemnius, Levinus. *The touchstone of complexions. Generallye appliable, expedient and profitable for all such, as be desirous & carefull of their bodylye health. Contayning most easie rules & ready tokens, whereby every one may perfectly try, and throughly know, as well the exacte state, habite, disposition, and constitution, of his owne body outwardly: as also the inclinations, affections motions, & desires of his mynd inwardly. First written in Latine, by Leuine Lemnie, and now englished by Thomas Newton.* London, 1576.

Letters and papers, foreign and domestic of the reign of Henry VIII preserved in the Public Record Office, the British Museum, and elsewhere. London: Her Majesty's Stationery Office, 1862–1920.

Letters of John Chamberlain, ed. Norman Egbert McClure. Philadelphia: American Philosophical Society, 1939.

Letters of King James VI & I, ed. G.P.V. Akrigg. Berkeley: University of California Press, 1984.

Lilly, William. *A groats worth of wit for a penny, or, The interpretation of dreams.* London, 1670.

Loyer, Pierre de. *A Treatise of Specters or straunge Sights, Visions and Apparitions appearing sensibly unto men. Wherein is delivered, the Nature of Spirites, Angels, and Divels: their power and properties: as also of Witches, Sorcerers, Enchanters, and such like,* newly done out of French into English by Zacharie Jones. London, 1605.

Marguerite, Queen Consort of Henry IV, *The History of M. de Valois,* trans. Robert Codrington. London, 1650.

Minor Prose Works of King James VI and I, ed. James Craigie. Edinburgh, UK: Scottish Text Society, 1982.

The Mirror for Magistrates, ed. Lily B. Campbell. Cambridge, UK: Cambridge University Press, 1938; republished New York: Barnes & Noble, 1960.

A Miscellaneous Collections of Recipes—Household, Medical & Veterinary (12 vol. Compiled ca. 1600 and bound together with an index ca. 1750), owned by the Folger Shakespeare Library.

More, Henry. *An Antidote Against Atheisme.* London, 1653.

More, Thomas. *The History of King Richard III and Selections from the English and Latin Poems,* ed. Richard S. Sylvester. New Haven, CT: Yale University Press, 1976.

The most strange and admirable discouerie of the three witches of Warboys arraigned, conuicted and executed at the last Assises at Huntington, for the bewitching of the fiue daughters of Robert Throckmorton Esquier, and diuers other persons, with sundrie diuelish and grieuous torments. And also for the bewitching to death of the Lady Crumwell, the like hath not bene heard of in this age. London, 1593.

Murdin, William, and Samuel Haynes, eds. *A Collection of State papers Relating to Affairs in the Reign of Queen Elizabeth from 1542 to 1596 by William Cecil, Lord Burghley.* London: William Bowyer, 1740–1759.

Nash, Thomas. *The terrors of the night. Or, A Discourse of apparitions.* London, 1594.

Nicols, Thomas. *Arcula Gemmea, or, A Cabinet of Jewels.* London, 1653.

Ocland, Christopher. *The Popes Farwel; or, Queen Ann's Dream. Containing a true Prognostick of her own Death, Written Originally in Latine Verse by Mr. Christopher Ocland, and Printed in the Year 1582.* London, 1680.

Palsgrave, John, Gulielmus Gnaphaeus, and P.L. Carver. *Acolastus: The Comedy of Acolastus Translated from Discourse of the Sight: Of Melancholike Diseases; of Rheumes, and of Old Age from the Latin of Fullonius,* ed. P. L. Carver. London: H. Milford, Oxford University Press, 1937.

Patten, W. Londoner. *The Expedicion into Scotlande of the most woorthely fortunate prince Edward, Duke of Soomerset, uncle unto our most noble sovereign lord the kinges majestie Edward the VI.* London, 1548.

Penington, Mary. *Experiences in the Life of Mary Penington* (written by Herself), edited with introduction and notes by Norman Penney. Philadelphia: Biddle Press, 1911; new edition 1992, with preface by Gil Skidmore.

Potts, Thomas. *The vvonderfull discouerie of witches in the countie of Lancaster VVith the arraignement and triall of nineteene notorious witches, at the assizes and general gaole deliuerie, holden at the castle of Lancaster, upon Munday, the seuenteenth of August last, 1612.* London, 1613.

Powell, Vavasour. *Spirituall experiences, of sundry beleevers Held forth by them at severall solemne meetings, and conferences to that end. With the recommendation of the sound, spiritual, and savoury worth of them, to the sober and spirituall reader, by Vavasor Powel, minister of the gospel.* London, 1653.

Pryme, Abraham de la. *The Diary of Abraham de la Pryme, the Yorkshire Antiquary,* ed. Charles Jackson. Publications of the Surtees Society, vol. 54. Durham, UK: Andrews, 1870.

Renou, Jean de. *A medical Dispensatory, containing the whole Body of Physick,* trans. Richard Tomlinson. London, 1657.

The returne of the knight of the poste from Hell. London, 1606.

Rogers, John. *Ohel Ohel or Beth-shemesh. A tabernacle for the sun: or Irenicum evangelicum. An idea of church-discipline, in the theorick and practick parts; which come forth first into the world as bridegroom and bride, hand in hand; by whom you will have the totum essentiale of a true Gospel-Church state, according to Christ's rules and order, left us when he ascended. In which you may finde the hidden mystery of whole Christ, in head, neck, and body. Hidden in former ages from the sons of men.* London, 1653.

Rye, Walter, ed. *Depositions taken before the mayor & aldermen of Norwich, 1549–1567 and Extracts from the Court Books of the City of Norwich, 1666–1688.* Norwich, UK: Printed for the Norfolk and Norwich Archaeological Society by A. H. Goose, 1905.

Saunders, Richard. *Physiognomie, and chiromancie, metoposcopie.* 2nd edn. London, 1671.

Scot, Reginald. *The Discovery of Witchcraft.* London, 1584.

Scribonius, Wilhelm Adolf. *Naturall philosophy: or, A description of the vvorld, and of the severall creatures therein contained viz. of angels, of mankinde, of the heavens, the starres, the planets, the foure elements, with their order, nature and government: as also of minerals, mettals, plants, and precious stones; with their colours, formes, and virtues,* trans. Daniel Widdowes. London, 1631.

Seyton, Andrew. *The Seytonian Dreamer's Sure Guide Collected from the Writings of Andrew Seyton, Celebrated Seer of Cumberland.* London: R. Walwyn, 1820.

Shakespeare, William. *The Complete Works of Shakespeare,* ed. David Bevington, 4th edn. New York: Harper Collins, 1992.

Stow, John. *The annales of England faithfully collected out of the most autenticall authors, records, and other monuments of antiquitie, lately corrected, encreased, and continued, from the first inhabitation vntill this present yeere 1600.* London, 1600.

———. *The Chronicle of England.* London, 1580.

Thornton, Alice Wandesford. *The autobiography of Mrs. Alice Thornton, of East Newton, Co. York,* ed. Charles Jackson. Durham, UK: Published for the Surtees Society by Andrew, 1875.

Topsell, Edward. *The historie of serpents.* 2nd edn. London, 1608.

Turner, William. *A Book of Wines,* ed. Sanford V. Larkey and Philip M. Wagner. New York: Scholars' Facsimiles & Reprints, 1941.

———. *The first and seconde partes of the herbal of William Turner Doctor in Phisick, lately ouersene, corrected and enlarged with the thirde parte,* 2nd edn. Collen, 1568.

Udal, John Symonds. *Dorsetshire Folklore.* Hertford, UK: Stephen Austins and Sons, 1922.

Valentine, L. *Picturesque England: Its Landmarks and Historical Haunts, As Described in Lay and Legend.* London: Frederick Warne, 1891.

Valois, Marguerite de. *Memoirs of Marguerite de Valois.* Available online: *The Project Gutenberg EBook of Memoirs of Marguerite de Valois, Complete by Marguerite de Valois, Queen of Navarre,* http://www.gutenberg.org/etext/3841 [Accessed: 10 Jan 2008].

Vaughan, W. *Directions for Health, Naturall and Artificiall,* the seventh edition reviewed by the author. London, 1633.

Vaux, Laurence. *A catechisme or christian doctrine necesssarie for children and ignorante people.* Louvain, 1583.

Verstegan, Richard. *A declaration of the true causes of the great troubles, presupposed to be intended against the realme of England VVherein the indifferent reader shall manifestly perceaue, by whome, and by what means, the realme is broughte into these pretented perils.* Antwerp, 1592.

Vicars, John. *November 5 1605: The Quintessence of Cruelty, or Master-piece of Treachery, the Popish Pouder-Plot, Invented by Hellish-Malice, Prevented by Heavenly-mercy. Truly related, and from the Latine of the Learned, Religious, and Reverend D. Herring, translated and very much dilated.* London, 1641.

Walkington, Thomas. *The optick glasse of humors or The touchstone of a golden temperature, or the Philosophers stone to make a golden temper Wherein the foure complections sanguine, cholericke, phligmaticke, melancholicke are succinctly painted forth and their externall intimates laid open to the purblind eye of ignorance it selfe, by which euery one may iudge, of what complection he is, and answerably learne what is most sutable to his nature, 1631,* a photoprint with an introduction by John A. Popplestone and Marion White McPherson. Delmar, NY: Scholars' Facsimiles & Reprints, 1981.

Webster, John. *The Displaying of Supposed Witchcraft.* London, 1677.

Whitelocke, Bulstrode. *The Diary of Bulstrode Whitelocke, 1605–1675*, ed. Ruth Spalding. Oxford, UK: Published for the British Academy by Oxford University Press, 1990.

William, Lord Bishop of Rochester. *The Sermon Preached at Paules Cross, the tenth day of November, being the next Sunday after the Discoverie of this late Horrible Treason.* London, 1606.

Wilson, Arthur. *The History of Great Britain, being the life and reign of King James the First, relating to what passed from his first accesse to the crown, till his death.* London, 1653.

Winstanley, William. *The new help to discourse: or, Wit, mirth, and jollity intermixt with more serious matters. Consisting of pleasant astrological, astronomical, philosophical, grammatical, physical, chyrurgical, historical, moral, and poetical questions and answers. As also histories, poems, songs, epitaphs, epigrams, anagrams, acrosticks, riddles, jests, poesies, complements, &c. With several other varieties intermixt.* London, 1672.

The Works of Sir Thomas Browne, ed. Charles Sayer. Edinburgh: John Grant, 1927.

Wotton, Sir Henry. *Reliquiae wottonianae.* London, 1651.

Wright, Thomas. *The Passions of the Minde in Generall.* London, 1620.

Secondary Sources

Akrigg, G.P.V. *Jacobean Pageant, or the Court of King James I.* Cambridge, MA: Harvard University Press, 1962.

Allen, Elizabeth. "Everard, John (ca. 1584–1640/41)," *Oxford Dictionary of National Biography* (Oxford University Press, 2004). Available online: http://www.oxforddnb.com/view/article/8998 [Accessed: 1 May 2007].

Almond, Philip C. *Demonic Possession and Exorcism in Early Modern England: Contemporary Texts and Their Cultural Contexts.* Cambridge, UK: Cambridge University Press, 2004.

Alwes, Derek. "Elizabethan Dreaming: Fictional Dreams from Gascoigne to Lodge," *Framing Elizabethan Fictions: Contemporary Approaches to Early Modern Narrative Prose*, ed. Constance C. Relihan. Kent, OH: The Kent State University Press, 1996.

Anderson, Judith H. *Biographical Truth: The Representation of Historical Persons in Tudor-Stuart Writing.* New Haven, CT: Yale University Press, 1984.

Anderson-Miller, Julia, and Bruce Joshua Miller. *Dreams of Bill: A Collection of Funny, Strange and Downright Peculiar Dreams about Our President.* Secaucus, NJ: Carol Pub. Group, 1994.

Andrachuk, Gregory Peter. "Calderón's View of the English Schism," in *Parallel Lives: Spanish and English National Drama, 1580–1680*, ed. Louise and Peter Fothergill-Payne. Lewisburg, PA: Bucknell University Press, 1991.

Babb, Lawrence. *The Elizabethan Malady: A Study of Melancholia in English Literature from 1580 to 1642.* East Lansing: Michigan State College Press, 1951.

Barbour, Reid. *Literature and Religious Culture in Seventeenth-Century England.* Cambridge, UK: Cambridge University Press, 2002.

Barlow, Frank. *William Rufus.* Berkeley and Los Angeles: University of California Press, 1983.

Baumgartner, Frederic J. *Henry II, King of France, 1547–1559.* Durham, NC and London: Duke University Press, 1988.

Bellamy, Elizabeth Jane. "Desires and Disavowals: Speculations on the Aftermath of Stephen Greenblatt's 'Psychoanalysis and Renaissance Culture,'" *Clio* 34, no. 3 (2005), 297–315.

Bellamy, John. *Strange, Inhuman Deaths: Murder in Tudor England*. Westport, CT: Praeger, 2006.

Bennett, Michael J. "Simnel, Lambert (*b.* 1476/7, *d.* after 1534)," *Oxford Dictionary of National Biography* (Oxford University Press, Sep 2004). Available online: http://0-www.oxforddnb.com.library.unl.edu:80/view/article/25569 [Accessed: 21 Oct 2007].

Beradt, Charlotte. *The Third Reich of Dreams*. Chicago: Quadrangle Books, 1968.

Bildhauer, Bettina. "Blood," in *Medieval Folklore: A Guide to Myths, Legends, Tales, Beliefs, and Customs,* ed. Carl Lindahl, John McNamara, and John Lindow. Oxford, UK and New York: Oxford University Press, 2002.

Bingham, Caroline. *The Making of a King: The Early Years of James VI and I*. London: Collins, 1968.

Birch, Thomas. *The Court and Times of James the First: Containing a series of Historical and confidential Letters*. London: Henry Colburn, 1849.

Bowerbank, Sylvia. *Speaking for Nature: Women and Ecologies of Early Modern England*. Baltimore: Johns Hopkins University Press, 2004.

Brinson, David. "Hesketh, Richard (1553–1593)," *Oxford Dictionary of National Biography* (Oxford University Press, 2004). Available online: http://www.oxforddnb.com/view/article/13126 [Accessed: 9 Feb 2007].

Brown, Peter, ed., *Reading Dreams: The Interpretation of Dreams from Chaucer to Shakespeare*. Oxford, UK: Oxford University Press, 1999.

Budra, Paul. *A mirror for magistrates and the de casibus tradition*. Toronto: University of Toronto Press, 2000.

Bynum, Caroline Walker. *Wonderful Blood: Theology and Practice in Late Medieval Northern Germany and Beyond*. Philadelphia: University of Pennsylvania Press, 2007.

———. *Fragmentation and Redemption: Essays on Gender and the Human Body in Medieval Religion*. New York: Zone, 1991.

Campion, Thomas. "Sleepe, Angry Beauty," in *Poems of Sleep and Dreams,* ed. Peter Washington. New York: Random House, 2004.

Carlton, Charles. *Archbishop William Laud*. London and New York: Routledge & Kegan Paul, 1987.

Clapham, John. *Elizabeth of England,* ed. Evelyn Plummer Read and Conyers Read. Philadelphia: University of Pennsylvania Press, 1951.

Coleman, Linda S. "Gender, Sect, and Circumstances: Quaker Mary Penington's Many Voices," in *Women's Life-Writing: Finding Voice/Building Community,* ed. Linda S. Coleman. Bowling Green, OH: Bowling Green State University Popular Press, 1997.

Como, David R. *Blown by the Spirit: Puritanism and the Emergence of an Antinomian Underground in Pre-Civil War England*. Stanford, CA: Stanford University Press, 2004.

Crawford, Patricia. *Women and Religion in England, 1500–1720*. London: Routledge, 1993.

Crawford, Patricia, and Laura Gowing, eds., *Women's Worlds in Seventeenth-Century England: A Sourcebook*. London and New York: Routledge, 2000.

Crouzet, Denis. *La nuit de la Saint-Barthélemy: un rêve perdu de la Renaissance*. Paris: Fayard, 1994.

Curry, Patrick. "Lilly, William (1602–1681)," *Oxford Dictionary of National Biography* (Oxford University Press, 2004). Available from: http://www.oxforddnb.com/view/article/16661 [Accessed: 6 Apr 2007].

Selwyn, David G. *The Library of Thomas Cranmer.* Oxford, UK: Oxford Bibliographical Society, 1996.

Davidson, H. R. Ellis. "Hostile Magic in the Icelandic Sagas," in *The Witch Figure: Folklore Essays by a Group of Scholars in England Honouring the 75th Birthday of Katharine M. Briggs,* ed. Venetia Newall. London and Boston: Routledge and Kegan Paul, 1973.

De Becker, Raymond. *The Understanding of Dreams and Their Influence on the History of Man,* trans. Michael Heron. New York: Bell, 1948.

Dement, William C. *The Promise of Sleep: A Pioneer in Sleep Medicine Explores the Vital Connection between Health, Happiness, and a Good Night's Sleep.* New York: Delacorte Press, 1999.

Devlin, Christopher. "The Earl and the Alchemist," *The Month* 1, no. 9 (1953).

Dolan, Frances. *Dangerous Familiars: Representations of Domestic Crime in England, 1550–1700.* Ithaca, NY: Cornell University Press, 1994.

Doran, Susan. "Revenge Her Foul and Most Unnatural Murder? The Impact of Mary Stewart's Execution on Anglo-Scottish Relations," *History* 85 (2000), 589–612.

Duncan-Jones, E. E. "Queen Katherine's Visions and Queen Margaret's Dreams," *Notes and Queries* 206 (1961), 142–43.

Durston, Gregory. *Crime & Justice in Early Modern England, 1500–1750.* Chichester, UK: Barry Rose Law Publishers, 2004.

Dutton, Paul Edward. *The Politics of Dreaming in the Carolingian Empire.* Lincoln: University of Nebraska Press, 1994.

Ekirch, A. Roger. *At Day's Close: Night in Times Past.* New York: W. W. Norton, 2005.

Ferrell, Lori Anne. *Government by Polemic: James I, the King's Preachers, and the Rhetorics of Conformity, 1603–1625.* Stanford: Stanford University Press, 1998.

Fischer, Steven R. *The Complete Medieval Dream Book.* Berne: Peter Lang, 1982.

Fox, Adam. *Oral and Literate Culture in England, 1500–1700.* Oxford, UK: Clarendon Press, 2000.

Fraser, Antonia. *The Gunpowder Plot: Terror & Faith in 1605.* London: Weidenfeld and Nicolson, 1996.

Gabrieli, Vittorio. *Sir Kenelm Digby: Un Inglese italianato nell'età della Controriforma.* Roma: Edizioni di storia e letteratura, 1957.

Garber, Marjorie B. *Dream in Shakespeare: From Metaphor to Metamorphosis.* New Haven, CT: Yale University Press, 1974.

Gerona, Carla. *Night Journeys: The Power of Dreams in Transatlantic Quaker Culture.* Charlottesville: University of Virginia Press, 2004.

Gordon, Bruce. "Malevolent Ghosts and Ministering Angels: Apparitions and Pastoral Care in the Swiss Reformation," in *The Place of the Dead: Death and Remembrance in Late Medieval and Early Modern Europe.* Cambridge, UK: Cambridge University Press, 2000.

Greaves, Richard L. *Dublin's Merchant-Quaker: Anthony Sharp and the Community of Friends, 1643–1707.* Stanford: Stanford University Press, 1998.

Greenblatt, Stephen. *Renaissance Self-Fashioning: From More to Shakespeare.* Chicago: University of Chicago Press, 1980.

———. *Hamlet in Purgatory.* Princeton, NJ: Princeton University Press, 2001.

———. "Psychoanalysis and Renaissance Culture," in *Literary Theory/Renaissance Texts,* ed. Patricia Parker and David Quint. Baltimore: Johns Hopkins University Press, 1986.

Grene, Nicholas. *Shakespeare's Serial History Plays.* Cambridge, UK: Cambridge University Press, 2002.

Gunn, J. "Wilford, Ralph (ca. 1479–1499)," *Oxford Dictionary of National Biography* (Oxford University Press, 2004). Available online: http://0-www.oxforddnb.com.library.unl.edu:80/view/article/30094 [Accessed: 22 Oct 2007].

Gwyn, Douglas. *Seekers Found: Atonement in Early Quaker Experience.* Walingford, PA: Pendle Hill, 2000.

Haley, Gail E. *Dream Peddler.* New York: Dutton, 1993.

Hammer, Paul E. J. "Devereux, Robert, second earl of Essex (1565–1601)," *Oxford Dictionary of National Biography* (Oxford University Press, Sep 2004); online edn., Oct 2007. Available online: http://0-www.oxforddnb.com.library.unl.edu:80/view/article/7565 [Accessed: 5 Dec 2007].

Hard, Frederick. "Richard Haydocke and Alexander Browne: Two Half-Forgotten Writers on the Art of Painting," *PMLA* 55, no. 3 (1940), 727–41.

Herbert, Anne Clifford. *Countess of Pembroke, Lives of Lady Anne Clifford Countess of Dorset, Pembroke and Montgomery (1590–1676) and of her parents,* with an introduction by J. P. Gibson. London: Printed for Presentation to the members of the Roxburghe Club by Hazell, Watson and Viney, 1916.

Herford, C.H., and Percy Simpson, eds., *Ben Jonson.* Oxford, UK: Clarendon Press, 1925.

Hill, David. "Dreams," Richard J. Clifford, "Joseph (son of Jacob)" in *The Oxford Companion to the Bible,* ed. Bruce M. Metzger and Michael D. Coogan. Oxford, NY and Oxford, UK: Oxford University Press, 1993.

Hodgkin, Katherine, Michelle O'Callaghan, and S. J. Wiseman, *Reading the Early Modern Dream: The Terrors of the Night.* New York and London: Routledge, 2008.

Hole, Christina. *Witchcraft in England.* Totowa, NJ: Rowman and Littlefield, 1977.

Hollister, C. Warren. "The Strange Death of William Rufus," *Speculum: A Journal of Medieval Studies* 48, no. 4 (1973), 637–53.

Hsia, R. Po-Chia. "Dreams and Conversions: A Comparative Analysis of Catholic and Buddhist Dreams in Ming and Qing China: Part 1," *Journal of Religious History* 29, no. 3 (2005), 223–40.

Hunter, Michael. "Ashmole, Elias (1617–1692)," *Oxford Dictionary of National Biography* (Oxford University Press, Sep 2004); online edn, May 2006. Available online: http://0-www.oxforddnb.com.library.unl.edu:80/view/article/764 [Accessed: 9 Feb 2007].

Hurstfield, Joel. "Gun-powder Plot and the Politics of Dissent," in *Early Stuart Studies: Essays in Honor of David Harris Willson.* Minneapolis: University of Minnesota Press, 1970.

Jenkyns, Henry, ed. *The Remains of Thomas Cranmer, D. D. Archbishop of Canterbury.* Oxford, UK: Oxford University Press, 1833.

Johnson, Francis R. "Thomas Hill: An Elizabethan Huxley," *The Huntington Library Quarterly* 4 (1944), 329–51.

Jones, Eldred. *The Elizabethan Image of Africa.* Charlottesville: Published for the Folger Shakespeare Library by the University Press of Virginia, 1971.

Jones, Emrys. *The Origins of Shakespeare.* Oxford, UK: Clarendon Press, 1977.

Jones, Michael K., and Malcolm G. Underwood, "Beaufort, Margaret, countess of Richmond and Derby (1443–1509)," *Oxford Dictionary of National Biography* (Oxford University Press, 2004). Available online: http://0-www.oxforddnb.com .library.unl.edu:80/view/article/1863 [Accessed: 21 Oct 2007].

Jones, Michael K., and Malcolm G. Underwood. *The King's Mother: Lady Margaret Beaufort, Countess of Richmond and Derby.* Cambridge, UK: Cambridge University Press, 1992.

Josten, C.H., ed. *Elias Ashmole (1617–1692): His Autobiographical and Historical Notes, his Correspondence, and Other Contemporary Sources Relating to his Life and Work.* Oxford, UK: Clarendon Press, 1966.

Just Tour Limited, "Swaffham Norfolk Tourist Information Guide," Tour UK. Available from: http://www.touruk.co.uk/norfolk/nor_swaf.html [Accessed: 9 Nov 2007].

Kagan, Richard. *Lucrecia's Dream: Politics and Prophecy in Sixteenth-Century Spain.* Berkeley: University of California Press, 1990.

Kassell, Lauren. *Medicine and magic in Elizabethan London: Simon Forman; astrologer, alchemist, and physician.* Oxford, UK: Clarendon Press, 2005.

Kathman, David. "Stanley, Ferdinando, fifth earl of Derby (ca. 1559–1594)," *Oxford Dictionary of National Biography* (Oxford University Press, Sep 2004); online edn., May 2006. Available online: http://0-www.oxforddnb.com.library.unl. edu:80/view/article/26269 [Accessed: 9 Sep 2007].

Keeble, N. H. "Margaret Baxter," *Oxford Dictionary of National Biography* (Oxford University Press, Sep 2004); online edn., May 2007. Available online: http:// 0-www.oxforddnb.com.library.unl.edu:80/view/article/1734 [Accessed: 31 Jul 2007].

Kinney, Arthur. *Lies Like Truth: Shakespeare, Macbeth, and the Cultural Moment.* Detroit, MI: Wayne State University Press, 2001.

Krippner, Stanley, and William Hughes. "Everybody Dreams Every Night," in *The New World of Dreams,* ed. Ralph L. Woods and Herbert B. Greenhouse. New York: Macmillan, 1974.

Steven F. Kruger, *Dreaming in the Middle Ages.* Cambridge, UK: Cambridge University Press, 1992.

Kruse, Elaine. "The Blood-Stained Hands of Catherine de Médicis," in *Political Rhetoric, Power, and Renaissance Women,* ed. Carole Levin and Patricia A. Sulivan. Albany, NY: SUNY Press, 1995.

———. "The Woman in Black: The Image of Catherine de Medici from Marlowe to Queen Margot," in *"High and Mighty Queens" of Early Modern England: Realities and Representations.* New York: Palgrave Macmillan, 2003.

Le Goff, Jacques. *The Medieval Imagination,* trans. Arthur Goldhammer. Chicago: University of Chicago Press, 1988.

Leather, Ella Mary. *The Folk-Lore of Herefordshire.* Hereford, UK: Jakeman and Carver, 1912.

Lemon, Rebecca. *Treason by Words: Literature, Law, and Rebellion in Shakespeare's England.* Ithaca, NY: Cornell University Press, 2006.

Levack, Brian P. *The Witch-hunt in Early Modern Europe.* London: Longman, 1987.

Levine, Nina. "The Case of Eleanor Cobham: Authorizing History in *2 Henry VI,*" *Shakespeare Studies* 22, no. 10 (1994), 104–21.

Liebler, Naomi C., and Lisa Scancella Shea. "Shakespeare's Queen Margaret: Unruly or Unruled," in *Henry VI: Critical Essays,* ed. Thomas Pendleton. New York: Routlege, 2001.

Lodge, Edmund. *Illustrations of British History*. London: John Childley, 1838.

Loomis, Catherine. "Elizabeth Southwell's Manuscript Account of the Death of Queen Elizabeth," *ELR* 26 (1996), 482–509.

Loughlin, Marie H. "Penington, Mary [*other married name* Mary Springett, Lady Springett] (*bap.* 1623, *d.* 1682)," *Oxford Dictionary of National Biography* [online] (Oxford, UK: Oxford University Press, Sep 2004). Available from: http://0-www.oxforddnb.com.library.unl.edu:80/view/article/45819 [Accessed: 7 Aug 2007].

Macdonald, Michael. "The Fearefull Estate of Francis Spira: Narrative, Identity, and Emotion in Early Modern England," *Journal of British Studies* 31, no. 1 (1992), 32–61.

MacFarlane, Alan. *The Family Life of Ralph Josselin, a Seventeenth-Century Clergyman: An Essay in Historical Anthropology*. Cambridge, UK: Cambridge University Press, 1970.

Mackay, Charles. *Extraordinary Popular Delusions and the Madness of Crowds*. Boston: L. C. Page, 1932.

Margeson, John. "Introduction," William Shakespeare, *King Henry VIII*, ed. John Margeson. Cambridge, UK: Cambridge University Press, 1990.

Mariscal, George. "Calderón and Shakespeare: The Subject of Henry VIII," *Bulletin of the Comediantes* 39, no. 2 (1987), 189–213.

Marotti, Arthur F. "The Catholic Martyrdom Account," in *Print, Manuscript, and Performance: The Changing Relations of the Media in Early Modern England*, ed. Arthur F. Marotti and Michael D. Bristol. Columbus: Ohio State University Press, 2000.

Masten, Jeffrey. "The Interpretation of Dreams, ca. 1610," *Historicism, Psychoanalysis, and Early Modern Culture*, ed. Carla Mazzio and Douglas Trevor. New York and London: Routledge, 2000.

Masters, Brian. *Dreams about H.M. the Queen and Other Members of the Royal Family*. London: Blond & Briggs, 1972.

McCullough, Peter E. "Out of Egypt: Richard Fletcher's Sermon before Elizabeth I after the Execution of Mary Queen of Scots," *Dissing Elizabeth: Negative Representations of Gloriana*, ed. Julia M. Walker. Durham, NC: Duke University Press, 1998.

McMullen, Gordon. "Introduction," William Shakespeare and John Fletcher, *King Henry VIII*, ed. Gordon McMullen. London: Thomson Learning, 2000.

Miller, David Lee. "Writing the Specular Son: Jonson, Freud, Lacan, and the (K)not of Masculinity," *Desire in the Renaissance: Psychoanalysis and Literature*, ed. Valeria Finucci and Regina Schwartz. Princeton, NJ: Princeton University Press, 1994.

Montrose, Louis. "Shaping Fantasies: Figurations of Gender and Power in Elizabethan Culture," *Representations* 1, no. 2 (1983), 61–94.

Moses, Stéphane. "The Cultural Index of Freud's Interpretation of Dreams," *Dream Cultures: Explorations in the Comparative History of Dreaming*, ed. David Shulman and Guy Stroumsa. Oxford, NY: Oxford University Press, 1999.

Neale, J. E. "The Sayings of Queen Elizabeth," *History* 10 (1925), 212–33.

Nicholl, Charles. *A Cup of News: The Life of Thomas Nashe*. London: Routledge & Kegan Paul, 1984.

Nicholls, Mark. *Investigating Gunpowder Plot*. Manchester: Manchester University Press, 1991.

Osborne, Roger. *The Dreamer of Calle de San Salvador: Visions of Sedition and Sacrilege in Sixteenth-Century Spain*. London: Jonathan Cape, 2001.

Oxford English Dictionary, 2nd edn. Oxford, UK: Oxford University Press, 1989.

P., A. F. "Thomas Wotton," *Dictionary of National Biography Archive,* first published 1900.

Paperno, Irina. "Dreams of Terror: Dreams from Stalinist Russia as a Historical Source," *Kritika: Explorations in Russian and Eurasian History* 7, no. 4 (2006), 793–824.

Parker, Derek. *Familiar to All: William Lilly and Astrology in the Seventeenth Century.* London: Jonathan Cape, 1973.

Paster, Gail Kern. *The Body Embarrassed: Drama and the Disciplines of Shame in Early Modern England.* Ithaca, NY: Cornell University Press, 1993.

Paul, Henry. *The Royal Play of Macbeth; When, Why, and How It Was Written by Shakespeare.* New York: Macmillan, 1950.

Phillips, James Emerson. *Images of a Queen: Mary Stuart in Sixteenth-Century Literature.* Berkeley and Los Angeles: University of California Press, 1964.

Pollen, John Hungerford. *Acts of English martyrs hitherto unpublished.* London: Burns and Oates, 1891.

Presson, Robert K. "Two Types of Dreams in Elizabethan Drama, and Their Heritage: Somnium Animale and the Prick-of-Conscience," *Studies in English Literature, 1500–1900* 7 (1967), 239–56.

Price, S.R.F. "The Future of Dreams: From Freud to Artemidorus," *Past and Present* 113 (1986), 3–37.

Purkiss, Diane. *The Witch in History: Early Modern and Twentieth-Century Representations.* London: Routledge, 1996.

Quaife, G. R. *Godly Zeal and Furious Rage: The Witch in Early Modern Europe.* London: Croom Helm, 1987.

Ratcliff, A.J.J. *A History of Dreams.* Boston: Small, Maynard, 1923.

Riggs, David. *Ben Jonson: A Life.* Cambridge, MA: Harvard University Press, 1989.

Robinson, Marsha S. *Writing the Reformation: Actes and Monuments and the Jacobean History Play.* Burlington, VT: Ashgate, 2002.

Rowse, A. L. *Simon Forman: Sex and Society in Shakespeare's Age.* London: Weidenfeld and Nicolson, 1974.

Scott, Harold Spencer, ed. "The Journal of Sir Roger Wilbraham, Solicitor-General in Ireland and Master of the Requests, for the Years 1593–1616" in *The Camden Miscellany: Volume the Tenth* (Camden Society, third series, 4, 1902).

Seafield, Frank. *The Literature and Curiosities of Dreams.* London: Chapman and Hall, 1865.

Seaver, Paul S. *Wallington's World.* Stanford: Stanford University Press, 1985.

Sharpe, James. *The Bewitching of Anne Gunter: A Horrible and True Story of Deception, Witchcraft, Murder, and the King of England.* New York: Routledge, 2000.

———. *Instruments of Darkness: Witchcraft in England, 1550–1750.*London: Hamish Hamilton, 1996.

———. *Remember, Remember: A Cultural History of Guy Fawkes Day.* Cambridge, MA: Harvard University Press, 2005.

———. "Introduction: the Lancashire Witches in Historical Context," in *The Lancashire Witches: Histories and Stories,* ed. Robert Poole. Manchester and New York: Manchester University Press, 2002.

Simon, Linda. *Of Virtue Rare: Margaret Beaufort, Matriarch of the House of Tudor.* Boston: Houghton Mifflin, 1982.

Simons, Eric N. *Henry VII: The First Tudor King.* New York: Barnes & Noble, 1968.

Smith, Nigel. *Perfection Proclaimed: Language and Literature in English Radical Religion, 1640–1660.* Oxford, UK: Clarendon Press, 1989.

204 BIBLIOGRAPHY

Sobel, Mechal. *Teach Me Dreams: The Search for Self in the Revolutionary Era.* Princeton, NJ: Princeton University Press, 2000.

Steiner, George. "The Historicity of Dreams (two questions to Freud)," *Salmagundi* 61 (1983), 6–21.

Stephens, Walter. *Demon Lovers: Witchcraft, Sex, and the Crisis of Belief.* Chicago and London: University of Chicago Press, 2000.

Stevens, Anthony. *Private Myths: Dreams and Dreaming.* Cambridge, MA: Harvard University Press, 1995.

Strickland, Agnes. *Lives of the Queens of England from the Norman Conquest,* new and revised edn. London: George Bells and Sons, 1888.

"The Swaffam Tinker," in *The World of Dreams,* ed. R. L. Woods. New York: Random House, 1974.

Tenison, E. M. *Elizabethan England,* vol. III: 1575–1580. Royal Leamington Spa, Warwick: issued by the author, 1933.

Thiselfton-Dyer, T. F. *Folklore of Women.* Chicago: A. C. McClurg, 1906.

Thomas, Keith. *Religion and the Decline of Magic.* London: Weidenfeld and Nicolson, 1971.

Traister, Barbara Howard. *The Notorious Astrological Physician of London: Works and Days of Simon Forman.* Chicago: University of Chicago Press, 2001.

Travers, James. *James I: The Masque of Monarchy.* Surrey: National Archives, 2003.

Udall, John Symonds. *Dorsetshire Folklore.* Hertford, UK: Stephen Austins and Sons, 1922.

Usher, Brett. "Fletcher, Richard (1544/5–1596)," *Oxford Dictionary of National Biography* (Oxford University Press, 2004). Available online: http://0-www .oxforddnb.com.library.unl.edu:80/view/article/9739 [Accessed: 25 Nov 2007].

Valentine, L. *Picturesque England: Its Landmarks and Historical Haunts, As Described in Lay and Legend.* London: Frederick Warne, 1891.

Van de Castle, Robert L. *Our Dreaming Mind.* New York: Ballantine Books, 1994.

Villani, Stefano. "Evans, Katharine (ca. 1618–1692)" (Oxford University Press, 2004). Available online: http://0-www.oxforddnb.com.library.unl.edu:80/view/article/45814 [Accessed: 11 Aug 2007].

Walker, Garthine. *Crime, Gender and Social Order in Early Modern England.* Cambridge, UK: Cambridge University Press, 2003.

Watkins, John. *Representing Elizabeth in Stuart England: Literature, History, Sovereignty.* Cambridge, UK: Cambridge University Press, 2002.

Westwood, Jennifer. *Albion: A Guide to Legendary Britain.* London: Granada, 1985.

Wiedermann, Gotthelf. "Alesius [Allane or Alan], Alexander (1500–1565)," *Oxford Dictionary of National Biography* (Oxford University Press, 2004). Available online: http://0-www.oxforddnb.com.library.unl.edu:80/view/article/320 [Accessed: 12 Nov 2007].

Williamson, Hugh Ross. *Catherine de' Medici.* London: Michael Joseph, 1973.

Wilson, Derek. *Sweet Robin: A Biography of Robert Dudley, Earl of Leicester.* London: Hamilton, 1981.

Wormald, Jenny. "Gunpowder, Treason, and Scots," *Journal of British Studies* 24 (1985), 141–68.

Wroe, Ann. *The Perfect Prince.* New York: Random House, 2003.

Wylie, James A. *The History of Protestantism.* London: Cassell Petter Galpin, 1870.

Ziegler, Georgianna. "Mary Stuart," in *Elizabeth I: Then and Now.* Washington, DC: The Folger Shakespeare Library, 2003.

INDEX

Page numbers in italics indicate illustrations.

CPSIA information can be obtained at www.ICGtesting.com
Printed in the USA
LVOW102321300712

292262LV00004B/41/P